When Beds Float

EXPLORING THE POLTERGEIST ENIGMA

MICHAEL CLARKSON

KEY PORTER BOOKS

Library and Archives Canada Cataloguing in Publication

Clarkson, Michael, 1948–
When beds float : examining the poltergeist enigma / Michael Clarkson.

ISBN 1-55263-708-5

1. Poltergeists. I. Title.

BF1483.C53 2005 133.1'42 C2005-902749-5

The Canada Council for the Arts since 1957 | Le Conseil des Arts du Canada depuis 1957

Ontario Arts Council
Conseil des Arts de l'Ontario

The publisher gratefully acknowledges the support of the Canada Council for the Arts and the Ontario Arts Council for its publishing program. We acknowledge the support of the Government of Ontario through the Ontario Media Development Corporation's Ontario Book Initiative.

We acknowledge the financial support of the Government of Canada through the Book Publishing Industry Development Program (BPIDP) for our publishing activities.

Key Porter Books Limited
Six Adelaide Street East, Tenth Floor
Toronto, Ontario
Canada M5C 1H6

www.keyporter.com

Text design: Ingrid Paulson
Electronic formatting: Jean Lightfoot Peters
Printed and bound in Canada

05 06 07 08 09 6 5 4 3 2 1

CONTENTS

Introduction 3

EXAMINING THE POLTERGEIST ENIGMA 9

CHAPTER 1 The Eyewitnesses 10
CHAPTER 2 The Theories 20
CHAPTER 3 The Electrical Connection 32
CHAPTER 4 The Frauds: Things That Go Sneak in the Night 39

SCARY BEGINNING, GOOD ENDING 51

CHAPTER 5 A Cop Goes Flying 52
CHAPTER 6 Our Only Visitor at Halloween 63
CHAPTER 7 Police Controversy in New England 72

THE FLYING PHONE 81

CHAPTER 8 The House of Styrofoam Cups 82
CHAPTER 9 The Circus Comes to Columbus 91
CHAPTER 10 Tragedy 100
CHAPTER 11 The Ghostbuster (William Roll) and the Mythbuster (James Randi) 103

PK IN THE UK 113
CHAPTER 12 Enfield: Watch out for the Lego Bricks 114
CHAPTER 13 Enfield: Strange Twists and Turns 122
CHAPTER 14 Enfield: The Voice 129
CHAPTER 15 Enfield: Epilogue 139
CHAPTER 16 The Irish Gal and Wee Hughie 143
CHAPTER 17 Lively Case in Cheshire 153

AROUND THE WORLD 163
CHAPTER 18 The Super-Static Girl and More Electricity 164
CHAPTER 19 The Detective Puzzler on Long Island 173
CHAPTER 20 Kentucky: The Poltergeist Who Moved Around 181
CHAPTER 21 Miami: Fire Sale at the Souvenir Place 186

POLTERGEISTS IN POP CULTURE AND THE FUTURE 195
CHAPTER 22 The New Frontier: Tapping Psychokinesis 196
CHAPTER 23 The Poltergeist in Popular Culture 206
CHAPTER 24 Show Me the Money 212

Sources and Recommended Reading 217

"It is possible that there exist emanations that are still unknown to us. Do you remember how electrical currents and unseen waves were laughed at?"

—ALBERT EINSTEIN

INTRODUCTION

As a daily newspaper reporter for thirty-eight years (recently retired) and author of four books on fear management and stress, I do not treat lightly the topic of poltergeists. Some of my colleagues, who know me as an investigator of everything from the AIDS epidemic to serial killers to nepotism in government hiring, may shudder at the thought of me now entering the shadowy world of the paranormal. Going senile in your old age, Clarkson?

In fact, I have been considering this topic for more than twenty-five years, but did not take action until now.

In 1980, a young man who had been the center of a poltergeist case came to my house to talk. Since then, I have been following with some interest as poltergeist cases pop up from time to time in the media and in scholarly publications. Some of them seem worthy of further examination. In the past couple of years, I have closely examined some of the cases in this book.

I am not an expert in poltergeists or paranormal phenomena, so you could probably call me a skeptic. As an investigative journalist, I'm always looking for reasonable proof for extrasensory perception, UFOs, or ghosts.

As a fear researcher, I believe we are just beginning to understand some of the amazing capabilities of the fight-or-flight system, which is hardwired into each of us by nature.

For this book, I have reviewed about fifty poltergeist cases and interviewed hundreds of witnesses, paranormal experts, psychologists, university professors, magicians, and skeptics.

Although I try to remain neutral, it is difficult not to arrive at some conclusions. I now suspect that poltergeists exist, or at least a type of poltergeist energy exists. That does not mean I believe they exist, just that I think there is enough evidence to suspect there is something going on from time to time that seems to defy the laws of physics. I remain skeptical, but not cynical, and you will see in my wording that I question the evidence. For example, when describing the supposed poltergeist events, I frequently use the words "reportedly" and "allegedly." "The table *reportedly* moved under its own power..."

Some of the cases may raise as many questions as they provide answers, while others may have flaws or be the result of trickery. But if we are too quick to dismiss cases, we might miss some intriguing stories and theories on the edge of science.

Poltergeists are hard to prove for a number of reasons. They often involve adolescents or teenagers, who may be prone to trickery or at least to drawing attention to themselves.

Nevertheless, I believe there is enough evidence to raise debate. Please join me in this unusual adventure to examine something out of the ordinary.

PEOPLE STILL BELIEVE

Probably hundreds of millions of people in America believe in some form of the supernatural. A 2003 Harris Poll of more than 2,000 Americans revealed that 90 percent believed in God, 89 percent in miracles, 68 percent in the devil, 51 percent in ghosts, 31 percent in astrology, and 27 percent in reincarnation. In Britain, a 2004 survey showed that 42 percent of people believed in ghosts.

A BRIEF HISTORY OF THE POLTERGEIST

Poltergeists have fascinated people from ancient times to the Amityville Horror case on Long Island in 1974 to the contemporary Harry Potter books and movies.

They were reported as early as 858 BC in a farmhouse in Rhine, Germany, where an unseen force reportedly threw stones, shook the walls, moved objects, and caused loud banging noises.

Other cases were reported in AD 530 in Roman Italy and AD 900 in China and they continue to be studied and documented around the world, although their definition is debatable and there is speculation about their existence.

The Spiritualism movement in America began in 1848 when it was reported that sisters Kate and Margaret Fox were creating disruptive, noisy energy in their home in Hydesville, New York. The belief of Spiritualism in the continued existence of the human soul remains popular around the world, particularly in Brazil.

In what has become known as the Epworth Poltergeist, the Wesley family of Epworth, Lincolnshire, England, said they heard loud rapping noises over two months in their parsonage in 1716. No explanation for this phenomenon was found.

The Borley Rectory is one of the most famous cases in England, in which mysterious footsteps, phantom stone throwing, and hauntings were reported throughout the 1920s and 1930s, but whether these activities might have been the result of fraud or natural causes is controversial.

Many people are skeptical about early poltergeist investigations, which were sometimes conducted by superstitious researchers, who might have too easily jumped to conclusions.

Even the celebrated murder and poltergeist/haunting case in a house in Amityville, which was made into the book and movie, the *Amityville Horror*, was considered by many to be fraudulent.

Three poltergeist movies of the 1980s were partly based on several poltergeist cases.

And poltergeists continue to be reported today. In 2000 in Tomika-cho, Japan, many families living in an apartment building claimed that a poltergeist was causing mysterious sounds, moving objects, apparitions, and electric tools to work without power supply.

Other recent documented cases were in Mexico in 2002, Florida in 2003, and Savannah, Georgia, in 2005. For an overview of poltergeists in Finland over the years, check the Internet at http://personal.inet.fi/tiede/poltergeist/English.htm.

In ancient times, many people believed that demons were behind poltergeist activity, then the theory generally turned to the idea that they were actually ghosts of the dead.

Beginning in the twentieth century, parapsychologists, such as Sir William Barrett, Federic Myers, Nador Fodor, and William Roll, suspected that poltergeist activity involved young people and teenagers, that the loud bumps and moving objects were caused by mischievous or angry youths (in these cases, of course, it was believed they did it subconsciously through a type of kinetic energy).

GLOSSARY OF MAJOR TERMS

levitation: The lifting of objects through PK or RSPK.

parapsychology: The study of general paranormal phenomena.

poltergeist: A disturbance or energy with bizarre physical effects of paranormal origin that suggest mischievous or destructive intent, such as breaking or moving objects and loud knocks or noises. The disturbance usually centers around an individual, often a child going through puberty in a stressful house. The term is German, meaning "noisy ghost."

poltergeist agent: A person around whom poltergeist activities seem to revolve.

psi: A term used to encompass all paranormal abilities.

psychokinesis (PK): The power of the mind to consciously affect matter without physical contact.

recurrent spontaneous psychokinesis (RSPK): Bizarre movement of objects, noises, and other paranormal effects caused unconsciously by a person, otherwise known as poltergeist activity. Unlike PK, it occurs spontaneously and repeatedly over a period of time.

telekinesis: Paranormal movement of objects. "Psychokinesis" is the modern term for this.

A TYPICAL POLTERGEIST CASE

If there is anything at all typical about a poltergeist case, here it is. Actually, there are many common denominators in the fifty cases I reviewed in writing this book. Although each case has its own characteristics and idiosyncrasies, here are the trends. The cases generally have:

- a poltergeist agent, usually an adolescent entering puberty and quite intelligent, around whom the strange activities occur
- some sort of repression or frustration of the poltergeist agent by others
- a high level of stress in the household prior to the start of the poltergeist activity that continues throughout the case
- poltergeist activity lasts one week to several months
- dramatic events, such as unexplained knocking, electrical malfunctions, and movement of objects and furniture; occasionally reported are levitation of objects, electrical appliances working without power, and stones falling apparently from nowhere; rarely reported are strange voices coming from the agent, apparitions, strange odors, cold spots, and puddles.
- a mischievous or destructive intent on the part of the agent rather than a downright malevolent intent, although about a dozen people have been injured, but none seriously, in the cases in this book

Examining the Poltergeist Enigma

In this section, we set out the issues, theories, and controversies of the poltergeist, raising questions about its possible existence, and setting the stage for the many case studies in the subsequent sections. Chapter 1 has eyewitness accounts from police officers and others. Chapter 2 tells the many theories of the complex poltergeist issue, from the fight-or-flight syndrome to adolescents using a rare type of sexual energy. In Chapter 3, a possible electrical connection is examined, while Chapter 4 exposes the fraudulent poltergeist cases, and why some people stoop to trickery.

CHAPTER 1

THE EYEWITNESSES

"You stay around here, you get hit by a lot of stuff."

—MRS. CHARLES DAUGHTERY TO A POLICE OFFICER, WHO HAD BEEN STRUCK IN THE LEG BY A FLYING "POLTERGEIST OBJECT" IN HER HOME IN PORTSMOUTH, VIRGINIA

At least thirty-five police officers around the world — in thirteen cases since 1952 — claim to have seen poltergeist activity up close. Nine of them were assaulted by what they say was a poltergeist, but none was seriously injured, and no one was charged. One officer even pulled a gun on the "unseen force."

Although there is no scientific proof that poltergeists exist, the eyewitness accounts of these officers, taken from published reports and from interviews I conducted, seem compelling. Gathering scientific proof is difficult because of the fleeting nature of their alleged existence. By the time a family suspects that they may have something paranormal on their hands, it is often too late for anyone to study it, or the family doesn't talk about it for fear of appearing crazy.

But if we go simply by eyewitness accounts of first-line responders, the police officers, even some skeptics may start to suspect there is something paranormal at work here, or at least something that science cannot explain.

Generally, police tend to be solid witnesses, trained and experienced in knowing how to focus when something is happening quickly. As believable witnesses for so-called paranormal events, they should be better than the average person because they tend to be skeptical and sometimes cynical about potential trickery. And if they are wrong about such a contentious subject, they lose credibility among their peers and the general public.

As an author of four books on fear and as a police reporter for daily newspapers for thirteen years, I tend to listen to police officers. I think I know how to read them and how to interpret what they say.

In this book, we have at least thirty-five cops who believe they saw — and had the guts to report to their superiors — what they believed to be poltergeist activity: furniture moving, kitchen utensils floating in the air, and chairs rising off the floor.

For example, in a middle-class home on Long Island, New York, in 1958, Detective Joseph Tozzi, one of the brightest gumshoes in the Nassau County Police Department, said he was hit in the back of the legs by a flying bronze horse that weighed nearly 100 pounds while he was walking down basement steps with a thirteen-year-old boy, Jimmy Herrmann. No one else was in the area, Tozzi said.

He said he saw other paranormal events, including a sugar bowl fall off a table and then he was nearly hit by an airborne globe of the world.

There were many other witnesses to events, which lasted more than four weeks, including John Gold, a photographer from the *London Evening News*, who said his flashbulbs moved by themselves off a table and flew into the air; Jimmy's father, James, who said he saw medicine and a bottle of shampoo move on their own; visitor Marie Murtha, who said she saw a porcelain figure rise off a table and hover in the air; and *Newsday* reporter David Kahn, who said the globe moved again. To have done some of the things suspected of him, Jimmy "would have had to have been extraordinarily strong and agile," Kahn said. "When statuettes [of the Virgin Mary] struck objects, they did so with an almost explosive sound." (For more, see Chapter 19.)

In another case, when Patrolman William Killin was told to go to a souvenir warehouse in Miami to investigate a ghost or poltergeist on January 14, 1967, he thought his coworkers were playing a joke on him. He reluctantly drove to the scene and quickly became a believer as he saw glasses and souvenirs fall off shelves, seemingly under their own power. Killin sent a radio dispatch back to his sergeant: "Get more men down here!"

Over the next two and a half weeks, police officers, newspaper reporters, television crews, and insurance agents claimed they saw cowbells, ashtrays, key chains, and rubber daggers fly or fall off shelves in the warehouse, sometimes at unusual angles and always while nineteen-year-old shipping clerk Julio Vasquez was nearby. However, Vasquez was never caught cheating, even though police and others were closely watching him. The building's owners brought in anyone they believed could solve the riddle, including magician Howard Brooks, who at first laughed off the goings-on as a cheap trick, but then admitted he could not explain them, even though he checked the entire warehouse for wires or secret mechanisms. “Something did move those things, and I couldn’t figure it out,” Brooks said. (See Chapter 21.)

Three years later in St. Catharines, Ontario, an entire shift of police officers said they believed in poltergeists after watching furniture move strangely around an eleven-year-old boy in his apartment. The crustiest cop among them, burly veteran Constable Bill Weir, said that an unknown, unseen force lifted a chair he was sitting in and flipped him onto his behind. The boy could not possibly have done it, Weir said. As well, the boy was reportedly thrown off a chair in a similar fashion about a dozen times over the course of a week while Weir was watching.

“These occurrences are phenomenal,” said Weir, who went home and slept with his service revolver and a glass of liquor at his bedside.

Over the course of more than a week, seven officers, an acting Crown attorney, and two priests say they witnessed paranormal events in the apartment, including a heavy bed that rose 2 feet off the floor. “It stayed that way, unsupported — I couldn’t believe my eyes,” Constable Scotty Crawford said in his official report.

The family, who did not want their name publicized in the media, had called police after ten days, only as a last resort. Over the course of the intense investigation, no one saw anyone, including the eleven-year-old boy, cheat. (See Chapters 5 and 6.)

In 1974, in the home of factory worker Gerald Goodin in Bridgeport, Connecticut, Officer John Holsworth swore he saw a heavy refrigerator “lift slowly off the floor, turn and then set down again. There was no one else around. Then the big TV set seemed to float in the air and crash to the floor.” Fellow officer Joe Tomek added, “Shelves fixed to the walls vibrated until they broke loose, then flew through the air.”

Paranormal investigator Lorraine Warren said she never saw so many police officers get down on their knees and ask for a priest’s blessing. (See Chapter 7.)

In a house in London, England, in 1977, Constable Carolyn Keeps said she saw a chair move 3 or 4 feet, apparently without the help of human hands. Constable Keeps was so convinced she had seen something unnatural and legitimate that she recounted it in her official report that night. “I looked at the chair and noticed that it was wobbling slightly from side to side. I then saw the chair slide across the floor towards the kitchen wall."

Also in the London case, Sergeant Bryan Hyams and another officer reported that toys began flying about the house. "Lego bricks just started to levitate, or move about, I should say, jump about like jumping beans," Hyams said. "There was a bird in a cage that started squawking. And suddenly, one or two Lego bricks started to fly towards us." Hyams and the officer became afraid and he ran out of the house.

Years later, Hyams would say, "I'm no hero. I went straight out of the door and I think there was a rush between us [as to] who got out the swiftest... in 28 years in the police service, that's the only time I've consciously become aware of something like that, and I think that it is so rare and few and far between. When I tell the story, people still look at me as much as to say, 'Is he or isn't he telling the truth?' and I say, 'Look, this is really what happened and what I saw.' "

The mysterious activity seemed to revolve around eleven-year-old Janet Hodgson, but police could not find any evidence of her or anyone else playing tricks.

On another day, a reporter for the British Broadcasting Corporation, Rosalind Morris, said she saw Janet's chair fly across the room and her bed shake up and down on its own power. In addition, parapsychologist Maurice Grosse said he saw a teapot next to a stove rock back and forth for about seven seconds, "doing a little dance right in front of my eyes." When he examined the pot, it was empty and quite cold. (See Chapters 12 through 15.)

Also in England, in 1952, police say they were witnesses, and also the victims, of strange incidents in Runcorn, Lancashire, in which seventeen-year-old John Glynn Jones, a quiet apprentice draftsman, was said to cause dressing tables and other things to move with his mind over a ten-week period, causing about $35,000 damage. It was said that three strong police officers were thrown off a chest.

In a test to see if he was pulling a prank, four people sat on Jones, yet the incidents reportedly continued. A local Methodist minister, Rev. W.H. Stevens, said he was hit on the head with a flying dictionary. (See Chapter 17.)

In the village of Druten, The Netherlands, in 1995, two police officers investigating poltergeist-like activities in a house say they had sand thrown in their faces. The only other person in the room was a fifteen-year-old boy who had his hands in his pockets. Later, one officer said she had sand thrown "forcefully" at her head while inside her police cruiser and also while standing outside the police cruiser when the boy was locked in the car. Researchers believe the boy was stressed while making the transition from an Islamic culture.

THE TEACHER AND THE MOVING DESK

As well as police officers, teachers are often good witnesses — and cognizant of potential trickery on the part of students.

At her home in Scotland and at a primary school in 1960, eleven-year-old Virginia Campbell was said to move objects, including a heavy desk, with her mind. During a class, her teacher, Margaret Stewart, said she observed Virginia trying to hold down her desk lid, which several times raised itself to an angle of 45 to 50 degrees.

Miss Stewart recalled: "The class was quiet, and writing away. We still had the old school desks, which had a lid top. Anyway, I looked over at Virginia and noticed she was sitting with both hands pressed firmly down on top of her desk lid. I saw the desk lid rise and fall, with Virginia trying her best to keep the lid shut with her hands." Miss Stewart said she could plainly see Virginia's hands flat on the lid of the desk and her legs were underneath the desk.

Later, when another student got up to bring a jotter to the teacher, Miss Stewart said that the unnamed student's unoccupied desk, which was located behind Virginia, slowly rose off the floor, and then settled down again. Still suspicious of a prank, Miss Stewart checked the desk for strings or wires, but found none.

On another day, while Virginia stood, hands clasped behind her back, the teacher said she saw a blackboard pointer lying on a table move across the table until it fell to the floor. Then the whole table reportedly swung away from the teacher in a counterclockwise motion. Virginia started crying and said she was not causing the disturbance. Miss Stewart recalls how the heavy table levitated right in front of her: "At first, it was vibrating slowly, then increased as the seconds wore on. I sat transfixed looking at this. Then the table, which was quite a heavy one, started to rise up very slowly into the air and also vibrate. I put my hands on the table and tried to push it back down, but with no success. I was quite horrified, but it did not stop there. The table continued to vibrate as it hovered a few inches off the floor. Then the table rotated 90 degrees so that, where I had moments before sat behind the long edge of the table, the table had rotated so that its narrow edge was now directly in front of my stomach. I looked up at Virginia and saw she was quite distressed, and I remember her saying, 'Please, Miss, I'm not doing that, honest I'm not.' Then I calmed her down."

Like many other poltergeist cases, it had its skeptics, but a parapsychologist, Dr. A.G. Owen, concluded that there were too many reliable witnesses to dismiss the case as fraud or accident. "The five main witnesses believed themselves to have heard certain sounds and seen certain movements of objects," he said. "It is just possible in principle to suppose that one person could be the victim of illusion or hallucination. It is, however, beyond all possibility that five responsible persons should be so deceived at various occasions over a period of two weeks. Thus we must conclude that they heard actual noises and saw actual motions of real objects." (See Chapter 16.)

Late in the nineteenth century in Amherst, Nova Scotia, physician Dr. Gene Carritte said he saw potatoes hurl themselves across a room and a thundering noise come from the roof of the house. He wrote of his experience to a colleague: "Honestly, skeptical persons were on all occasions soon convinced that there was no fraud or deception in the case. Were I to publish the case in the medical journals, as you suggest, I doubt if it would be believed by physicians generally. I am certain I could not have believed such apparent miracles — had I not witnessed them."

We also have numerous accounts of parapsychologists who claim to have seen poltergeist activity, although neutral people might be more skeptical of their claims because parapsychologists might have a vested interest in having a paranormal event actually happen, or they might tend to believe in the paranormal, which might affect their interpretation of the events.

Nevertheless, parapsychologist William Roll of Duke University and psychology student/paranormal researcher John P. Stump say they both saw amazing occurrences at a home in Olive Hill, Kentucky, in 1968 while in the presence of twelve-year-old Roger Callihan.

Roll recalls: "At one point, I was following Roger, walking right behind him, into the kitchen when the kitchen table jumped up in the air, rotated 45 degrees and fell down on the backs of the chairs that stood around it, its four legs off the floor. Roger and the table were in full view when this happened. Later, when I was standing in the doorway between the living room and the children's bedroom, I saw a bottle fly off the dresser and land 4 feet away. It did not slide off and roll into the room, but was clearly airborne. When this took place, Roger was in my peripheral vision on my right in the living room, walking away. His sister was standing slightly behind me on my left. There was no one else in the room. I could discover no way in which the event could have been faked."

Altogether, Roll counted ten similar incidents while he and/or Stump were present and keeping an eye on Roger. "It is the only case I know of where two parapsychologists saw the beginning stages of movements of several objects," Roll said. (See Chapter 20.)

This book is filled with similar stories and eyewitness accounts. Most scientists will not accept eyewitness accounts or anecdotal evidence as proof that poltergeists exist. And, of course, why should they? People sometimes can be fooled or can hallucinate.

Unfortunately, it is very hard to prove that recurrent spontaneous psychokinesis (RSPK) and poltergeists are real, says a respected scientist, Professor Robert Jahn, dean emeritus of the School of Engineering and Applied Sciences at Princeton University, who believes he has proven in laboratory experiments that psychokinesis exists, at least on a small scale. (See Chapter 22).

Prof. Jahn says: "The [poltergeist] cases are so rare and happen under such awkward circumstances, it is hard to set up research to investigate them. There's no doubt, however, that they do exist. William Roll has investigated them and I trust his work. The effects seen in his cases are substantial. You can't dismiss it."

TESTING THE POLTERGEIST AGENTS

On a more scientific basis, some youths suspected as being the center or "agent" of poltergeist activity have been tested under scientific conditions at laboratories, but the results have not been spectacular or even conclusive. However, perhaps the laboratory is the wrong place to test a person. Most poltergeist incidents are reported in homes, possibly because of family tension, and removing the poltergeist "agent" from the home may dissipate the unusual energy needed for such a paranormal event (see the following chapter). Or in some cases, perhaps the unusual energy has run its course by the time the agent is sent off for testing.

In the Miami warehouse case, William Roll persuaded shipping clerk Julio Vasquez to go with him to a psychical research foundation in Durham, North Carolina. Under controlled conditions, researchers say they saw a bottle fall off a table while Vasquez was nearby and, in another instance, a vase allegedly move while he was standing with researchers. He was also tested with a dice-throwing machine and apparently showed better-than-chance averages, Roll said.

Otherwise, poltergeist events are "the most elusive and problematic to access for controlled research, despite their severe anomalous effects," Jahn said.

As mentioned earlier, Prof. Jahn believes that he and his colleagues at the Princeton Anomalies Research (PEAR) Laboratory (www.princeton.edu/~pear/) have produced good experimental data to support the existence of PK, or mind over matter. They say that some people have been able to influence the movement of small balls and pendulums by using their minds.

Possibly the most compelling evidence for psychokinesis was Nina Kulagina of Russia, who was also given the pseudonym Nelya Mikhailova by the government of the Soviet Union during the Cold War in the 1950s and 1960s because they believed she possessed a new and powerful mental force. Initially, poltergeist activity was reported around her in her apartment—objects moved and lights flickered on and off.

Then, for three decades, respected Soviet scientists, including two Nobel laureates, tested her—often in closely controlled laboratory conditions—and they claimed that she could move things by concentrating with her mind. Kulagina was sometimes put into a cage to prevent trickery or she was forced to move things placed in a Plexiglas cube while video cameras recorded everything. No one ever caught her cheating.

The chairman of theoretical physics at Moscow University, Dr. Ya. Terletsky, said that Kulagina "displays a new and unknown form of energy."

In Poland in 1985, a biophysicist, a metallurgist, a psychologist, and other scientists studied fifteen-year-old Joasia Gajewski, who two years earlier was reportedly at the center of poltergeist activity in her home, which was witnessed by police Sergeant Tadeusz Slowik. In the laboratory tests, the scientists said they saw an armchair start to move with Joasia sitting in it, cross-legged. The chair continued to move when she got out of it, they said, and it took a sharp turn in the air and rotated. Three of them reportedly could not hold the chair down.

PHOTOS AND VIDEOS

There is not a lot of poltergeist evidence in videos and photographs, partly because the events are so unpredictable and partly because those who try to record the events say they often have mysterious electrical problems while trying to document the cases. Electrical malfunctions and power failures are said to be common in poltergeist cases.

However, parapsychologist Dr. Hans Bender said he got videotapes of pictures rotating on the walls after nineteen-year-old Annemarie Schneider had breezed into an office in 1967 in Bavaria. He also got a photograph of a swaying lamp, which is reproduced in the book *Poltergeists* by A.D. Cornell and Alan Gauld. Over a period of several weeks, many electrical disturbances were reported, mostly revolving around Schneider.

In 1955, photographer Gerrard Lestienne of the newspaper *Samedi Soir*. snapped a stunning picture of what appears to be several household items swirling in the air in the kitchen of the Costa family in the French village of St. Jean-de-Maurienne on the France–Italy border. Lestienne and reporter Michel Agallet were sent to the home on reports of a poltergeist. At first, they say they examined the home without finding any evidence of a poltergeist, but after about ninety minutes, various pots and cutlery started floating around the kitchen under their own power. The photographer said he saw the objects "slide from their places, make a semi-circle in the air and fall in different locations." This occurred over a prolonged period of time, he added.

In Lestienne's photo, which can be seen on the Internet at www.ufopsi.com/ufopsigallery/g-poltergeists.html, the woman of the house, Madame Teresa Costa, is looking concerned, while protecting her baby in a blanket and watching a saucepan, a pot lid, a pair of scissors, and what seems to be a box of matches float in the air. The photograph shows either an elaborate hoax or a true poltergeist event.

Perhaps the most famous poltergeist photograph was taken on March 5, 1984, in a home in Columbus, Ohio. After several weeks of reported incidents, photographer Fred Shannon of the *Columbus Dispatch* took a series of shots of a telephone moving across the lap of fourteen-year-old Tina Resch, who had been suspected of making many objects move or break in the home, either by trickery or by using her mind. One of the photos, which appeared on the front page of the *Dispatch* the following day and has subsequently been reproduced in periodicals around the world, shows the Princess phone in flight, either by sleight of hand or recurrent spontaneous psychokinesis.

Several witnesses said no one touched the phone before it went flying. "[Tina] wasn't touching anything," a friend of her mother, Joyce Beaumont, said. "She was sitting there with her arms crossed."

Shannon, who was sitting on a couch nearby, said he saw the phone fly about seven different times. "Each time the receiver flew like a projectile, rapidly and with great force," Shannon said. Several people in the room, including Shannon and *Dispatch* reporter Mike Harden, said they didn't think Tina could have picked up the phone and tossed it so many times without them seeing her do it. Said Harden, "I was seated across the room facing Tina...I saw [the phone] in motion without it being aided in any way on her part. It moved on a level trajectory from Tina's left to right."

A short time later, two friends of the Resch family from the Franklin County Children's Services, Kathy Goeff and Lee Arnold, said they saw the phone jump again and fly into a nearby loveseat. Arnold said she was watching Tina and believed it was not possible for the girl to have tossed the phone.

Also that day, Shannon took a picture that reportedly shows a loveseat moving toward Resch. Several witnesses in the room said that as Tina sat on the side of a reclining chair, a loveseat about 4 feet away moved approximately 18 inches out from a wall. Shannon managed to take two pictures, one showing Tina looking stunned and appearing to brace herself for the loveseat moving toward her and a second showing her seemingly losing her balance and ready to fall backwards into the recliner. "I saw this with my own eyes," Shannon said. (For reported evidence of psychokinesis, see Chapter 22.)

CHAPTER 2

THE THEORIES

"There is no mystery greater than that posed by the poltergeist. The noisy ghosts of folklore and legend represent some of the most complex phenomena known to science."

—LATE PARAPSYCHOLOGIST D. SCOTT ROGO

We have seen in the previous chapter that there are enough credible eyewitness accounts to suspect that poltergeist activity may exist, however rare it may be. If it does exist, what is behind it? How could objects possibly move without being touched by human hands?

Many skeptics and scientists do not understand how it is possible to move things with the mind, which is called psychokinesis (PK) or, in poltergeist cases, recurrent spontaneous psychokinesis (RSPK). Leading this charge are Paul Kurtz, a professor of philosophy at the State University of New York at Buffalo, and professional magician James (The Amazing) Randi, who are leading members of the Committee for the Scientific Investigation of Claims of the Paranormal (www.csicop.org). The organization's magazine, published six times a year, is the *Skeptical Inquirer*.

Randi, who offers $1 million if anyone can prove the existence of such paranormal events, says that if people can make things move off the ground with their minds, it would amount to "a repeal of the basic laws of physics." But perhaps there are forces in the universe and inside the complex human brain that we still do not understand or have not been able to identify or document.

Certainly, we are discovering things all the time that we once thought were highly improbably. Demonstrations of the first phonograph of Thomas Edison were laughed at by some early scientists, who thought it was a cheap ventriloquist's trick. Other groundbreakers were ridiculed, such as French chemist Louis Pasteur. Even the famous British mathematician Lord Kelvin once said that X-rays would prove to be a hoax and that air flight was impossible. And, of course, Albert Einstein's general theory of relativity was scoffed at by leading scientists of his day (it has now been proven).

"Science, then, is not a set of immutable truths, but rather a method of inquiry," writes investigator reporter Michael Schmicker in his 2002 book *Best Evidence*. "Scientific theories and hypothesis change as new evidence appears to challenge existing views of reality, as it always does."

American parapsychologist William Roll disagrees with Randi's theory about the laws of physics. "Physics does not say that objects cannot be affected without tangible contact — the moon revolves around the earth and magnets attract pieces of iron — recurrent spontaneous psychokinesis requires an extension of the laws of physics, not their repeal."

Of course, many poltergeist cases turn out to come from traditional causes or hoaxes. (See Chapter 4.) But there seems to be a small number of cases that defy explanation, reported throughout history in every country while exhibiting similar characteristics — mysterious loud noises and movement of objects and furniture, usually happening in the presence of a young person, even though that person is closely watched by others and is cleared of tomfoolery.

While these genuine cases seem to be rare, there is no way of estimating their number because often they are not reported or documented. "I expect it's happening every day. It certainly isn't a frequent occurrence, though," Roll says. "Reporting of the occurrences is rare because people tend to think they are possessed or they are afraid of being accused of being crazy. So you don't get people coming forward."

According to Stephen Mera, founder of Manchester's Association of Paranormal Investigators and Training (MAPIT), located in Manchester, England, only about 12 percent of poltergeist cases are investigated by parapsychologists. One reason these cases are hard to investigate, or even to document, is that they usually do not last long, generally from one week to several months, although some have lasted more than a year.

If we are to believe that there are such things as poltergeists, how do we get past the basic questions of how things move under their own power, or how somebody moves something without touching it, particularly when we hear incredible reports of chairs rising into the air and glasses flying through a kitchen?

Even the most ardent parapsychologists don't profess to have proof of mind over matter on such a large scale, nor can they explain it. However, there are many theories and much speculation. One theory is that agents have unusual brains, with an ability to tap into outside energy sources, perhaps tension in a home or an electrical power source.

William Roll, who has likely spent more time than anyone studying poltergeists in recent times, believes that some people unconsciously unleash a rare and mysterious force to interfere with gravity. Some people call this the zero point theory. According to Roll, there is a brief suspension of gravity during the actual movement or levitation of objects. "It's still just speculation," he said in 2005. "But I think something interferes with inertia and gravity, allowing objects to gravitate. Scientists have found an electromagnetic field that fills the universe, but it's hard to detect. But it is detected in experiments. It's called zero point energy and it interacts with gravity and inertia. The theory in cases of RSPK is the weak electromagnetic signals from the brain affect this field. It's temporary and it cancels gravity and inertia."

In this unproven theory, the person who has the mysterious energy — the poltergeist agent — causes the zero point energy to cohere and thereby loosen the hold on gravity and inertia that ordinary keeps things grounded, according to Dr. Harold Puthoff, director of the Institute for Advanced Studies in Austin, Texas, who conducts theoretical studies in gravitation, energy generation, and space propulsion.

Puthoff says that inertia is the effect that causes stationary objects to remain at rest and moving objects to remain in motion: "If you stand on a train at a station and it leaves with a jerk, inertia may cause you to topple backwards, and lurch forward if the train suddenly stops." It is thought that inertia is due to pressure from the zero point energy.

Poltergeist agents may have something unusual about their brain, which causes this temporary suspension of gravity, Roll and others suggest. In ninety-two poltergeist cases, Roll found that four agents were diagnosed as epileptic. That's higher than the world average of 0.5 percent of people who have epilepsy.

After studying Roll's work, another parapsychologist, Andrew Green of London, agreed that some of the agents suffered from front temporal lobe epilepsy, a brain disorder in which people can suffer blackouts lasting from one minute to half an hour. During these blackouts, an unknown power of the mind may be released that can cause objects to move, Roll and Green said.

Green also suspects that a higher than average number of poltergeist agents suffer from schizophrenia, which may also lead to unusual mental powers. In 1956, Green investigated the case of a fifteen-year-old girl in London, Shirley Hitching, who was said to cause loud rapping noises with her mind. She had been diagnosed as schizophrenic.

It is possible that some agents suffer a type of partial seizure in which their brains are subject to sudden electromagnetic discharges and thus interfere with gravity and stationary objects, Roll said. (In the next chapter, we will examine the possibility that electricity within the brain or body, as well as electric fields, may influence poltergeist activity.) Other agents are said to be susceptible to hysteria, phobias, and high anxiety.

"TELEKINETIC TEMPER TANTRUMS"

These days, most parapsychologists believe that poltergeists are *haunted people*, usually young people of above-average intelligence. Most often the phenomena happen in the agent's home, but if he or she leaves the home, it sometimes follows the agent.

"Research indicates that poltergeists are not caused by spirits or demons, but are creations released by the human mind," the late parapsychologist and author Scott Rogo said. "Psychological research indicates that poltergeists focus on unhappy families who tend to repress and sublimate massive amounts of their inner aggressions and anger. This anger tends to build within the unconscious mind of one of the family members until it explodes outward in the form of the poltergeist. This theory, called the 'projected repression hypothesis,' is the standard accepted explanation of the poltergeist and has been long honored by parapsychologists. But is it the whole answer?" Rogo said.

Rogo, Roll, and others say they've found trends in their investigations. They have even come up with a psychological profile — typically the agent is an adolescent with a low tolerance for frustration, repressing feelings of aggression, and hostility. However, Andrew Green says he knows of poltergeist cases involving people from three to forty years old, and usually they have suffered some sort of mental trauma.

In fact, in many (if not most) poltergeist cases, there seems to be a buildup of stress, fear, frustration, or anger in a household and/or in the poltergeist agent. Often these emotional issues are said to be unresolved. There is a theory for this called repressed psychokinetic energy, which was put forward in the early part of the twentieth century. Prior to that, agents were thought to be possessed by demons or attacked by ghosts.

"Agents can be people who typically have no method of dealing with the stress on any normal level, so the subconscious takes advantage of the psychokinetic ability to blow off steam," says California parapsychologist Lloyd Auerbach. "You can think of a poltergeist scenario as a type of telekinetic temper tantrum." This can even occur with adults, Auerbach said. "If a husband doesn't want his wife to work, instead of asking her to stay home with a new baby, kitchen appliances may act strangely when the subject is brought up in discussion. Water bursts may be representative of pent-up guilt."

Some poltergeist cases may be mass delusions or hallucinations by several people in a stressed-out household, according to Allentown, Pennsylvania, psychologist Robert Gordon. He believes a type of hysteria may take over, similar to that prevalent in the Salem witch trials.

A Hungarian-American psychic investigator, Nandor Fodor, said that repression of creativity can on rare occasions lead to paranormal events.

In the house of retired firefighter Edgar Jones in Baltimore, Maryland, in 1960, Jones's seventeen-year-old grandson, Ted Pauls, was suspected of causing soda bottles to burst from within, piles of firewood to explode, pictures to fall, and windows to break by subconsciously willing them to do so with his mind. At one point, while the whole family watched, a ceramic flower pot reportedly rose from a shelf and crashed through a window and a sugar bowl floated up to an overhead ceiling light and dumped its contents all over a table. Fodor investigated and suspected that the shy, brooding Ted, who had dropped out of high school because he was bored, was a brilliant, frustrated writer with no outlet for his talents. And he apparently felt he was not getting enough attention from others. "He had created a psychic disassociation," Fodor speculated. "The human body is capable of releasing energy in a matter similar to atomic bombardments as this force was apparently able to enter soda bottles that had not been uncapped and to burst them from within." (See Chapter 19.)

Hate seems a trigger for some agents. In the 1980s in Bournemouth, England, a house was plagued for years by the mysterious breaking of windows and the upturning of paint cans. Parapsychologist Mary Rose Barrington suspected it was caused subconsciously by a young man who lived with his cousin and his aunt, both of whom he apparently hated. The incidents stopped when he left the house. Said Barrington, "If this attribution is well founded, it certainly broadens the scope of poltergeist investigation by adding the routine question, 'And is there anyone who hates you?'" (Of course, hatred and hostility can be shown in physical ways, as well. In fact, it's possible that poltergeist agents directing hostility could do it in psychokinetic ways and the good, old-fashioned way — by throwing things around.)

According to Rogo, the poltergeist agent often focuses his or her energies toward authority figures, such as parents or employers, "There is an abnormally strong use of such defenses as repression, sublimation, and denial in order to deal with frustrations. They push this strong underlying anger out of the conscious mind and into the mysterious realms of the unconscious... when the [agent] can no longer control his intense anger, the psychokinesis is unleashed as a safety valve and as [a] means of venting the pent-up frustration." In this way, the child can also maintain a conscious innocence about the events, Rogo and others believe.

And so it's possible that the poltergeist agent may not even realize he or she is causing a disturbance. "The puzzling thing is how it's possible for someone to be the cause of destructive activities and yet be unaware that he or she is responsible," said Stephen Mera.

But secretly, they may be pleased with the irritation or damage it is causing in a home or to people, said Roll, who studied written reports of 116 suspected poltergeist cases spanning four centuries and more than 100 countries.

OUR AMAZING FEAR ENERGY

Perhaps poltergeist activity is not black magic but stress magic. Perhaps PK or RSPK are rare weapons (or byproducts) of the magnificent fight-or-flight system, which is hardwired into our bodies and has helped our species survive on a harsh planet for hundreds of thousands of years.

I have written four books on fear and fight-or-flight. The more I study our fear reaction, the more I realize how little we understand it, and what amazing powers we all possess, many of them probably still untapped.

When you feel afraid or angry, your body goes through chemical changes that effectively turn you briefly into a different person and give you substantial new powers. This occurs through your sympathetic nervous system, or what I call the emergency fear system.

Here are some of the changes (which may or may not occur, depending on the severity of the threat, or what you perceive as a threat):

- Your heart goes from pumping 1 gallon of blood per minute to 5 gallons per minute.
- Pupils dilate for maximum visual perception.
- Arteries constrict for maximum pressure to pump blood to the heart and other muscles.
- Blood is rerouted away from skin and internal organs toward the brain and skeletal muscles. Your muscles tense and you feel stronger.
- Breathing becomes more rapid and nostrils flare, causing an increased supply of air.
- Pain threshold increases.
- Your concentration can sharpen to the point that a phenomenon known as *tachypsychia* (Greek for "speed of the mind") occurs and all the action in front of you seems to happen in slow motion, allowing you to increase your ability to deal with a threat.

At its peak, the emergency fear system produces a big-bang response known as fight-or-flight as potent hormones — such as adrenaline, dopamine, testosterone, and endorphin — come to your aid. For example, occasionally people perform superhuman feats of strength to rescue relatives; in Montana's Glacier Park, 5-foot-3-inch grandmother Lorraine Lengkeek used binoculars to beat off a 500-pound grizzly bear that was mauling her husband.

At times, this fear energy produces altered states of consciousness. For example, tachypsychia is reported by many police officers and soldiers when they are faced with death.

Corporal Ron Thompson reported reaching a twilight zone of superior focus while he was in a gun battle with a suspect in 1984 in Woodstock, Ontario. He recalled: "A gray mantle, like a blanket, was rolled down. Suddenly everything was gone — the street, the traffic, the moon, my partner. All that was left was the gunman and me. His head was transformed into a white oval egg. Very sharp. I shot him between the eyes... and killed him."

Altered states are also reported in less-threatening circumstances. Barbara Brown, a brain and behavior researcher, recalls giving an important speech at the University of California at Los Angeles: "As I began to speak, my consciousness split completely. My perceptions and conscious sensations found themselves in a pastoral image, where I was resting on a green lawn under a tree, calm and totally relaxed. I was faintly aware that something related to me was on a platform and was speaking with words and thoughts, as if inspired. The separate 'I' had no idea what the other 'I' was talking about, far away." The audience said it was a remarkable speech.

This sounds similar to what may be another fight-or-flight symptom, the out-of-body experience, in which people say they saw themselves floating above their bodies to watch surgeons operate on them.

As an athlete and a journalist writing to deadline, I have had similar experiences with being able to expand time, or at least expand my ability to deal with time constraints. During basketball games in the 1990s, I summoned an altered state to produce perfect shooting performances. While shooting, I saw (in a sort of split-screen) a version of the ball leave my hand about one-quarter of a second before it actually did, then I saw the real ball. And then I saw the split-screen ball enter the basket shortly before it actually did. Some athletes call this a part of being in the zone.

When I queried some biochemists and psychologists about this afterward, they suggested I had had a type of mini seizure.

I have been in this zone about forty times in my life and every time it was only when I trusted myself and did things unconsciously.

What does all this have to do with RSPK or PK? I'm not sure, but I suspect both are rare symptoms of fear energy and the fight-or-flight system. In most of the poltergeist cases in this book, the poltergeist agent is suffering from stress, anger, fear, or trauma. It follows that the person's sympathetic nervous system, and perhaps fight-or-flight, would kick in. Physical examinations of some poltergeist agents often show high levels of adrenaline and noradrenaline in their nervous systems, which are traditional fight-or-flight hormones.

If the agent is showing unconscious hostility toward someone in the home, as parapsychologists speculate, then the agent's fear energy would be directed at that person.

If the agent has PK powers, then it might manifest itself in moving objects.

In the Columbus, Ohio, case, fourteen-year-old Tina Resch was said to move things with her mind because she was frustrated with her home life. "It usually happens when I'm really mad," Tina said.

British parapsychologist and author John Spencer suspects there is a connection between fight-or-flight and RSPK. When people are in their normal mode, they cannot do superhuman things physically or mentally, he said. But when they are really fearful or angry, "when their unconscious and sometimes irrational mind takes over, it appears to be able to call on more extreme resources than otherwise. There are accounts of parents performing incredible feats of strength, physically lifting objects in order to rescue or safeguard their children, when, in normal conditions, they would not be able to show such extreme strength."

Spencer believes this may also be true of mental strength. "Perhaps RSPK is generated by a part of the brain beyond conscious or rational control, where much greater potential lurks. Indeed, maybe those parents were being assisted by some form of PK or RSPK when they acted in those extreme situations."

But how could fear energy project itself outside the body? That, of course, is unproven, and yet great athletes and performers have shown they use their mind and their willpower to influence physical results, such as golfer Tiger Woods and former basketball great Michael Jordan, who have used controlled anger to vault themselves into the "zone." In 1993, an amateur bowler, Troy Ockerman, raised his adrenaline levels through heavy metal music and anger at his opponent and got his fear energy working to the point that he bowled three consecutive perfect games in Corunna, Michigan.

Perhaps PK and RSPK are anomalies that have been lost in our evolution as human beings, or perhaps they are yet to be discovered or developed.

THE PUBERTY ANGLE

A popular theory about poltergeist agents is that they are youths just entering or going through puberty, which somehow triggers an unknown energy force and perhaps transformations in brain chemistry. Or perhaps it is released by suppression of sexual energy.

Certainly, in a general sense, sex can be a powerful force and many superachievers say they redirect their sexual energy into creative production. The complex, multifaceted period of puberty usually begins in girls between ten and eleven and in boys between eleven and twelve. The children go through a series of profound psychological, emotional, and physical changes. And if they live in a stressful home during that time, it could alter their behavior or brain chemistry, change the way they view themselves and others, and perhaps make them more aggressive.

In the Enfield case in London in 1977, researcher Guy Lyon Playfair traced the problems of the poltergeist agent, said to be eleven-year-old Janet Hodgson, partly to the fact she was entering puberty. Playfair believed this was related to her pineal gland. Located at the center of the brain, the gland is responsible for controlling the release of sexual hormones. Playfair believes that during puberty the gland can secrete a type of creative energy. "When a child suddenly acquires this new force, there is a need for an outlet. If this outlet is lacking, the energy will be available for marauding entities (a poltergeist force) to steal and put to their own purposes." Playfair compares this energy to what he calls psychic football. "Along come spirits who do what any group of schoolboys would do — they go and kick it around, smashing windows and generally creating havoc." And yet, Playfair admits there are many things we do not know about puberty, never mind RSPK.

In 1961 in Sauchie, Scotland, eleven-year-old Virginia Campbell caused paranormal actions that may have been related to her twenty-eight-day "quasi-menstrual cycle, occurring as a result of exceptionally rapid pubescence," according to Dr. A.R.G. Owen, a fellow at Trinity College in Cambridge, England.

Many other researchers believe there is a link between puberty and sex and possible rare cases of RSPK.

Sometimes sexual trauma may be a factor. In the Amherst case in the nineteenth century, Esther Cox was said to have been sexually threatened by a gun-toting man. And Tina Resch said she had been sexually assaulted by a relative (whose name does not appear in this book) prior to the reported RSPK events in her home.

THE DWINDLING SPIRITS THEORY

Some parapsychologists, including psychiatrist Dr. Ian Stevenson, a professor at the University of Virginia, still believe there is a link between spirits of the dead and poltergeist activity, and they sometimes suggest to victimized families that a séance be held to "cleanse" a home. Others believe that a poltergeist agent is possessed by a spirit or a demon and they may suggest a type of exorcism to try to bring the person back to himself or herself.

Some people find it easier to believe in RSPK as an unexplained energy force than to believe in ghosts because with the latter, one must consider that there is life after death.

Parapsychologist Lloyd Auerbach suggests that rare instances of apparitions in poltergeist cases are due to a "projection of stress, guilt, anger, fear or frustration from the subconscious."

In Gravesend, England, in 1985, the Tom Johnson family told Andrew Green that their son was seeing the ghost of a monk, which seemed connected to strange sounds in their house, movement of small objects, and electrical malfunctions. Green concluded that the boy was the subject of RSPK because he felt neglected and unloved.

There are a handful of cases in this book in which people involved in so-called poltergeist cases say they see an apparition. That does not necessarily mean that there is life after death, but possibly that the people are hallucinating. In fact, hallucinations of ghosts are relatively common in people undergoing trauma. Michael Persinger, a neuroscientist at Laurentian University in Sudbury, Ontario, has done studies that show many people who claim they see ghosts are activating a part of their brain's fight-or-flight system in order to deal with a situation that they cannot fathom, such as the death of a loved one. (See Chapter 4.)

William Roll does not know of any case in which a spirit was responsible for a poltergeist incident. "We should close our minds to that possibility, but they always seem to occur around a living person," he said.

In England, poltergeist investigations are being hampered by researchers and parapsychologists who too quickly jump to the conclusion that spirits are responsible, according to Wayne Pickrell, investigations coordinator for the Black Country Paranormal Society. "In all my years of being interested in the paranormal, I have never seen so much rubbish flying about," he said in 2004. "We dealt with some people having poltergeist activity. Psychics had been in and exorcised the spirit. To add insult to injury, they charged the poor family for their services. And guess what? The spirit was back the next night. Yes, I do believe in ghosts, but sometimes other more plausible explanations are found."

In the end, despite all the above theories and speculations, many parapsychologists and mainstream scientists often throw up their hands in dismay when asked to pinpoint the cause of poltergeist activity. As he continues to investigate the subject into his eighties, parapsychologist Maurice Grosse says he's convinced that society is far from understanding the poltergeist. "There are many theories, and I've heard them all," he said in 2005. "Nobody has come up with a convincing theory. All this talk about electrical disturbances behind poltergeists... we just don't understand [it] yet. I think it's a type of mind force, perhaps with something else attached to it. It's an intriguing phenomena."

TRAUMA VICTIMS

People who have suffered extreme trauma may be at risk for paranormal events.

Psychologist Joel L. Whitton, professor of psychiatry at the University of Toronto Medical School, believes that some cases may have a link to post-traumatic stress disorder. He says the agent may unconsciously recreate stressful situations from infancy, explaining why there is a large number of poltergeist cases involving bottles, food, and eating utensils, all of which might relate to the powerful oral needs of infants.

In 1961 in the Felix Fuld Housing Project in Newark, New Jersey, Mabelle Clark shared an apartment with her thirteen-year-old grandson Ernest Rivers. It was said that over a two-week period, cups, bowls, and ashtrays sailed across the small apartment. Clark apparently tried to keep it secret because she had lived in the home for twenty years and didn't want to be evicted, but the neighbors complained and housing officials investigated.

The officials and several other people reportedly saw a string of unexplained events, including a heavy steam iron floating from a linen closet into a bedroom.

A team of parapsychologists investigated and the incidents stopped when Ernest was removed from the building. It turned out he was highly stressed after his mother was murdered by his abusive prizefighter father five years earlier. And just before the phenomena began, the boy's mother had escaped from a women's reformatory.

CHAPTER 3

THE ELECTRICAL CONNECTION

"...we can now enter realms of real scientific possibilities...some very strange doors begin to open."

—ALBERT BUDDEN, AN INVESTIGATOR SPECIALIZING IN THE SCIENTIFIC STUDY OF THE PARANORMAL AS WELL AS ELECTROMAGNETICS AND HEALTH

In the previous chapter, we saw that some parapsychologists believe that poltergeist agents may have unusual brains that are subject to sudden electromagnetic discharges. These discharges may somehow interact with physical energies, including electromagnetic energy, to set off poltergeist activity, also known as recurrent spontaneous psychokinesis.

Let us now examine an overall electrical theory a little further and the possibility that throughout the human brain and body, electricity could spark RSPK. This theory was suspected as early as the mid-1800s.

In 1846 in La Perriere, France, a fourteen-year-old peasant girl, Angelique Cottin, was weaving gloves on an oak loom with other girls when the loom suddenly began to shake. Many witnesses said the loom shook only when Cottin was near it, although she was not touching it. After she was checked by a minister and a doctor, her effect on things accelerated and it was reported that a 60-pound chair rose from the floor in her presence, a bed rocked, and she gave people electric shocks.

When doctors examined her, they established that her heart rate rose to 120 beats a minute during the mysterious activity, she sometimes suffered convulsions, and she ran away from the scene, quite frightened. Observers noted that she had more effect on objects around her when she was standing on bare earth and less when she stood on a carpet or waxed cloth. Her powers were said to be intermittent and sometimes would be dormant for several days.

She was tested at an observatory in Paris by a group of scientists appointed by the Academy of Sciences, and they said that her powers were genuine and perhaps somehow related to the electrical makeup of her body.

(In general terms, there is electricity in the beat of the human heart and electrical signals also move along your nerve cells. When you walk across a carpet, your body can pick up or rub off extra electrons that slightly change your body's electrical potential. Then, when you touch a doorknob, the small electrical shock you get is the electrons leaving your body.)

A respected physicist, Dr. Francois Arago, published a report in the *Journal des Debats* (February 1846) in which he called Angelique's power "a kind of electromagnetism." He said the force seemed to be coming more from the left side of her body, which was warmer than the right. She was also affected by unusual movements and shakings and her power was more prevalent from 7 p.m. to 9 p.m. A pen or light object on a table would fly off when Angelique moved her left hand toward it. On one occasion, two strong men tried to hold down a chair, but when she came near it, it reportedly shattered in their hands.

Arago said the girl was very sensitive to magnets. Needles reportedly swung quickly when her arm was near it, but not touching it, and she often got a strong shock when she approached the north pole of a magnet.

Electricity (bodily or otherwise) seemed to be involved in the case of the celebrated Nina Kulagina (pseudonym Nelya Mikhailova) during the 1950s, 1960s, and 1970s in the Soviet Union. It was said that as a young woman, Kulagina was the center of poltergeist activity in her apartment. She was tested for thirty years by top Soviet scientists, who said she often was able to move things with her mind in laboratory conditions through sheer focus.

A military physiologist, Dr. Genady Sergeyev, studied the electrical potentials in her brain, which, he said, had strong voltages and could expose undeveloped photos in a sealed envelope. In addition, he said that the usual force field around Nina was ten times weaker than the magnetic field of the earth.

Dr. Sergeyev added that Nina's abilities seemed to diminish during stormy weather.

The chairman of theoretical physics at Moscow University, Dr. Ya. Terletsky, said that Kulagina "displays a new and unknown form of energy." With this focused energy, scientists said, she was able to move things as her pulse rate soared to about 240 beats per minute at the peak of the psychokinesis.

Another unusual girl was thirteen-year-old Joasia Gajewski of Poland (see the previous chapter and also Chapter 18), who was said to cause objects to move in her home and during laboratory tests. Her family and friends said she was sometimes highly charged with static electricity and was described as "crackling" with sounds similar to finger snapping. During extensive medical tests, Gajewski developed high static electrical charges on her body that would not dissipate when she was grounded.

Unusual noises were also heard coming from an eleven-year-old girl in Scotland in 1960. Strange movements of furniture were reported at home and school around Virginia Campbell. When a physician, Dr. William Logan, examined Virginia, he reported noises coming from her, similar to sounds heard during a magnetic resonance imaging (MRI) scan. (See Chapter 16.)

Parapsychologists are not sure whether such a poltergeist agent generates internal energy to make objects move or whether the person's energy interacts with outside sources.

The late German paranormal researcher Hans Bender, who investigated many poltergeist cases, developed a theory that in some or many instances, poltergeist agents tap into alternate sources of energy, such as electrical supplies. He said it doesn't seem possible for such agents to generate the power they need to move heavy furniture, so they somehow, perhaps without knowing they are doing it, "organize energy sources rather than project their own energy."

Controversial Uri Geller, a psychic from Israel, whose claim to fame was bending spoons with his mind, said he got his unusual powers from a strong electric shock. Geller said that when he was five years old, he saw a blue spark coming out of his mother's sewing machine and when he tried to touch it, he received a severe shock and was knocked off his feet. He said that after that, he was able to read his mother's mind and could make the hands speed up on a watch by focusing on it.

In 1972 at the Stanford Research Institute in California, Geller impressed scientists by correctly identifying numbers hidden from him, although tests to prove his metal-bending abilities were inconclusive.

Another psychic, Matthew Manning of Cambridge, England, was tested in 1972 in Toronto at the age of seventeen. Measurements of his brain waves while he was reportedly bending cutlery suggested that he produced unusual patterns of electrical energy from his limbic system. As a child, Manning was purportedly the agent for poltergeist activity in his home.

MAGNETIC FIELDS

One theory for poltergeist activity is that it sometimes occurs on or near unusual magnetic fields.

"Magnetic field strengths of some locations of unexplained phenomena are significantly different from magnetic field strengths in other areas," says Andrew Nichols of the American Institute of Parapsychology and City College in Gainesville, Florida.

In 1996, Nichols investigated movement of objects, rapping noises, and bizarre appearances of water in a home in Jacksonville, Florida. Tension between an eleven-year-old girl and her grandmother was cited as one of the reasons for the disturbances, but also electrical interferences may have come into play. High-voltage transmission towers were located near the family home and a naval air station was close by with its radar transmitters and other high-tech equipment. Nichols suspected this electrical interference may have affected the eleven-year-old girl, whose brain may have been wired in an unusual manner.

Mysterious outpourings of water were reported in another case in a home in Rochdale, England, in 1995. Occurrences, which reportedly included flying objects, seemed to follow a thirty-three-year-old woman. (See Chapter 17.) Investigators from the North West Water Laboratories said that there were significant differences in samples of water, which mysteriously appeared from the ceiling, and water from the bathroom tap. Calcium, sodium, and chloride percentages were higher in the "paranormal" water. And the electrical content of the two samples also differed — the tap water had a conductivity of 181, compared to 1,323 for the mysterious water.

In the end, some parapsychologists believe, energies from poltergeist agents and/or from outside sources create a zero point energy, which temporarily suspends gravity. People suspected as agents for the poltergeist activity may have something unusual about their brains, which causes this temporary suspension of gravity, William Roll and others suggest. "The theory in cases of RSPK is, the weak electromagnetic signals from the brain affect this field," Roll said. "It's temporary and it cancels gravity and inertia."

The idea of gravity being temporarily suspended on earth is not a new one. World powers have reportedly been investigating the possibility for many years, beginning with the Nazis in the Second World War, with hopes of using such a force for lightning-fast aircraft and weapons.

Many, if not most, scientists are skeptical that anti-gravity can be achieved. However, if the possibility is realized, the answer might have something to do with electricity; in 1996, a Finnish scientist said he could partially "shield" objects from gravity by using spinning superconductors. For a further look at this subject, read the 2002 book *The Hunt for Zero Point* by Nick Cook, who was editor for ten years of *Jane's Defense Weekly*, the bible of the defense establishment.

THE POLTERGEIST MACHINE

A Canadian electromagnetics pioneer, John Hutchinson, claims to have reached a type of zero point energy during experiments in British Columbia. And with it, many people believe, he created what has been called the poltergeist machine because it reportedly triggers poltergeist-like phenomena.

Hutchinson says he came upon his findings by accident during an experiment. He crammed into a room a variety of devices that emit electromagnetic fields, such as Tesla coils, Van de Graaff generators, RF transmitters, and signal generators. After they had been operating for a while, bizarre things reportedly began to occur: Objects levitated and hovered in the air, or moved about and then fell; fires broke out around the building; a mirror smashed 80 feet away; metal distorted and broke; water spontaneously swirled in containers; lights appeared in the air and then vanished; and metal became white hot, but did not burn surrounding materials.

And yet, just like in poltergeist cases, the phenomena were unpredictable. Hutchinson watched the room for days and nothing would occur, but suddenly coins would fly into the air, water would act strangely, and transformers would blow.

On a video taken in the room, a 19-pound bronze cylinder is seen to rise into the air.

Of course, this machine is not at work in any of the cases in this book, but perhaps electricity and magnetism are important parts of some poltergeist puzzles.

"This certainly does not mean that if we identify poltergeists as electromagnetic in nature, we can all pack up and go home, mystery solved," said Albert Budden, an investigator specializing in the scientific study of the paranormal as well as electromagnetics and health. "In fact, the situation is the reverse as we can now enter realms of real scientific possibilities... some very strange doors begin to open."

Budden speculates that the bodies of some poltergeist agents may act as electrical apparatus to interact in an unknown way with electromagnetic pollution from power lines or transmitters near their homes, thus causing objects to move and household appliances to be disrupted.

These energies could also interact with earth energies (geomagnetic and geoelectric fields) at "hot-spot" locations inadvertently built over fault lines, said Budden, author of several books.

In 2003–2004 in Leawood, Kansas, strange disturbances were occurring in a house — jiggling doorknobs, electrical malfunctions, cold spots, opening and shutting doors, and strange footsteps, according to Kelli Patrick (www.ghost-investigators.com). After an investigation, her group concluded that a girl in the home was just entering puberty. (Some parapsychologists believe that youths entering puberty may have an unusual sexual energy that interacts with other energy to create RSPK.)

In addition, there was an unsettled geomagnetic field around the Kansas home that constantly set off electromagnetic field detectors and gave some people migraine headaches. The occurrences subsided a few months after the girl had entered puberty. "They were a really nice and sane family," Patrick said. "They definitely didn't make anything up."

There are many instances in this book in which household electricity and appliances reportedly worked in weird ways.

In Columbus, Ohio, in 1984, electrical problems followed fourteen-year-old Tina Resch. The numbers on her digital clock radio were said to race without power and numerous malfunctions were reported with a baby monitor, a television, telephones, and a hair dryer in her home. A utility company checked the house, but could not find any problems with the electricity or wiring.

In the Enfield case, there were reports of metal bending, teapots rocking, electrical equipment malfunctioning, and "an entire frame of the gas fire wrenched out of the wall." Investigators at Enfield reported that their magnetometer registered "deflections" as objects moved across a room. But Budden suggested that researchers at the site did not investigate the electromagnetic possibilities thoroughly enough because perhaps it was "not a welcome explanation for the phenomena they witnessed."

In the Virginia Campbell case, it is possible that Virginia caused the events subconsciously through a type of psychokinesis or recurrent spontaneous psychokinesis, several observers noted. At one point, Dr. Logan made a curious finding when he checked Virginia while she was in an agitated state "both physically and emotionally." Despite the agitation, her pulse rate remained normal and quite slow. "I thought this rather unusual, but I can't explain it," Dr. Logan said. "It was as if the subconscious part of her brain was aware that the phenomena was emanating from her and there was nothing to fear, and the irrational side was producing a standard fear response."

In the following chapter, we will see that one respected scientist believes paranormal experiences are actually hallucinations sparked by electromagnetic signals in the brain.

CHAPTER 4

THE FRAUDS: THINGS THAT GO SNEAK IN THE NIGHT

"Well, mate, you don't know my daughter-in-law."
—A LONDON MAN'S EXCUSE FOR SCARING HIS FAMILY OUT OF A HOUSE BY PRETENDING TO BE A POLTERGEIST

Some poltergeists are outright frauds. "Many suspected cases of poltergeists have proved to be no more than the fantasies of distraught minds or the actions of jokers," says British parapsychologist Maurice Grosse, who has investigated many cases over the years, some of them the result of trickery.

In fact, many of the serious paranormal researchers in this book, including Grosse, William Roll, and Tony Cornell, have admitted they have been duped by people, especially youths, from time to time.

Cornell, considered one of England's leading paranormal experts and the author of a book on poltergeists, once caught a cheater with a video camera.

The fisherman, who lived in Kent, England, said that a poltergeist had been cutting him with an invisible razor blade and he showed hundreds of cuts on his body to prove it.

Cornell installed a camera in the man's home and it showed that he always went to the lavatory before the attacks occurred. It also showed a razor blade and a pin fall out of his jacket.

A few months later, the man claimed the poltergeist was setting fires in his house, but by this time, Cornell suspected he was starting the fires himself to get attention because his second wife's children did not like him. Shortly after, the man was convicted of burning down a barn and was jailed for two and a half years.

In another case in London, Cornell became suspicious of an elderly man, whose Victorian house was said to have loud, poltergeist-type noises that had driven away his son, daughter-in-law, and grandchild. After investigating, Cornell discovered the man had rigged an ingenious device in which he created the peculiar noises. At night with his relatives in bed, the man would pull on a wire at the side of a downstairs fireplace, setting off a noisy contraption hidden under floorboards, which consisted of two tin mugs, an iron bar, and a biscuit tin with two wooden balls in it. When the wire was pulled, it started the noises, which became amplified in two upstairs bedrooms.

It turned out his motivation was not to get attention from authorities or the media, but to be rid of his kin. "Well, mate," he told Cornell, "you don't know my daughter-in-law... my wife did not like her, and neither did I, but it was not our right to interfere. Then my wife goes and dies and [my son] says he and [the daughter-in-law] ought to live with me for company and to look after the house for me... I was in the way and she was trying to make it seem that I was funny in the head and ought to be in an old people's home. Well, I knew what to do. She was scared stiff of ghosts."

Skeptic Paul Kurtz says that some people are predisposed to believe in a paranormal explanation and may be easily fooled by a smart trickster. "If the situation is charged with drama and emotion, it is more likely to arouse an affirmative response," he said.

Although many people, including psychic observers, were perhaps more superstitious and gullible in the past, the late Hans Driesch warned of fakes in the early part of the twentieth century. "What human being, however meticulously conscientious, is not liable to be deceived?" said Driesch, an embryologist, professor of philosophy, and president of the Society of Psychical Research in England from 1926 to 1927. "Even the greatest men of science have sometimes made mistakes and fell victims to deception... now in psychical research, in which the subject of the investigation can himself actively contribute to the deception, in which there is not, as in the normal natural sciences, a determined state of affairs itself incapable of active deception, everything is infinitely more difficult."

And, in modern times, there are hoaxes played on the Internet. If you go to http://paranormal.about.com/library/weekly/aa040599.htm?once=true&terms=poltergeist, you will find the "Strange Case of Katrina Landrou." It claims that "a 14-year-old Long Island girl is the focus of mystifying and terrifying poltergeist activity." The story, accompanied by a photo showing a girl being accompanied by a floating loaf of bread over her shoulder, is quite a clever cliché of many poltergeist cases, including rapping on windows, ping-pong balls dropping down a chimney, and Tom Jones's songs coming from inside a toilet, apparently all caused by Katrina in her entry into puberty.

"All I gotta say is, don't get her mad," her brother was quoted as saying. At the end of the article is the punch line — April Fool. It is on the web site of Stephen Wagner ("Your Guide to Paranormal Phenomena"), who isn't afraid to poke fun at himself and his genre from time to time. For other spoofs, check out Wagner's page at http://paranormal.about.com/cs/paranormalezines/a/aa042803.htm.

Apart from an April Fool's joke, why would someone pretend to be a poltergeist? There seems to be lots of reasons, including those from people who are looking for a way to move out of their house, to get someone to relocate them, or to lower property value. As far back as the eighteenth century, fraudulent poltergeist activities were suspected. In Bristol, England, in 1761, it was said that Richard Giles's two daughters were terrorized by a poltergeist. No satisfactory explanation was discovered, but one theory was that it was a hoax, set up to lower the value of the property.

According to a state's attorney, thirteen-year-old Wanet McNeil set fires at her uncle's farm in Macomb, Illinois, in 1948, while posing as a poltergeist because "she was unhappy, didn't like the farm, wanted to see her mother, who was living elsewhere, and most of all she didn't have pretty clothes."

But many members of the local fire department did not believe her confession, claiming to have seen numerous mysterious fires and other unexplained occurrences, which they say Wanet could not have faked.

In recent times, landlords of British council houses have claimed that some tenants have faked poltergeist incidents in order to be moved to a better home.

And then there are good, old-fashioned grudges. In 2005, a Polish woman, who apparently harbored a grudge against her husband's boss, was sentenced to four months in jail for pretending to be a ghost or poltergeist in the boss's castle estate in Innsbruck, Austria.

The forty-two-year-old woman, whose name was not released in court proceedings, allegedly terrorized the boss by slamming doors late at night. She was shown on videotape creating the disturbances.

FIELD DAY FOR SKEPTICS

The skeptics often have a field day when frauds are caught. See, we told you! But should the exposure of a cheat mean that all poltergeist cases are fraudulent? Should we close our minds to paranormal possibilities?

In 2004, I sent an e-mail to the ultimate skeptic of the paranormal and of poltergeists, James Randi. Attached was a synopsis of this book with sample chapters about the St. Catharines case in which numerous police officers swore they saw poltergeist activity involving an eleven-year-old boy. (See Chapters 5 and 6.) One officer said he was flipped onto his behind by an unknown force while watching the boy. I had hoped Randi would read the synopsis and eventually get back to me with his thoughts.

But he replied the same day and I suspect he didn't read my stuff, except for the introduction, which asked him if it was possible the St. Catharines boy was indeed a poltergeist agent. "I dunno," Randi snapped. "I wasn't there, and neither were you. I've heard similar reports of what [alleged spoon-bending psychic Uri] Geller has done — until the stories fell apart under investigation."

I quickly replied to Randi: "Is it possible there is such a thing (however rare) as psychokinesis?"

Seven minutes later, his e-mail came back: "Yes. But there is also the possibility (however unlikely) that Richard Nixon is alive and living in Argentina with Martin Borman..."

According to Randi, it's no coincidence that poltergeist cases almost always revolve around young people. "It's a way of these kids getting attention," he said. "They either move the objects themselves or pretend they have seen them moving."

"If we are to get to the bottom of the poltergeist issue, we cannot let the frauds turn us off and we cannot throw out the cases that seem to be legitimate because of those that are not," says Maurice Grosse.

THE LITTLE DEVIL

In 1993, in the foothills of the Rocky Mountains, I saw something that at the time made me question my beliefs about reality, or at least the laws of physics. At a friend's home in Okotoks, Alberta, I watched a demonstration by Linda, a forty-nine-year-old woman, that defied logic. She sat on the living room floor with a little wooden figure lying face-down on the carpet between her legs. She called it the

Little Devil, a neat wooden toy with hinges connecting its limbs, allowing the arms and legs to move.

Staring down intensely at the Little Devil, Linda waved two sticks above its head over and over again while Elvis Presley music played in the background. Suddenly, and to everyone's amazement in the room, the Little Devil rose off the floor and started dancing to "Jailhouse Rock." He quickly fell down, but was resurrected as Linda waved the sticks harder and harder. The room wasn't that well lit, but I could not see any strings or any way in which she could have faked the crazy dance.

I queried Linda about her skill, but all she said was it was related to focus, the music, and perhaps a small ball necklace around her neck, which she claimed helped her to relieve stress. Linda's ability was well known in her large family and the Little Devil had become something of a legend over the years.

Impressed, I took the Little Devil home with me for a week and, when no one was around, tried to get him to jive to Elvis, but without success. (At this point in my life, I don't consider myself to have psychic abilities.)

A few months later, Linda was at it again, performing at a family party in an auditorium near Edmonton, Alberta. Her many nieces, nephews, and grandchildren gathered around in awe. Santa Claus and the tooth fairy may be fictitious, but the Little Devil was alive! This time, there was better lighting and I snapped a photograph of the wooden doll. When the photo was developed, it showed a fine thread attached to the strings and to Linda's sweater, allowing her deft fingers to give the wooden toy some energy. So much for her psychokinesis.

I said nothing about it to anyone until one of her relatives in the Maritimes confirmed that it was a friendly hoax.

When I mentioned it to Linda's son-in-law, he was quite upset about being duped for so many years.

WHEN THE CIRCUS COMES TO TOWN

We have established that there are many cases of fraud in poltergeist investigations, but there may also be instances of fraud and genuine paranormal activity within the same case.

In at least a half-dozen scenarios in this book, youths who were said to have paranormal powers were either caught cheating at some point or confessed to using trickery. But that does not necessarily mean other occurrences that happened in their presence were phony. Sound confusing? Not really, if you examine human nature.

Let's say a young boy unconsciously uses his mind to move objects. Police, family members, and parapsychologists all testify to the legitimacy of the events because they have been closely watching the boy and rule out trickery. But genuine poltergeist events are fleeting and seemingly difficult to produce, so if his abilities start to wane, he may not want to give up center stage because he has become enamored with all the attention he had been getting. Most children like attention and being stroked by adults, especially if journalists come to their home and publicize it in the newspapers and on television. But if they cannot immediately reproduce the genuine events, the children may resort to cheating to keep the attention on themselves. They may nudge a chair when they think no one is watching or bang on a wall around a corner. Some parapsychologists call this imitative fraud.

In the big picture, let us call this the "When the Circus Comes to Town Syndrome" because, in many of these well-documented cases, that is exactly what happens: the local media sniff out the story and go to a home with their notepads and cameras, and sometimes the national media get involved. Pretty soon, police, neighbors, parapsychologists, and the nosy woman across the street are trampling through the home. It really does become a circus.

In the highly celebrated Enfield case of 1977–1978, many witnesses, including police, reported seeing furniture and toys move on their own power when eleven-year-old Janet Hodgson was present. As the case dragged on and the girl became a mini-celebrity, the voice of an old man started coming out of her mouth. Janet's sister reportedly told a newspaper that she and Janet had played tricks to fool observers in order to keep the case from dying out in the media.

"It's very sad," journalist Ray Alan said. "But these little girls obviously loved all the attention they got when objects were mysteriously moved round the house, and they decided to keep the whole thing going by inventing the voice."

Another investigator said that a video camera had caught Janet attempting to bend spoons and an iron bar and practising levitation by bouncing up and down on her bed. When faced with this evidence, Janet admitting to faking some of the events, but not all of them, because she said she "wanted to see if the investigators would catch [her]. They always did."

"Where children are involved, accusations of trickery flow thick and fast," said parapsychologist Maurice Grosse, who was in charge of the case. He claimed that numerous legitimate paranormal events took place prior to the trickery, "but the real experience cannot be confused with their pranks." (See Chapters 12 through 15.)

A similar situation occurred in the Columbus, Ohio, case of Tina Resch, who witnesses said used her mind to move many objects, including a telephone, but then a video camera caught her cheating when she pulled down a lamp. Resch said she did it to give journalists something to write about after they refused to leave her parents' house after a vigil of more than nine hours.

It is also possible that in some of these cases, the disturbances are both paranormal and traditional; in other words, a youth may take his or her hostility out on family members by moving things with the mind and the body.

William Roll agrees. "It may help us understand the psychological process which results in genuine phenomena if we know that this can also result in ordinary destructive behavior," Roll said. "And vice-versa. It is important to know that destructive impulses in a person can not only find an outlet in ordinary acts of aggression, but also in [psychokinetic] activities.

However, once cheating is discovered, everything that happened prior to that can be called into question. "If a person is once caught cheating, then the further display of his or her powers should be highly suspect," said Paul Kurtz. He suspected that Tina Resch was a con artist who fooled everyone right from the beginning in order to get attention and perhaps because she was jealous of others in the house.

Kurtz believes that Tina cheated several times, although he was never in the Resch house, and that Roll and others were duped because they had a predisposition to believe in a poltergeist. And yet Kurtz left a small window open for the possibility of the paranormal: "Perhaps [Tina] does have these marvelous powers and perhaps it is the skeptics' will to disbelieve that causes them to refuse to accept the testimony of others."

Like James Randi, however, Kurtz tends not to believe in poltergeists. When I asked him in 2004 if poltergeists might actually exist, he said it was "very doubtful."

Apart from the lamp incident, Resch denied cheating in other instances and, indeed, Roll said that she went on to move objects with her mind later under test conditions at his lab in North Carolina.

Confessions have been elicited from youths in some other celebrated poltergeist cases. But not everyone was buying the confessions.

In 1960–1961, on a farm near Mena, Arkansas, many members of the Ed and Birdie Shinn family and their neighbors reported seeing kitchen utensils, books, and chairs float in the air on numerous occasions in the presence of fifteen-year-old Charles Elbert Shaeffer, the Shinns' grandson, a gawky, overweight boy with thick glasses.

"People will think we're crazy," said Ed, after being hit in the head with a figurine that reportedly flew off a shelf.

After about eleven months of mysterious events, Shaeffer confessed to police that he overturned chairs and lamps and tapped on his bed frame with steel pliers because his grandfather had been picking on him.

But Charles Albright, a columnist for the *Arkansas Gazette*, who covered the story, rejected the confession. "Elbert can't make biscuits float through the air anymore than we can!" he said. "Our theory is that he took the rap so that everybody could get some peace." Indeed, during all the rumors and publicity over the case, the Shinn farm had been overrun with curiosity seekers, police, and investigators, who all left once the confession was published in the papers.

Although the media is often quick to embrace a poltergeist story for its unusual qualities and potential human interest angles, journalists can also quickly turn against a case at the hint of a hoax.

That was true even in more superstitious times in the early twentieth century, Hans Driesch said. But he added that the press was often too quick to come to conclusions. "There are journals that empty whole buckets of sarcasm as soon as psychical research, which they usually confuse with the specific spiritualistic hypothesis, is so much as mentioned, without having made any attempt even to glance at the serious literature of the subject."

NATURAL CAUSES

Not all poltergeist cases are real or fraudulent. There is often a natural explanation for unusual bumps and noises — faulty pipes, raccoons in the attic, or seismic disturbances.

In 2003 in Marathon County, Wisconsin, strange knockings, gushing water taps, and the peculiar movements of a helium balloon were reported in a home, along with a radio that, for no apparent reason, suddenly played big band music. Members of the Wausau Paranormal Research Society said they could not rule out the possibility of paranormal phenomena, but they believed that some of the occurrences were caused by a pump connected to the plumbing, causing fluctuations in the magnet field; by temperature changes that caused drafts; by faulty faucet valves; and by a weak radio signal that allowed the big band station to slip in and out.

In 2002, what was initially called an outbreak of poltergeist activity in the village of Boquate Ha Sofonia in the African country of Lesotho (a large stone smashed into a cooking area in a village) turned out to have a heavenly source. One of the village residents, Malino Mantsoe, blamed a *thokolosi* (poltergeist) and sprinkled holy water around her house and on the stone. Another resident had pieces of rock bounce off her roof.

It turned out to be a meteorite weighing a ton, which had been circling the sun for 4,600 million years and had exploded into thousands of pieces when it hit the earth's atmosphere.

In 1999 in Sandwell, England, a family had their home exorcised to get rid of a poltergeist. John and Jackie Bambrick said they were forced out of their home on Lansbury Road by loud bangs and scratching noises that seem to shake the house. It turned out to be a wild cat that had become stuck up their chimney.

THE SKEPTICS' VIEW OF WHY PEOPLE BELIEVE

As stated in the introduction, millions of people believe in ghosts and the paranormal. Why do so many of us believe? Perhaps there really are ghosts, poltergeists, UFOs, and all sorts of supernatural events.

But there may be other reasons, according to Michael Shermer, founder of *Skeptic Magazine*, in his 1997 book *Why People Believe in Weird Things*. In that book, he listed a number of reasons:

- *Credo consolans (it feels good):* It is comforting to believe that there is a god and an afterlife.
- *Immediate gratification:* People call psychics for comfort over their personal lives, their careers, or their future, but they tend to remember only the positive or comforting answers they get.
- *Simple explanations:* They want simple answers for a complex world. Superstition and belief in fate provide a simple explanation to complex science.
- *Mortality and meaning:* Without a belief in a higher power, why be moral? What is the meaning of life? Science often seems cold, but pseudoscience, superstition, magic, and religion offer simple and consoling meaning.

As far as poltergeists or ghosts are concerned, a large segment of the public and the media are "far more fascinated by demons and ghosts than the possibility of a prank or fraud," Paul Kurtz said.

Some parapsychologists agree. Tony Cornell warns that if people can find no logical explanation for a poltergeist case, they often automatically believe that the paranormal is at work. "It is as if all the age-old beliefs developed in less enlightened times lie dormant in the unconscious, awaiting revival," he said. "This is particularly liable to happen when such beliefs are given a nudge by the intervention of a clergyman or a spiritualist medium."

A predisposition to believe may be in our hard-wiring. In fact, paranormal experiences may be partly, or wholly, hallucinations or altered states of consciousness, some scientists believe.

Michael Persinger, Ph.D., a neuroscientist and professor of psychology at Laurentian University, believes that mystical experiences, such as poltergeists, ghosts, out-of-body experiences, alien abductions, and psychic and religious experiences, are somehow linked to excessive bursts of electrical activity in temporal lobes, the area of the brain responsible for the regulation of emotions, the fight-or-flight response, and motivated behaviors.

People with sensitive temporal lobes, or "temporal lobe lability," get frequent bursts of electrical activity and may be more susceptible to paranormal hallucinations than others, he said. They may also be creative and have experiences "resembling those of epileptics." Persinger believes that these people are particularly susceptible to hallucinations when they are near an electromagnetic field.

Persinger says he has been able to prove his theories in the laboratory by putting helmets on people and exposing them to electromagnetic signals. Four of five people, he said, report a "mystical experience, the feeling that there is a sentient being or entity standing behind them or near them." Some weep and some feel God has touched them, but others say they feel the presence of demons or evil spirits.

"That's in the laboratory, and they know they are in the laboratory," Persinger said. "Can you imagine what would happen if that happened late at night in a pew or mosque or synagogue?"

Meditation can also cause these effects, he added. "Individuals prone to paranormal experiences are sensitive to weak magnetic fields and to man-made electrical fields, which are becoming more prominent in the communication age," Persinger said.

THE ELECTRIC FAMILY

Parasearch, a group that investigates paranormal activity in England, suspects that a family with two small children in the West Midlands was predisposed to ghost and poltergeist activity because of personal and household electricity.

In 2002, the family reported apparitions, electrical disturbances, loud banging on the ceiling of their home, and a child's protective gate swinging back and forth on its own.

Parasearch discovered that the father had been hit by lightning as a child and had received two severe electrical shocks as an adult.

Their home had high readings for electromagnetic fields and ultrasonic sources, and one child's cot was made of metal and was near a satellite dish. As well, the central heating system was suspected of acting as both a receiving and transmitting antenna for radio signals. After the heating system was replaced, the family reported that the phenomena dissipated.

Parasearch speculated that the family hallucinated the phenomena because of the complex electrical connections between their brains and their environment.

IN THE DARK?

A lack of exposure to science may be another reason so many people believe in the paranormal.

Karen Lohman, a former teacher, said she joined the Cleveland, Ohio-based South Shore Skeptics, a group of scientists and science buffs, because "America just doesn't have scientific literacy. We don't have an understanding of even the most basic principles about why the sun comes up in the east and sets in the west... we want magic to exist, whether it's clairvoyance or crystals, because it's an awfully cold and cruel universe and we want to control the uncontrollable."

The late astronomer/author Carl Sagan said that science has "beauty and power and majesty that can provide spiritual as well as practical fulfillment. But superstition and pseudoscience keep getting in the way, providing easy answers, casually pressing our awe buttons, and cheapening the experience."

Sagan added that pseudoscience speaks to powerful emotional needs that science often leaves unfulfilled. "It caters to fantasies about personal powers we lack and long for."

Then, again, maybe some or all poltergeists, ghosts, and UFOs are real?

Indeed, Sagan tried to stay somewhat neutral on the subject of the paranormal and called for both skeptics and believers to remain open-minded to the possibility of other ideas.

"It seems to me what is called for is an exquisite balance between two conflicting needs: the most skeptical of all hypothesis that are served up to us and at the same time a great openness to new ideas," Sagan said. "If you are only skeptical, then no new ideas make it through to you... you become a crotchy old person convinced that nonsense is ruling the world. There is, of course, much data to support you. On the other hand, if you are not open to the point of gullibility and have not an ounce of skeptical sense in you, then you cannot distinguish useful ideas from worthless ones."

Bernard Carr, professor of mathematics and astronomy at Queen Mary University in London, England, says that there remain enough questions about the paranormal that science should not close the book on it. "Although we don't fully understand these phenomena, scientists should investigate them," he said.

Scary Beginning, Good Ending

Two of the three chapters in this section focus on a case in St. Catharines, Ontario, in 1970, which probably did not get the recognition it deserved as these cases go, partly because the stressed-out family did not allow paranormal investigators into their home. The chapters tell the story of an eleven-year-old boy, who was reportedly at the epicenter of poltergeist activity, which left many police officers befuddled and even scared. But it has a good ending as the boy grew into a successful adult, if somewhat shy about his unusual past. Chapter 7 details a similar case in Bridgeport, Connecticut, in which many police officers give compelling testimony about moving furniture, although their superior officers seemed to have pulled the plug on the investigation after accusing a young girl of trickery.

CHAPTER 5

A COP GOES FLYING

The only visitor we had at Halloween in 1980 came at midnight. He had no mask, and he didn't need one. His name was John Mulvey (pseudonym) and in some people's eyes, his story was a strong case for the existence of the supernatural, or at least the paranormal.

We had never met, but he knew that I was a newspaper reporter interested in his story, which had taken place in 1970 in St. Catharines, Ontario, where it was said a poltergeist had inhabited his body as an eleven-year-old, causing, among other things, pictures to move and raising a chair with a police officer sitting on it.

The cops swore it all happened over a period of several weeks, and so did two priests and two lawyers. Even comedian Johnny Carson had joked about it on the *Tonight Show*. ("How scary was it?" chuckled Carson's sidekick Ed McMahon. "It was soooo scary, the cops went to bed with their revolvers under their pillows." And so it had been, at least for one of them.)

Mulvey's family had been so paranoid about publicity that they had managed to keep their identities secret for ten years after the incidents.

And now he was coming over to my house at midnight. As his sleek, black sports car slowly crushed the brittle leaves down our long, narrow driveway, which a few weeks previously had been a tunnel under friendly catalpa trees, I peered through a small square in my living room window and started to shake a little. Why had I invited him to our house as my wife and two children slept?

It had always seemed safe, out here in the country on the edge of Niagara Falls, removed from the tourists and the neon lights of the wax museums. We even had a cherry orchard in the backyard, leading to a windswept hydro field. There was no hiding now on the last naked night of October.

I had talked to John Mulvey briefly over the phone several days earlier to get a quote for a ten-year anniversary story in my daily newspaper, the *St. Catharines Standard*. His name, of course, had been omitted and I was one of the few people in the Niagara Peninsula who knew who he was. "You asked me to call you when I was ready to give you the story...," he had said.

Prior to his phone call, I had been sitting in the kitchen at 10:30 p.m., toying with wrapped candy and wondering why no kids had come trick or treating. Huge, damn country — there were too many distances between people. You hardly knew your own neighbors.

John Mulvey's car stopped near my front door and no one got out for what seemed like a full minute. It had not been a long drive for Mulvey, who lived 8 miles away in St. Catharines.

And then the doorbell rang. There is something about a doorbell at 12:03 a.m. that rocks the framing of a house. I should have simply opened the door before he pulled it, but I guess I kind of froze.

His broad-shouldered frame filled my doorway. He was no boy anymore. He looked different, certainly not pure white like most of us in Niagara Region. His hand reached for mine in the yellow of the porch light. "Sorry for bothering you this time of night," he said in a calm voice as he stepped inside. A smile broke his swarthy face, and then he made a sudden move: I thought he was reaching for something, but he simply and quietly removed his shoes, looked around for somewhere to put them, and settled on a corner. He was the most polite person in our house in a month — big, and yet trying to keep himself small.

Suddenly, my wife Jennifer appeared at the top of the stairs in a nightgown and a guarded smile. She shuffled down the steps and shook John Mulvey's hand. It broke the ice for me and I felt safer. As John and I walked up the stairs to my office, the details of 1970 raced through my head.

THE WINTER OF 1970

It had all started in late January 1970, approaching the final part of a long Canadian winter.

Reportedly, there were bizarre goings-on in the Mulvey apartment, one of four units in an old downtown building above a little cleaning store, where John Mulvey Sr., an immigrant who worked with his hands and had moved up the ladder at his company to become a supervisor, lived with his wife, Barbara, and their two sons, eleven-year-old John and his eight-year-old brother Jeff.

The family was puzzled and scared as furniture shifted and paintings crashed down, seemingly under their own power.

The Mulveys, who had lived there for many years without such problems, at first summoned the city's engineering department to check for structural failings, or perhaps wood shrinking and expanding from fluctuation in temperatures. Engineers went over the place with a fine-toothed comb, but found nothing out of the ordinary.

"There was a problem with certain noises and items of furniture which appeared to be moving around," said Mel Holenski, assistant city engineer. "But, after checking, we satisfied ourselves that there were no problems with the building."

But the occurrences continued, and so the provincial gas company got involved on January 28 and February 2, but there were no faults in the building's gas furnace. Next to the rescue came the St. Catharines Fire Department and the Public Utilities Commission. They found nothing.

John Sr. and Barbara were embarrassed about having to explain the goings-on and having strangers walk through their apartment, checking everything. One of the few things that comforted them was the presence of two Roman Catholic priests.

It was only as a last resort that they summoned the St. Catharines Police Department, and even then it happened only by chance; officers were at the apartment building on another matter and Mrs. Mulvey saw the opportunity and called one of them inside her unit.

This was the very last thing the family wanted — cops and media releases every day. As soon as police started to investigate, the Mulveys asked for a media ban on the story, but there were leaks within the police department and bits and pieces of the strange tale got into the *St. Catharines Standard* and the local radio stations. What newspaper or radio station could resist these details: a chair allegedly sliding across a room to the boy's bedside, a footstool turning upside-down, a framed photo of young John and his parents becoming a *moving* picture. In another occurrence, an officer was sitting in a chair when an unseen force reportedly flipped him onto his behind. Other alleged phenomena included the boy being pinned against a wall by a chair too heavy for one man to move, and a heavy bed being raised 6 inches off the floor. All of the events occurred when little John was in the vicinity.

"At first, I thought the family must be mental, but, believe me, what I saw was done by no human hands," said Constable Robert (Scotty) Crawford, a salty cop who spoke with a thick Scottish brogue and was already a veteran of bar brawls on Bridge Street.

As he sent other officers to the Mulvey home, dispatcher Bob Little shook his head in disbelief. "You get a lot of funny calls in this business, and this seemed like a really funny one," Little said.

Four of the first five officers submitted reports to their superiors about what they saw. A fifth refused to hand one in because "they would have thought me crazy." In fact, at first, some officers thought it was a British joke concocted by the first three constables — two Scots and an Irish constable — to reach the scene. "Our superiors thought we were pulling a joke on them," said Constable Mike McMenamin, who was quite sobered by the experience. Other witnesses to the mysterious events were two doctors, two Roman Catholic priests, and two pinstriped lawyers. To this day, some of the officials refuse to speak to the media or even to be identified with the case and asked about what they saw.

Here is a sampling of some of the reported occurrences in the Mulvey apartment:

- *Wednesday, February 4, approximately 7 p.m.:* A bed that reportedly moved away from a wall was pushed back by Father Melvin Stevens, an assistant at the St. Catharines (Roman Catholic) Cathedral, but the bed almost immediately moved back by itself. Witnesses were Father Stevens and Barbara Mulvey.
- *Friday, February 6, sometime in the evening:* The St. Catharines Police Department became involved, but only by accident. Constable Crawford was attending the Mulvey apartment building to investigate a domestic complaint in another unit. As he was about to leave the building, he was summoned by Mrs. Mulvey and brought into her apartment. She showed him a heavy chest of drawers lying on its side in the kitchen. She explained that in the past ten days or so, many pieces of furniture had been moved by an unknown, unseen force. It was inexplicable, she told the officer. "She was starting to think both her and her husband were mental," Crawford said. Father Stevens came into the apartment, and he verified the strange occurrences, some of which he had witnessed. A day or two before, the priest said he had seen a bed move away from a wall. He pushed it back to the wall, turned to calm Mrs. Mulvey, and turned around to find that the bed had moved away from the wall again. After interviewing Mrs. Mulvey

and Father Stevens, Constable Crawford told them to go into the living room and he would join them. On his way out, the officer put a chair under the kitchen table and walked into the living room. He said he had just succeeded in calming down a very upset Mrs. Mulvey when he heard what sounded like footsteps moving from the living room toward the kitchen, even though no one was walking in that direction. When the officer and the priest went back into the kitchen, they found that the chair was mysteriously out in the middle of the room. There was no one around. Father Stevens said this was typical of the occurrences in the apartment over the past ten days. Constable Crawford logged all of this information in an official police report, which he entitled "house phenomena."

- *Friday, February 7, 10 p.m.:* Constable Crawford returned to the Mulveys' apartment to find that a heavy bed had reportedly been raised 2 feet off the floor by an unseen force. It was reported by Mrs. Baines, who told police she had seen it rise off the floor in the boys' bedroom. Constable Crawford rushed into the room and he said he saw the bed approximately 2 feet off the floor at one end — unsupported. "Not believing my eyes, I summoned Constable (Dick) Colledge, who was outside the apartment. On our return, the bed was in the same position, but it was now supported by two chairs. At this time, there were two other ladies present (one was Shirley McKinnon, thirty-two, manager of a hair salon, who was also the daughter of the landlord of the Mulveys' apartment building). As well, Colledge said he was standing just outside a bedroom when he saw a picture in the bedroom come off the wall forcefully, arch in the air across a bed, and fall to the floor. "With its trajectory, there was no way it could have simply fallen off a nail or it would have dropped onto the bed," Colledge said. "It was as if someone or something had ripped it off the wall and thrown it, but there was no one in the room... very strange."
- *Saturday, February 7, evening:* Shirley McKinnon said she saw a heavy rocking chair move from one side of a room to another and tip onto its back "without too much of a thump." At the same time, there was a knocking sound coming from the children's bedroom, as though something had fallen to the floor. Constable Crawford said he went into the bedroom and turned on the light to find that a doll he had earlier seen hanging on a wall about 6 feet from a bed was on the floor, not far from John Mulvey, who was still in bed. His younger brother, Jeff, was asleep nearby. Mrs. Mulvey entered the room and became very upset and was shaking. How could this

happen to one of her children? Was the family being punished for something? Was it the work of the devil? How long would this go on? And what will friends and family think?

At this point, Constable McMenamin arrived, along with local residents Lorne and Janet Asher, who were visiting the apartment. Most of the people in the house went into the living room, along with Constable Crawford, who watched through a door into the adjoining children's bedroom. He was keeping an eye on John Mulvey when a small picture frame fell from a wall onto John's head, the officer said in his official report.

Several minutes later, there was a rapid succession of events in the bedroom, Constable Crawford said: a table lamp in the bedroom fell over, a large heavy chest of drawers moved from a wall and then back again, a chair was raised in the air and slammed forcefully to the floor, and numerous objects on a dressing table in another part of the bedroom were hurled to the floor. All of the objects on the dressing table moved in the same direction, except for an alarm clock, which flew in the opposite direction, the officer reported. Constable McMenamin added his observations: "The boy was sitting on a chair and it rose off the floor and it started bouncing up and down... plaques and a painting on the wall started moving and falling and a bookcase toppled." Needless to say, the people in the house, which also included Monsignor M. Herbert Delaney of the St. Catharines Cathedral and Mr. Baines, were upset and very puzzled.

- *Sunday, February 8, afternoon:* Furniture was said to have moved about the apartment on its own accord. The witnesses were Monsignor Delaney, Mrs. McKinnon, and Father Stevens.
- *Tuesday, February 10:* For about the twelfth time in almost two weeks, Constable Bill Weir said he saw John Mulvey thrown off a chair. Weir wrote in his official report: "I attended [the apartment] in the morning and was assisted by Constable Eddie Batorski. While I was there, I witnessed some phenomenal occurrences which I have attached to this report. At 9 p.m., I proceeded to the residence again with Constable Crawford, where we again witnessed some very unusual things taking place. Between the time of the two calls, I contacted Mr. Bradley, the city building inspector. We both agreed that the causes of these weird occurrences were in no way connected to the building structure itself. My only solution to these

occurrences is that the boy [John], whom all the occurrences surround, has been inhabited by a spirit of a poltergeist. This is the spirit which inhabits the body of a young child that does not generally seriously harm anyone. People who have witnessed these occurrences are Constables Weir, Crawford, McMenamin and Colledge and other officers. Briefly, this boy can't sit on a chair without being thrown off and items are hitting him for no apparent reason. I, the writer [Weir], witnessed the boy being thrown on at last a dozen occasions, including while I was there with Constable Crawford."

Weir's report was later signed and authorized by his commanding officer, Sergeant Buck Taylor. On the official report, entitled "house phenomena," police marked THIS ITEM IS NOT FOR PRESS... REPEAT: NOT FOR PRESS.

Constable Weir said he also got the treatment from the unseen force. Although he apparently did not write it on his police report, Weir told Constable Harry Fox that the poltergeist force picked up a chair he was sitting in and, according to Fox, "tipped him on his ass." Now, if little John Mulvey had really done that physically, that would be a tough one to explain to the boys back at the station — a burly cop overpowered by an eleven-year-old!

- *Wednesday, February 11, at about suppertime:* A chair containing John Mulvey reportedly lifted itself 6 inches off the floor and slammed down. Constable Robert (Nobby) Richardson reported that he was sitting in the living room with John Mulvey and his younger brother, Mr. and Mrs. Mulvey, Constable Crawford, Detective Sandy Sandison, two physicians, and Monsignor Delaney. At about 5 p.m., as several people walked into the boys' bedroom, the chair that John Mulvey was sitting in "lifted abruptly about 6 inches off the floor, and then slammed down again," said Richardson, adding he witnessed the event while standing in the doorway of the master bedroom close to John. The casters under the legs of the chair fell away onto the floor, the officer said. "On examining the chair, there was no reason for this happening," recounted Constable Richardson. Another witness was Andrew McQuilken of the law firm Ross-McQuilken, which was acting on behalf of the owner of the building and also as a liaison between the Mulvey family and the public. Later that evening, McQuilken reported to police he saw incidents at the apartment similar to the one at suppertime. "The family do not want any publicity with regards to this, particularly with the child going to school," Richardson wrote on his report. "If it happened, the family feel they would have to leave town."

- *Date unknown:* John Mulvey was sitting on his bed in his nightclothes and being watched by Constable Crawford. Because of the stress in the house and the disturbances, police asked Mr. Mulvey to make arrangements for the two boys to stay with friends for the night. When the boys began to dress in the living room, a bookcase suddenly tipped over and fell from the wall near Mr. Asher, who was visiting the apartment, and onto the floor. The witnesses were Constables Crawford, Colledge, McMenamin, and Weir along with Mr. and Mrs. Asher, Father Stevens, Mrs. Baines, and Mrs. McKinnon.
- *Date unknown (early February):* Constable Harry Fox was talking to Mrs. Mulvey while sitting in an easy chair. "[The poltergeist] must like you," Mrs. Mulvey said, referring to the fact that the chair was the favorite of the poltergeist, and that it had not tried to throw Fox off. But the action was just to Fox's left, where John Mulvey was lying on a small chesterfield couch, about 7 feet long, when the couch suddenly flipped the boy onto the floor, the officer said. "The back legs of the chesterfield came a foot or more off the ground; there was no way the boy could have done it." According to Fox, John did not seem scared. "I guess he was used to this sort of thing by then. But it certainly surprised me. I had no idea what did that."

The police officers in the above occurrences stood by their reports, even though some people at the St. Catharines Police Department remained skeptical. "Some of the guys didn't even write reports on what they saw," Colledge said. "They didn't want to be called nuts." But Crawford and others signed their reports. "All persons interviewed were sober and responsible people," he wrote.

Later, the crusty, no-nonsense Weir said: "These occurrences are phenomenal."

"It was goddam scary," Fox said. "And yet [John Mulvey] didn't seem scared. Of course, I got there [about two weeks] after it started and [John Mulvey] by this time was probably taking everything for granted." However, Constable McMenamin had a different observation of John Mulvey and saw him more often than Fox did. "[John] seemed okay at the start [of the occurrences in late January], but then he got scared and was crying," McMenamin said. "Overall, the whole family was very upset."

Fox added that, "It was one of the scariest things I've ever been involved with. At least in your normal work, if you're confronted with a big man, you can defend yourself. But this was different, unpredictable. I think it was some sort of invisible energy which you couldn't see." Later, the mild-mannered, level-headed Fox would openly lecture about the case to his supervisors at the Ontario Police College. "As it turned out, I think the spirit was playful, not harmful," Fox said.

One of the few officers who went to the apartment and did not see anything unusual was Batorski. "I can't figure out why nothing happened when I went there, but all the other guys swore things were moving," he said. "I don't doubt they could have happened," he said. "I liked the family. They were clean living."

Some of the details of the Mulvey case made it into the three local papers, the *St. Catharines Standard*, the *Niagara Falls Review*, and the *Welland Tribune*, as well as onto some radio stations, and eventually the wire services carried them to Toronto and around the country, then into the United States and around the world over Associated Press. That's apparently how the producers of the "Tonight Show" heard about it, and it became part of Johnny Carson's monologue.

To try to appease the family, who shuddered at the thought of such publicity, the police brass issued an executive order on February 12 to ensure that officers who had been in the apartment would not give comments to the media. (By the mid-1990s, the official police reports had somehow had made it onto the Internet.)

During the course of the investigation, some researchers were prevented from getting into the Mulvey apartment, including several psychics and Sister Justa Smith, director of the Human Dimensions Division of Rosary Hill College in Buffalo, New York, which investigated psychic, spiritual, and paranormal phenomena. She said she did not intend to perform an exorcism, but was there only to study the case. Perhaps the most respected researcher into this type of phenomena, Dr. William Roll of North Carolina, author of a book on parapsychology and a university professor, was also banned. And so there was no official paranormal investigation or documentation of the case, as there has been on many other such cases.

But there were lots of theories. A Hamilton, Ontario, parapsychologist, Nellie Nielson, speculated that John Mulvey had unleashed a type of psychic energy because he was entering puberty and was feeling frustrated, perhaps at his family. "These youngsters, when they are reaching puberty, have a lot of emotion and energy, which may vent itself on the surroundings if the child is under pressure or frustrated," she said.

"Frustrations can only aggravate the situation." Nielson suggested that Mulvey had taken on a secondary, psychic personality "and he's probably unaware of it, and I don't believe his family is aware of it, either. The longer he's bothered, the longer it will last."

Many others had their own theories about what, or who, was behind the events, from the devil to ghosts to John Mulvey himself, because some of the events were similar to pranks a young boy might try. But the police had kept a close eye on him and they contended that a boy could not have fooled them. "To me, he just seemed like an average boy," Colledge said.

John's elementary school principal called him "an above-average student, who didn't cause any problems and was not unusual in any way. What happened came as a surprise to us."

Apparently, no events occurred at school — only when Mulvey was in the apartment with his parents. When the family left the apartment, nothing happened to them. And nothing seemed to involve the boy's younger brother. The Mulvey family was reportedly close, although it was said the children were to be seen and not heard, as in many families of a European background in that era. John had been named after his father and his grandfather.

Altogether, the events lasted several weeks until the family took a vacation in Montreal to get away from it all, especially from the publicity. Some media outlets were becoming frustrated because the family would not grant them interviews. Apparently nothing out of the ordinary happened while they were in Montreal and when they returned, all was quiet. A short time later, Constable Fox met the mother on the street and she nearly broke down in tears. "Thank God it's finally over," she said. "It went away."

In his later years in high school, John seemed to be a smart, popular teenager with a broad smile, sometimes flashy clothes, and perhaps an eye in the future toward politics. He was known for speaking his mind and standing up for his beliefs. He won an achievement award for his work outside school just five years after the mysterious occurrences.

To this day, no one has been able to shake the credibility of this compelling story or rattle John Mulvey's credibility. "We were all skeptical at first," said Constable Fox. "After all, we were all adult police officers. But, after those weeks and all those incidents, not one of us thought it was trickery."

The family was, and still is, hard working and respected in the St. Catharines community. The case remained sensitive to some people for decades. "I made a solemn promise to the family that I would never speak about it, and I intend to keep it. I'm a man of my word," Constable Bill Weir told me in the 1980s after he had been promoted to sergeant. "Some of my friends from the media have been angry with me about this." Weir was shaken by what he saw and slept at night with his police service revolver close to his pillow and a glass of liquor on a small table. (*Note:* The names of the John Mulvey family are pseudonyms.)

SHOWER OF APPLES

Although seemingly rare, the John Mulvey case was not the first reported case of poltergeist activity in the Niagara area. Decades earlier, a nine-year-old boy, John Kenneth Logan, was said to have acquired the ability to propel apples and pears through the air up to a distance of 20 yards. "It was as if the fruit suddenly became charged with electricity," reported the *St. Catharines Standard.* The boy's father, Alex, a respected member of the community, said that one time his son caused a tree to shake, bringing a shower of golden russet apples upon both of them.

CHAPTER 6

OUR ONLY VISITOR AT HALLOWEEN

And so, John Mulvey came to my house in Niagara Falls in 1980, apparently to explain some of the weird things that had happened ten years earlier.

We climbed the stairs and I ushered him into my office, a spare bedroom across the hall from where my two sons were sleeping, corn candies in their tummies from the Halloween night of trick-or-treating.

John eased into a comfortable rocking chair in the corner of the room while I sat on a chair by my desk, a couple of steps away.

"Nice place," he said. Right from the beginning, this guy seemed inoffensive and obliging — boy, was I relieved. In fact, he was very clean cut, from his round face (boyish by twenty-one-year-old standards) to his neat leather jacket, football shirt, and high school ring. I cracked a meaningless joke. He laughed. He was cheerful. There seemed nothing frightening about him at all; he could have been my younger brother. Here I was, expecting *Rosemary's Baby* and who shows up but a chap from *Leave It to Beaver*, rocking quietly in the night.

I offered him tea and cookies, but he declined. He talked pleasantly, gesturing with his hands, about things that other people might recount in anger.

"Why did you print the article in today's paper?" he said, referring to my ten-year anniversary story that recapped the famous case. "It caused me problems at home." He was still living with his parents in St. Catharines. (My managing editor at the *Standard*, Murray Thomson, liked stories on the supernatural from time to time. "Anybody who doesn't believe in ghosts is foolish," he once said.)

I explained to John that his experience of 1970 had fascinated a continent. "I suppose people want to know how this could happen in a place like

St. Catharines, and if there is anything new, and if the situation completely went away. They want to know about you."

"They wouldn't understand," he said, still civil. "Boy, oh, boy, I thought this was all over. I wanted it to just die." Suddenly, his wide hands became more animated, and his brows darkened. "Today, after your article appeared, somebody put a ghost on my locker at work. People are starting to get close again. Ten years later and it's starting all over again! Hardly anybody knows. My neighbors don't know who I am. My friends at high school never knew who I was."

St. Catharines is a nice, cozy place of 125,000 people with a low crime rate. It would be irresponsible to blame the people of such a city for what happened in the John Mulvey case. However, it could have been one of numerous causes. Many researchers believe that suppression is one of the factors in a poltergeist case. The suppression is often provoked by the parents of a young boy or girl, who is said to unconsciously act out through rare psychokinetic powers to move furniture and household objects. It seems to be an unconscious form of getting feelings out, researchers such as William Roll believe. Of course, other factors are usually involved, including other stresses in a household and often the onset of puberty in the child's life. And there may be something different about the brain of the poltergeist agent.

But back to John Mulvey and his upbringing in St. Catharines, a city in which I worked for a decade as a reporter for *The Standard*. In my view, the people of St. Catharines tended to be conservative by politics and lifestyle, reserved and slow to change. The world's ships passed through the city on the Welland Canal, part of the St. Lawrence Seaway, but who really knew its residents? In a way, it was like there was a bubble over the city, protecting it from the rest of the world. The residents' poor record of voting in elections seemed to reflect apathy and they rarely reacted to anything, unless the English clock above the old courthouse forgot to chime on the hour. As a reporter, I became frustrated at *The Standard*'s readers for their lack of response to anything creative or different. To get their attention, it seemed, you had to bang on their door. To get their emotions going, you almost had to threaten their privacy.

In my articles over the years, I revealed a lot of well-kept secrets in St. Catharines, including one in which a man described as a cornerstone of the community — a successful salesman, father of two young children, a Sunday school teacher, soccer coach, and "perfect neighbor"— set himself ablaze and died in his station wagon because he would not face the shame of being charged in a washroom sex scandal involving other men at a local shopping mall.

And yet John Mulvey sat in my rocking chair and said he wanted to stay home in St. Catharines and blend in. "I want a normal life. My life now is what's important. I don't want to do anything to jeopardize it. I have a good job. I earn more than my father."

"Yes, that makes sense," I said. There was no easy way for me to back into what had happened in that tormented apartment in 1970. "I understand from the old press reports that the occurrences went away after two or three weeks." I did not use the word "poltergeist" or even "supernatural" or "paranormal."

"I'm no different now than I was then," he snapped. "I haven't changed. But in people's eyes, I'm a human being again. I don't want to be different. When I got home from work tonight [after my anniversary story had appeared in *The Standard*], my father pulled the phone out of the wall. He's having it disconnected. When I called you, it was from a phone booth. Can you imagine that? This year, for the first time [since 1970], our telephone was listed in the phone book — and look what happens! It's like waving a red flag: 'Here I am!'" The rocking chair was moving quicker now, slightly toward me. "I've had ulcers," he sighed. He looked down at the floor and repeated it: "I've had ulcers."

How many times had I heard that type of thing lately? Stories about ulcers, high blood pressure, anxiety, and stress-related conditions were seemingly becoming common in society. "Since the day it happened, I'm not allowed to discuss it at home," John said. "You have no idea. My father gets upset... my parents can get emotional. We never talk about it. We're not allowed. We haven't talked about it since it happened."

He kept looking down at the floor, and then up at me. His voice started to shake through quivering lips and I was afraid he was about to clam up, so I mentioned something about my own family. When I had been a youth in the 1960s, I had penned several unpublished books and short stories that I had hoped my father would want to see and to share. He never did. Prior to his death in 2003, my father still had not bothered to read them. The papers are now under a mound somewhere at a city dump.

My sad little tale seemed to get him going again. "Why did you allow me to come here in the middle of the night?" he said. "I could have come with a knife."

"Maybe we have a little bit in common," I said.

"Well, since it happened, very few people have known I was involved. But some people who know me have become suspicious over the years. I've had to lie to them, believe it or not, about who I am. Why do I have to lie about who I am? Some people found out I had lived in that [apartment] building, so I told them, yes, but that I actually lived in one of the other apartments."

Out of nowhere, something happened in the rocking chair. John Mulvey broke down crying. One moment he was talking with a wry, adult smile and the next second he was sobbing like a child. It was almost like another person inside him had emerged. He cried long and hard and it was a bit discomfiting to see a man sob so much, especially a big man. It was like an uptight decade had burst.

I offered him a box of Kleenex, but he found a hankie in his pocket and tried awkwardly to dry his tears, his breathing sounding jerky. Perhaps it was my imagination, but the room seemed to crackle with electricity. I expected framed photos of my family and a map of downtown St. Catharines to fall off the walls or my desk to move. But in reality, the only thing that jumped was my heart.

I wanted to reach out and be emotional with him. I recalled the times I had wanted to let the emotional side of my personality out, just for a few minutes, and do something to move my father. (Ironically, I had always wanted to move people, but John Mulvey wanted things to stop moving.) But my dad always had to go into the cellar when moments like that came up. I never found out what was in the cellar that was so important, except for a few cigarette butts, hidden from my mother.

Once his tears had subsided, John started talking to me again. He seemed relieved that he had cried so hard. In recent years, he said, he had become a factory worker and he had also found an outlet for his passion with a business organization, ironically working with young people to help them reach their potential.

"I was just thinking," I said. "Of all the people you chose to open up to and it's a reporter!"

But he was not ready to reveal everything. In fact, he asked if our conversation was being recorded. He got up from the chair and checked under my desk and other areas of the office to see if there was a hidden tape recorder.

"I don't want to take the chance you're doing a story for *The Standard* again tomorrow," he said. "Everything today is for a buck." In 1970, some authors, museum officials, and even some of his old neighbors had tried to make money on the strange happenings, he said. "I thought about telling my story, but it's not worth the price." He looked upon Halloween stories as hokey and "just stories for children."

John did not give details of the 1970 occurrences, although he said he remembered them well. "I was an intelligent kid; I could read when I was five. The papers didn't get the story right — they were guessing." For the record, the papers had inferred that a ghost or demonic possession was to blame. "Since then, I've done some reading, some investigating of my own. I have my own theories, but it's nobody's business."

"There was a rumor that you were into magic, and that you went to California to become a professional magician," I said.

"I don't know anything about magic," he said sternly.

Finally, after nearly two hours of conversation, John Mulvey got out of the rocking chair and said he was feeling better. I offered him a bed for the night, but he shrugged, "No, I'll be OK. I'm going home." He apologized for "acting like a baby," but I told him he should be thankful he could let go.

People still continued to talk about the case. Not long after the occurrences at the Mulvey apartment, a rumor emerged that it had involved a satanic cult of voodoo men from Haiti, who had lived in the building. The Niagara region, rich in military history, has its share of ghost and paranormal stories, as well as many mediums and psychics. One of them, self-proclaimed white witch Joanna Honsberger, believed that as a boy, John Mulvey had been affected by restless spirits of the dead in his apartment.

The apartment is gone now, the victim of a wrecker's ball, but John Mulvey still lives in St. Catharines and now has a family and a son of his own.

One day in the early 1980s, I accidentally ran into him walking downtown. He was holding hands with an attractive blonde woman. As we approached one another on the sidewalk, his eyes met mine, but he looked quickly away from me, as though he had glanced into the hot sun. The couple blended in nicely with the crowds strolling in the sunshine, peering into store windows. He was a little older and his hair a little shorter. Otherwise, he hadn't changed. And, like his shirt, his emotions were tucked in.

EPILOGUE

Let us fast forward twenty-five years. From 1980 to 2005, I had written nothing about the case. The Mulvey story appears in this book because I think it is a compelling one, which might help us better understanding our complex human species.

Since I saw him in 1980, it appears as though John Mulvey has lived a relatively normal life, raising a family, living a middle-class lifestyle, and doing his best for his community. He has found an outlet for his passion in helping others. I would love to fill you in on the joys and pains of his life into his thirties and forties, but I must hold back most of the details because I do not want to identify him. Those are his wishes. I realize that by publishing the information that I am, people around him who did not know he was that poltergeist boy from 1970 will put two and two together, but I think he will be okay. The people who are that close to him will understand. They know that he did nothing wrong and that something perhaps paranormal transpired, but that does not mean that he is anti-social or a danger to anyone.

Some of that may have already happened. In 1995, the radio show the "X-Zone" aired a program on the St. Catharines poltergeist and interviewed several of the original police officers in the case, who had retired from the force. Producers of the show put some of the police reports on the Internet, blanking out the family names to protect their privacy.

By the year 2005, John Mulvey had moved up the ladder at his workplace (the same place he worked when he came to my house in 1980) and had been honored with several awards for his work over the years, particularly while working with young people. (At one awards ceremony as a young man, he showed up in a bright plaid sports jacket with long hair and a bowtie. Another award was a national one. And his superiors now refer to him as a role model.)

Over the years, his name and picture have appeared in the *St. Catharines Standard* for a variety of business and community events, and photographs have shown him smiling and enjoying himself with others — quite ironic, since he has done so much to suppress his story of 1970.

There was one close call. In 2002, at the age of forty-four, John suffered a heart attack and was admitted to hospital with his wife; his son; a young adult; and his younger brother, Jeff, at his side. (His son has also flourished in his job and in the community.) But he recovered.

It is no surprise that there has been stress in John's life — the pressure of keeping a controversial part of his life secret must be considerable — but he relaxes with soft music, company picnics, and golf. ("The world can be a crazy place," he told someone.) In fact, on one occasion, I ran into him on a golf course. When he spotted me behind him, he didn't seem too relaxed. Poor guy — I've never seen a golfer tee off so fast and hustle up the fairway.

Otherwise, if you saw him on the street, he's just one of the guys, and he smiles a lot. And his telephone number is listed again.

In late 2004, I decided to try to contact John again. I wanted to tell him about this book and to offer him a way to contribute to it, without using his name. I was hoping he would open up to me more this time about the details of 1970.

There were lots of questions I wanted to ask him:

- How did he feel during the occurrences? Was he aware that perhaps he caused them to happen?
- Did he have any conscious control over the incidents?
- Since 1970, has he felt he had any special mental or emotional powers? Has he tried to develop them? How about his children? Do they have any special abilities or stress manifestations?
- Did the incident change him or his view of the world?
- Has he kept the secret from his friends and family, and why? Does he have a confidante?
- How hard has it been to keep it secret? Would he ever tell his full story?

After talking with parapsychologist William Roll, I had a list of such questions prepared, should I get the chance to meet with John Mulvey again. I found out John's home address, his phone number, and his e-mail address. Just deciding how to contact him took weeks of planning because I didn't know how much his family knew of his past, if anything. Should I phone, e-mail, or just show up at his door?

In the end, I sent him a late-night, very dry e-mail, which did not tip off anyone who might read it:

> Hi John:
> You might remember me. At one time, I worked at *The Standard*, and you came to my home in Niagara Falls one night in 1980.
> I'm hoping we could get together again soon.
> Cheers,
> Michael Clarkson,
> Toronto

His response was swift, the first thing the very next day, with his intentions underscored:

> Good Morning
> Thank you for the e-mail.
> I would not be interested in meeting at this time.
> Thank you
> John Mulvey

Then I sent him a follow-up email:

> Hi John
> I understand completely. Since we met, I have written four books. I am writing another book and I wanted to give you a chance to contribute to it anonymously.
> Michael Clarkson

Once again, I wrote the e-mail so it would not tip off anyone else who read it. He never did respond to that second e-mail. I did not hear from him again, and I have not tried to contact him since.

When I told another parapsychologist, Maurice Grosse of London, England, about the Mulvey case, he was sad. "Society..." he sighed. "There is so much to know and find out, but we can't study this phenomena properly, because of the stigma."

I'm sure that I will monitor how John is doing through the years. The good thing is that his life seems to have turned out well.

MEET THE CRITICS

I would now like to introduce two regular voices in this book, Skeptic Sammy and Rebutt Al. At the end of chapters or sections, they will add brief comments on many of the cases. With a contentious, unproven, and often controversial subject such as poltergeists, we could use a little levity to break the ice. Sammy likely reflects some of the skepticism, and even cynicism, that some of us undoubtedly feel toward some of the stories and characters in this book. Rebutt Al tends to act as a devil's advocate to Sammy and is more middle of the road in his comments. At times, Al is slightly apologetic, depending on Sammy's tone. Readers, I'm sure you will have your own two cents and opinions to add!

Skeptic Sammy: Okay, author Mr. Clarkson, I understand you have written four previous books on fear management and stress. Why on earth would you jeopardize any credibility you have with a book on poltergeists! Hey, why not crop circles, alien abductions, or Elvis living as a vegetable in an apartment above a 7-Eleven?

Rebutt Al: I suspect there is something real about many poltergeist cases. I think it's worth taking a risk. If I'm wrong, I'm wrong.

Skeptic Sammy: I must admit that the police testimony in the St. Catharines case seems compelling, but cops makes mistakes, too.

Rebutt Al: You can probably fool some of the police some of the time, but all of the police all of the time? If this was simply a case of a boy throwing a tantrum, the family would not have brought all these people into their home.

CHAPTER 7

POLICE CONTROVERSY IN NEW ENGLAND

"We're investigating. We would hope to find out what's causing this. I think we might come up with some logical explanation."

—POLICE CAPTAIN JOHN O'LEARY

Indeed, the Bridgeport, Connecticut, Police Department did come up with a logical explanation as to what caused the strange goings-on in a small house at 966 Lindley Street in Bridgeport on a late November weekend in 1974.

After furniture had moved, plaster of Paris cherubs had fallen off the wall to the floor, and ashtrays had reportedly flown, Police Superintendent Joseph A. Walsh scoffed at the testimonies of eight of his officers. "Everything has a rational explanation," he announced. "This is the work of human powers. I don't believe in that supernatural stuff... there are not ghosts in Bridgeport."

The following day, Walsh announced at a Board of Police Commissioners meeting that the case was closed. He said that a ten-year-old girl in the house, Marcia Goodin, had confessed to staging a series of incidents.

"Oh, really?" many officers on his force said behind his back and in the newspapers.

How about the testimony, Supt. Walsh, of your Patrolman John Holsworth, who said he saw a 450-pound refrigerator "lift slowly off the floor, turn and then set down again. There was no one else around. Then the big TV set seemed to float in the air and crash to the floor. I checked to see what had caused it to fall, but I saw nothing."

And then there was Patrolman Joseph Tomek: "I just couldn't believe what I saw. Shelves fixed to the wall began to vibrate until they were loose, then flew through the air. I looked for evidence that someone was making it happen, but I couldn't find anything — no wires, nothing. Then I watched as the big TV fell over." Of course, there was a suspect nearby — Marcia Goodin, all 4 feet, 6 inches and 70 pounds of her, soaking wet.

Not only did this highly publicized case cause a rift in the police department, it was championed by a number of people to show either that paranormal events actually exist, or that people will go to any lengths in order to get attention.

Gerald and Laura Goodin, the owners of 966 Lindley Street, in a lower middle-class area of town, had bought the four-room bungalow fourteen years earlier. It was modest and box-like, yet quaint. The house had been built around 1915 for a shirt manufacturer, but none of the previous occupants had reported any unusual problems.

The heavy-set Gerald was a factory worker at the Harvey Hubbell (manufacturing) Company while Laura was described as a high-strung, devout Roman Catholic.

After their seven-year-old son had died of an illness, the Goodins adopted Marcia, a Canadian from the Iroquois tribe, in 1970. She was described as being intelligent, attractive, and shy, yet friendly, but she was having problems at school, where she had been teased and eventually beaten because of her Native heritage.

Gerald and Laura apparently became overprotective of Marcia and they walked her to school every day and would not allow her to leave the house alone.

Marcia had been home from school for about five weeks, partly to recuperate from the beating, when the occurrences began on Friday night, November 22, with loud poundings on the walls, objects dropping from shelves, tables overturning, and chairs reportedly levitating.

On the following day, Laura Goodin was injured when a television set, which allegedly moved under its own power, fell on her, said Special Constable Jack Bracken, an emergency ambulance driver, who took her to St. Vincent's Hospital. She suffered injuries to two toes (one of them suspected as being broken) on her right foot, he said.

Sunday, November 24, was the most hectic day of the case. At about dawn, Mrs. Goodin said that several easy chairs mysteriously moved and a kitchen table flipped over. Her husband said he saw another table rise and turn over. "Chairs picked themselves up and started going every which way. And there was nobody in the room but me," Gerald said. "Other things started happening in other rooms [when Marcia was with me]. A knife holder above the kitchen sink flew off the wall towards me and I caught it. Marcia was with me and she could not have done this."

The Goodins called for help from their friends, Harold and Mary Hofmann. Harold recalls entering the Goodin home: "The place was a mess...tables were overturned and there were knives, forks, and dishes all over. The big TV was on its side. When I put it back, a smaller TV began rocking back and forth by itself." Hofmann said there was no one else in the room.

Another neighbor, off-duty police officer Holsworth, was summoned to the home.

Holsworth ran into the home and saw the refrigerator rise off the floor, turn at right angles, and then set itself down, bumping into his right elbow, but not injuring him. He also said he saw three reclining chairs start to shake. After checking the house, including the cellar, for possible explanations or trickery, he found none. "There has got to be a logical explanation for the things I saw, but whatever it is, I don't have it," he said. "I doubt that the Goodins could have caused these things to move. They weren't near them when they moved."

THE ACTION HEATS UP

Patrolman Tomek then arrived with three other officers and made his observation about the flying shelves, noted earlier in this chapter. Almost immediately, several officers saw a lamp start to shake inexplicably.

"When we got there, we thought we were investigating a burglary, the way [the house] was messed up," Tomek said. "Only later did we find out [it was an alleged case of the paranormal]. What we saw there was totally unexpected and some of the policemen were really frightened. I was told I would see a lot of things in the police force, but I never expected this."

Shelves were reportedly shaking with high-pitched sounds and Patrolman Leroy Lawson said he was nearly struck by a picture falling off the wall.

Patrolman George F. Wilson Jr. said he saw the refrigerator move a few feet along the kitchen floor toward him and then a brass crucifix on a wall reportedly vibrated, rattled, and fell to the floor. Wilson also said he saw a 21-inch portable television turn itself around and face the wall and a bureau fall to the floor and bounce several times. Three chairs also bounced around and changed their positions in the room, he added.

"Everything was unreal in the house when we came in there," Patrolman Cal Leonzi said. "Everything was moving. A picture fell off the wall. The TV set shook."

At one juncture, a crying Mrs. Goodin was wearing a crucifix around her neck and clutching rosary beads.

Leonzi said he had been watching Marcia and was certain she was not moving anything. And yet Leonzi said he saw "pictures fly off the walls and a heavy wooden table start moving... I saw the little girl in a heavy, brown armchair fly backwards three times. We tried to make that chair do the same thing, but even a guy 235 pounds couldn't make it move like that."

Holsworth said that, apart from the kitchen, there were rugs in every room in the house, making it difficult to move chairs and objects with sleight of hand without getting caught.

Then the puzzled, even spooked, police officers called in the Bridgeport Fire Department to check the foundations of the house and for malfunctioning gas lines or electric lines. Nothing out of the ordinary was found, although Deputy Fire Chief of Operations Fred Zwerlein did see something that left him shaken: "A kitchen chair jumped in front of me, several inches into the air, and fell over backwards. And there was no one near it."

A short time later, when he was in the living room, Zwerlein said he saw a large recliner floating "a couple of inches off the ground." In addition, Fire Chief John Gleason said his men saw dinner plates "rattling, pictures jumping off the wall, a television set falling over, and a heavy leather chair jumping at least 6 inches off the floor." A crucifix was said to have fallen off a wall. (Later, Professor John Nicholas, head of the geology department at the University of Bridgeport, ruled out earthquakes or tremors as the cause of the events.)

But firemen offered no theories as to the cause. "We are not very good at chasing devils," Gleason said.

Three firemen and a radio newsman said they saw an overstuffed reclining chair somersault, a television set spin, and chairs levitate, all without the help of human hands.

Tim Quinn, a newsman for WNAB Radio, said he saw little Marcia slammed into a wall 5 feet away "like someone had a rope on her and pulled her into the wall." She suffered a bump to her head.

Quinn said he also saw a leather chair sitting on a thin rug, the sort that leaves a mark when you step on it. "Suddenly, the back went down and the chair moved a few feet," he said. "But there was no mark on the carpet from the runners underneath the chair."

If little Marcia was causing havoc, she was doing it with a sore back, which had been in a brace after she had been beaten and kicked at school.

Rev. William Charbonneau, an assistant pastor of St. John of the Cross Roman Catholic Church in Middlebury, who taught a course in the occult at St. Joseph College in West Hartford, Connecticut, said that during the ten hours he was at the home on Sunday and early Monday, he saw a TV and a chest of drawers fall over. "This is no hoax," he said.

Rev. Charbonneau said he checked for any evidence of fraud, such as strings or wires, but found nothing. He kept a close eye on Marcia, who was holding the family's white and orange calico cat, Sam, for comfort during some of the occurrences.

"At one point, [Marcia] was next to me, showing me a bracelet, when a heavy dresser moved off a table and whizzed by," the assistant pastor said.

Rev. Charbonneau said he saw several strange occurrences, including a bureau crash to the floor behind the girl. "This is a classic case of a poltergeist. It comes from some kind of psychic energy, but what causes that energy, I don't know."

Also on Sunday, Rev. Edward Doyle of St. Patrick's Church, the fire department chaplain, blessed all the rooms in the Goodin home with holy water. But he said he saw nothing to suggest that evil spirits were present.

As the weekend dragged on, requests for interviews became so persistent that the family stopped the media from entering the house.

To add to the carnival-like atmosphere, the family called in two demonologists, Ed and Lorraine Warren of Monroe, Connecticut, members of the New England Society for Paranormal Research, who had seen thirty-six exorcisms over the years and had investigated everything from werewolves to ghosts.

Lorraine Warren said that police officers were humbled by what they saw. "Never in my life did I see so many police officers get down on their knees and ask for a priest's blessing as in that house," she said.

"Exorcism must be performed in this house to learn what is causing these happenings," her husband said. Later, he said the paranormal force in the house was "something inhuman," but no exorcism was performed in the home.

THE HOAX THEORY

On Monday, November 25, Barbara Carter, Marcia's tutor, said she saw a television set fall over and chairs move, but the occurrences were getting few and far between.

At a press conference on Tuesday, November 26, Supt. Walsh declared it all a hoax.

Walsh said that Marcia was responsible for moving all the objects in the house while others were distracted, and that she had confessed as much to police. "She had been the one who had done the banging on the walls and floors, knocked a crucifix to the floor, threw pictures down, and caused other unusual things to happen," Walsh said.

One of the incidents that Marcia allegedly confessed to was throwing her voice as a ventriloquist through her pet cat, Sam, making it appear the animal was talking.

Then Walsh repeated his earlier statement in the investigation: "There are no ghosts in Bridgeport."

But Marcia told the media she did not fake anything, although she apparently did not give extensive interviews.

Walsh himself did not investigate the Goodin house, but one of his officers, Patrolman Michael Costello, believed that some of his fellow officers might have been tricked by ten-year-old Marcia, perhaps because they had been expecting to see something supernatural and quickly became "believers."

"I think it was as phony as a $3 bill," said Costello, who admitted he had not seen anyone in the house fake an incident.

But, despite skepticism from many of their superiors back at the police department, most of the officers stood by their earlier claims that what they saw was a poltergeist, ghost, or some other type of paranormal event.

Sergeant Bernard Mangiamele, who had twenty-two years of experience on the force, absolved Marcia of any blame. "I stood and watched a heavy wooden bureau slowly start to vibrate," he said. "Then it lifted itself up and moved around. If I hadn't seen it with my own eyes, I wouldn't have believed it.... What I saw amazed me."

Police Lieutenant Leonard Cocco trusted the reports of his four patrolmen and a sergeant, who said they saw phenomena, including a moving refrigerator, flying ashtrays, and a slamming door. "Together, they have more than 100 years of experience," Cocco said. "If they said they saw something, they saw something. I just don't know what it was."

Gerald Goodin refuted Walsh's claim about a hoax and said the police wanted to close the case and settle all the commotion. He and others said that no one had caught Marcia cheating and there had been more than forty witnesses to the events. But Gerald and Laura Goodin said they did not believe in a supernatural explanation and that there had to be a logical one, although they did not know what it was.

The Warrens said the police brass officially called the case a hoax because it was getting too hot to handle in the community and in the media, and many officers were looking silly in some people's eyes because of their comments.

"If the whole thing is a hoax, it's one of the biggest hoaxes I've ever seen," said Ed Warren, who claimed to have seen a number of unusual events in the home, including a mirror smash and a large chest of drawers fall down. "No 10-year-old child, who weighs 70 pounds, could create a hoax in full view of police, firemen and investigators for that length of time."

Walsh refuted Warren's statement, believing that the Warrens were out to make money on the case. The Warrens said they were not charging the Goodins for their services, but were making money lecturing on the paranormal.

Years later, Rev. Charbonneau would say, "I know the things I saw and the police saw in my presence, and it was real. It definitely wasn't a hoax."

Supt. Walsh and several other superior officers had a theory that Marcia was using deception or some sort of magic with the support of her family so they could make money out of the case, which was attracting national publicity. Outside the home, the crowd swelled to about 1,500 people on Sunday night, including journalists from as far away as New York City, causing a major traffic jam.

One man was arrested for disorderly conduct as armed police and guard dogs surrounded the home.

By Tuesday night, the occurrences inside the home had waned, along with the crowd outside.

A POLTERGEIST THEORY

If the case was not a hoax, what might have been behind it?

A psychic investigator, Boyce Batey, of Bloomfield, Connecticut, said he was in the Goodin home for some of the occurrences and made a detailed study of the case after interviewing many witnesses.

He concluded that some of incidents were poltergeist phenomenon, but he suspected that other incidents might have been "simulated" by Marcia or other family members. Batey believed the activity was caused by "unresolved and unexpressed tensions and emotions, especially the feelings of hostility and fear. The tensions that accompany the preadolescent phase of development [in Marcia] are also involved. Not finding expression and resolution normally, these tensions were released paranormally [and subconsciously]."

Another parapsychologist, Jerry Sawyer of Fairfield, Connecticut, who said he saw a television fall while Marcia was on the opposite side of the room, also leaned toward the poltergeist theory and he believed it was caused by intense stress in the Goodin house.

Long after the occurrences had ceased, the Goodin family continued to live in the house on Lindley Street and by 1976, Marcia was reportedly doing well in school.

A real estate company tried to sell the house for them for $21,500. Ten families were taken through the home, but no one bought it. "I have been to the house and it appears to be clean and neat, but small," said the owner of the real estate firm, George Brown.

In 1995, radio reporter Tim Quinn recalled of the case: "I'm a simple kind of guy. I'm not particularly deep, but there was definitely something... toward the end, I wondered if all of the things that supposedly happened really did, and if they did were they man-made or child-made events. But I have no proof."

It is not known what became of Marcia Goodin. Her adoptive mother, Laura, died in a car crash in 1994. In 1995, Gerald Goodin was still living in the small house at 966 Lindley Street and he died several years later. The house had a weathered look, with peeling paint, an American flag, a Catholic symbol on the door, and a whole lot of stories.

Skeptic Sammy: I'm really pleased these police officers aren't investigating a break and enter at my place. How about that Patrolman Costello, who stood up to the hallucinations of his fellow officers! I'd like to know how long the friction lasted at that cop shop. It's one thing to have sharp public disagreements about a Murder One case, but Moving Fridge One?

Rebutt Al: This case seems to have a ring of truth to it. Otherwise, I fail to see how so many experienced cops got it so wrong at the hands of a ten-year-old girl. If their observations were so poor, if they made mistakes that obvious, they should have been fired and replaced by one smarter than them—that little girl. She probably could have had the superintendent's job within a few years. But I can't see how the police were that mistaken.

The Flying Phone

The Tina Resch case of Columbus, Ohio, in 1984 takes up this entire section. It is perhaps the most famous and widely publicized poltergeist case of modern times, and not without controversy. Members of the Resch household and many of their friends reported airborne glasses, moving tables, and a Princess telephone, which was photographed in mid-air and shown around the world in newspapers the following day.

This chapter also formally introduces two of the main people in this book, Dr. William Roll, perhaps the most respected poltergeist investigator of recent times, and the world's number one skeptic of the paranormal, James (The Amazing) Randi.

CHAPTER 8

THE HOUSE OF STYROFOAM CUPS

"The extent to which it is possible to observe poltergeist events under good conditions will determine whether or not science can take them seriously."

—PARAPSYCHOLOGIST WILLIAM ROLL

When a family packs up and moves to a motel near their home for three days, leaving all the lights blazing, you know something is amiss. And so it was for John and Joan Resch and their daughter, Tina, in March 1984.

Home life could simply not go on the way it had been for even one more day in their house in Columbus, Ohio. For starters, the phone was acting up like you wouldn't believe, making a screeching noise every time someone tried to use it.

In the kitchen, there was juice on the walls and cheese and eggs on the floor. All but one glass was broken. The valuables were hidden away. Nerves were frayed and no one could sleep. Everybody was afraid of what had become known as The Force.

The Force, they said, was responsible for the broken household items and for moving furniture and scaring everyone half to death.

And so, it was off to the motel to seek sanctuary in perhaps the most famous and controversial case of an alleged poltergeist in American history. The story would have some spectacular moments, as a photographer captured a flying phone on film, and end badly years later with Tina being sent to jail after pleading guilty to killing her own daughter.

Let us set the stage for this story. The Resches lived in an ordinary brick and stucco home at 5242 Blue Ash Road on a quiet street in north Columbus.

It was well kept, and through the years, the family had taken in about 250 foster children. And it was a well-known residence — the city's largest newspaper, the *Columbus Dispatch*, had published a column on the family for outstanding community service.

In some ways, it was a traditional middle-class backdrop furnished with lots of Sears merchandise. Before The Force moved in, it had been a homey haven of couches and live plants, collages of family photos, and wall-to-wall carpets. Who wouldn't want to live here?

At that time, John and Joan had six children living in their house — their natural son, Craig, twenty-four; their adopted daughter Tina, fourteen; and four foster kids, from six years old to a few months. And there was a huge Siberian husky, Pete.

The focus of this story, Christina Elaine (Tina), was born on October 26, 1969, and abandoned shortly after by her mother. Joan Resch adopted her at a hospital when she was less than a year old. Tina was a busy, at times restless child, who had some trouble with projects in elementary school and was described as hyperactive. Joan suspected she had a learning disability and even attention deficit disorder (however, she showed talent in Girl Scouts, winning an achievement award). By Grade 3, her parents started giving her the drug Ritalin to relax her, but other students and even teachers reportedly teased her. She was beaten by bullies and on one occasion was left tied up by other students in the schoolyard.

Tina was insecure and slept with many teddy bears and other stuffed animals in her bed at night to comfort her.

Finally, Joan pulled Tina out of school and decided to have her tutored at home. At home, Tina helped with the foster children, but this tended to make her feel bottled up in the crowded Resch house.

By age fourteen, according to her family photos on the wall, Tina looked like she might be a people pleaser, seemingly forcing herself to smile in some shots. Like many girls, she liked perfume, music, and sometimes Bible study, and she developed crushes on older guys. She was also having problems with her parents.

Tina was tall for her age — about 5 feet, 8 inches — a brunette who was not quite beautiful, and yet attractive. There was most often a sparkle, an energy, a brightness in her eyes, and she seemed like someone you would like to spend time with. She looked like she had something to offer. Jim Corrigan, a neurologist who had visited with Tina, called her "kinetic, frenetic, bright eyed and bushy-tailed and darting all over."

If Tina was at times restless, she was also coy, even shy. Yes, she seemed to want to give to others — she warmed quickly to visitors — and yet she held something back. For example, her wristwatch was worn with its face under her wrist, so only she could see it.

By 1984, Tina's energy was becoming negative — she was starting to talk back to her parents and even became angry. Sometimes she refused to do her share of the housework.

John and Joan were strict parents and not afraid to spank their kids. They believed that unless they were firm, they could not have managed 250 foster children for the Franklin County Children's Services. But Tina said the corporal punishment got too much at times. On one occasion, she said, she was beaten by John and threatened him with a knife if he hit her again.

One of her frustrations, Tina said, was that she did not know her birth parents and she was not allowed to find out who they were.

Another source of sadness was that one of her best friends, Tina Scott, had been killed in a car crash in 1983. Scott, who was eleven years older than Tina, had been her confidante, her big sister.

Tina Resch's adoptive father, John Resch, was fifty-seven and described by those who knew him as a strong, well-built man, but not big on conversation. He spoke through his actions, gestured frequently, and was said to be a perfectionist when building and fixing things.

John, who had recently retired as a superintendent for a sheet metal firm, had not been well lately after suffering a heart attack. His full-time job had become helping Joan with Tina, Craig, and the four foster children.

As his wife, Joan Resch seemed to complement him well with her friendly, ever-smiling demeanor and easy ways. She was in her mid-fifties and quite neat in her dress and appearance.

THE INCIDENTS BEGIN

The first reported so-called paranormal incident in the house was claimed by Tina herself. She said that on Thursday, March 1, 1984, the day John allegedly beat her and she threatened him with a knife, she went to bed early. When she looked at her digital clock radio in the bedroom, the numbers began racing on their own without her touching the clock, she said. Then the radio came on by itself, and, after she turned it off, it came on again, she said. The only way to stop it was by unplugging it, which she did.

And then, the following morning, there was a mysterious problem with the heart monitor of one of the foster children, six-month old Anne. According to Joan, it kept giving false alarms. After Joan unplugged it, the alarm kept going off without any power or batteries, she said.

On Saturday morning, March 3, the television was reportedly malfunctioning as Tina and the children watched cartoons. Joan blamed Tina, which irritated the teenager. The family did not believe in a paranormal explanation for the occurrences, similar to those in the popular movie of two years earlier, *Poltergeist*. Tina then said she was developing a headache and a stomach ache and that she was tired of being blamed for things she did not do.

When Joan asked Tina to help her set her hair, a dryer reportedly slammed shut and started up on its own in another room, Joan said. Then, according to a puzzled and even frightened Joan, the garbage disposal in the kitchen came on with no one around, the minute hand of a battery-operated wall clock in the family room started spinning around, lights were coming off and on all over the house, and water began pouring out of faucets in an upstairs bathroom. Tina could not have been responsible for this mess because she had been with her, Joan said.

The Columbus and Southern utility company checked the wiring and power in the house, but found nothing unusual. While workers were in the house, a stereo system came on loudly and a television set, which was unplugged, came on, Joan said. And then her husband John reported unusual incidents involving household appliances.

Joan then called a friend, electrician Bruce Claggett, fifty-four, who had problems hearing her over the telephone. "There was an unearthly howling over the phone, like someone or something was preventing us from communicating," Claggett later recalled. At the Resch home, Claggett could find no electrical problems, hot spots, or loose joints and he thought the family was kidding him when they recounted the wacky occurrences.

But before he left, Claggett saw something unusual himself — the lights started going on and off. And he immediately found the source — the light switches on the walls were turning on and off of their own accord, he said. As well, while Claggett was in the kitchen with Tina and Joan, the garbage disposal came on under its own volition, he said. Baffled but not beaten, Claggett and Joan then taped down all the light switches to the walls with Scotch tape.

Suddenly, two ceiling lights in the kitchen activated, despite tape over their switches, so Claggett re-taped them. But they soon came on again, with no one near the switches.

"There was no way that [Tina] or anybody else could have turned those switches on... I felt the hair stand up on the back of my head," said Claggett, described as a cool, collected man.

This bizarre scenario repeated itself many times over the next several hours with the Scotch tape popping off the light switches and the bulbs coming on. The witnesses were Claggett, Tina, John, and Joan. Tina's reaction seemed to be one of excitement, but after her apparent glee subsided, she complained again of pains in her head and stomach. And she moaned, "I guess I'll get blamed for this, too."

Claggett was certain that Tina had not staged the scenario because he had been watching her closely. "I knew in my own heart and my own mind that nobody was playing tricks," he said. The only others in the house were the four small foster children, six and under, and they were not in a position to affect the lights, the electrician said.

Her father John was still not sure about Tina and later he blamed her when the water faucets in a bathroom suddenly came on and a picture on the living room wall swung to and fro. However, Tina's stepbrother, twenty-four-year-old Craig, said he saw the swinging picture and that Tina had not touched it. Prior to that, Craig had suspected Tina of trickery and was trying to catch her.

A short time later, John could not blame Tina for a painting, which swung in a similar fashion on a wall. She wasn't close enough to touch it, he said. John stopped it from swinging, but it started up again, he said. He checked for string, but found nothing. And when he put the painting under the couch, it slid out of its own accord, he said. Tina reportedly laughed.

Finally, still on the long, crazy day of March 3, John called the police. Two officers arrived and checked the house. At one point, while Tina led a cautious officer upstairs, a metal pan suddenly flew from a bathroom behind her. The officer drew his gun and pointed into the room, but he did not shoot. The cops did not stay for long and apparently later back at the station, they suggested in their brief report that the Resches were mentally ill.

And so the unexplained activity began and would continue for six weeks and become somewhat violent.

On Sunday, March 4, a friend of the Resch family, Joyce Beaumont, described as a levelheaded payroll clerk at Rockwell International, arrived at the home, suspecting Tina of trickery. But almost immediately, Beaumont absolved Tina of any blame when she said she saw several occurrences, including two sticks of butter slide up a cabinet door. She said she saw Tina get hit in the back of the head by a candlestick while sitting in the family room. It had reportedly flown from the kitchen and it was the first time someone in the house had been hit.

Beaumont said she also saw a clock fall on Tina's head and later the teenager was reportedly pinned to the floor by a table that fell on her. By this time, Tina was screaming and crying in pain, Beaumont said. As Joyce tried to free her, she said a telephone hit her (Joyce) on the back of the head. There was no one else in the room. "The phone was coming out from behind and hitting me while Tina was underneath the table," Beaumont said.

Later that day, two of Tina's stepbrothers said they saw kitchen chairs and a couch move by themselves. Joan and John, wondering if the cause was of a spiritual nature, called the minister of their Lutheran church, Pastor Heinz, who blessed each room in the house with a lit candle and told the evil to leave. But when he tried to sit on a couch, it lurched toward him, he said. No children were close enough to have touched it, he said.

On Monday, March 5, Mike Harden, a reporter for the *Columbus Dispatch*, said he saw a doll's cradle flip into the air and other similar occurrences while Tina was not close enough to have affected them. "I'm seeing something I can't understand," he said.

THE PHOTO SEEN AROUND THE WORLD

Also on March 5, *Dispatch* photographer Fred Shannon went to the Resch home. A veteran photographer for thirty years, Shannon thought he had seen everything, but he would soon change his mind. His first shot in the house was of the only wineglass left unsmashed. He took a shot of Tina holding it away from her body. A few minutes later, while he and Tina were in another room, the glass mysteriously smashed back in the dining room, he said. Shannon also said that six metal coasters had crashed against the dining room wall.

Then the action turned to the family room. While Tina sat on a chair, a Princess telephone flew across her lap, according to her stepbrother Craig. (It was not the first incident involving a phone. On March 4, Joyce Beaumont said a phone had flown across Tina's lap as the latter was crying. There was no way Tina could have thrown the phone, said Beaumont, who came to the conclusion there was an unknown force at work in the house.)

Craig said he also saw an afghan fly up from the carpet and land on Tina's head. Shannon took a photo of the afghan draped over her, then a room divider reportedly fell over. Shannon checked the room for strings, but found nothing.

At this point, Shannon was ready to shoot anything that moved, and he got his wish. As Tina sat on the side of a reclining chair, a loveseat situated about 4 feet away against a wall moved out from the wall about 18 inches, Shannon said. He got two pictures, one of them showing Tina looking a little surprised and appearing to brace herself for the loveseat moving toward her and a second showing her appearing to lose her balance and fall backwards into the recliner. "I saw this with my own eyes," Shannon said.

Then there was a loud noise and a large candlestick, which had been on the floor next to the loveseat, reportedly moved into the hallway.

Then the Princess phone really took center stage. As Tina sat on the reclining chair with the phone on a small table to her left, the phone started making airborne trips across her lap or repeatedly striking her in the side. It was attached to a cord and sometimes the flying cord would stretch out 6 feet across the room. "[Tina] wasn't touching anything," Joyce Beaumont said. "She was sitting there with her arms crossed."

Shannon, who was sitting on a couch nearby, said he saw this happen about seven times, but the flights were so fast and so unpredictable that it was difficult to capture them on film. "Each time the receiver flew like a projectile, rapidly and with great force," Shannon said. Several people in the room, including Shannon and reporter Mike Harden, said they did not think that Tina could have picked up the phone and tossed it so many times without them seeing her do it.

Finally, while he was focusing on the phone, Shannon got what he wanted — a picture of the phone flying about 6 feet across Tina's lap. Tina looked surprised and was holding her hands backward as though she had touched something hot.

Harden saw the phone fly. "I was seated across the room facing Tina . . . I saw [the phone] in motion without it being aided in any way on her part. It moved on a level trajectory from Tina's left to right."

Before Shannon got the film developed, two of Joan's friends from the Franklin County Children's Services, Kathy Goeff and Lee Arnold, who was Tina's caseworker, showed up to see if they could help the family. They said they saw the phone jump and crash into the loveseat. Arnold said she was watching Tina and believed it was not possible for the girl to have tossed the phone, especially at such high acceleration. "Three different times I saw it," Goeff said. "It was really interesting."

On the following day, March 6, Shannon's photo of Tina and the flying phone appeared on the front page of the *Columbus Dispatch*, then the photo was picked up by other newspapers and media around the United States and abroad. After that, reporter Harden received about 150 requests for the family to be interviewed from other media.

With all the publicity, the occurrences, and the increasing stress, family life was deteriorating in the Resch home. The four foster children were sent to other homes, which upset Joan and particularly John, who had become close to the kids. And Tina said she was getting harassed at school. "Kids would knock me down stairs and tell me to fly or they'd throw things at me and ask about *The Twilight Zone* [television show]," she said.

And so, John, Joan, and Tina packed up and went to a motel for three days and two nights. They didn't have much choice, since there were few glasses, cups, and dishes left unbroken and they were eating out of paper plates and Styrofoam cups.

No incidents were reported at the motel, but things got back to normal when they returned to 5242 Blue Ash Road. As soon as Tina walked through the door, several items reportedly moved, including a soft drink bottle, a candle, and a glass.

Tina said she didn't know what was happening. "I didn't know what to think," she said. "I thought the house was haunted, or it had something to do with the devil. People told me I was possessed." (However, at another time, Tina admitted to reporter Harden that she had been arguing with her mother Joan lately and when Tina got angry, the occurrences escalated. "It usually happens when I'm really mad," Tina said.)

On March 7, the Hughes family came to offer their emotional support to the Resches. Barbara Hughes, a foster mother, and her husband, Ted, a schoolteacher, brought their two adopted children with them. They were all born-again Christians, bearing a crucifix on a chain for Tina. What they say they saw smacked of the devil's work — four metal coasters flying of their own accord, a soap dish spinning in circles, and a glass shattering. Barbara said she was struck by kitchen chairs and one of their adoptive children was allegedly hit by a phone

Once again, the people in the house claimed that Tina could not physically have caused the damage. "Tina and I were standing in the doorway," Barbara said. "[The coasters] took off— one, two, three, four. The first one I saw in the air and then the others took off. One at a time, they just lifted off the pile and went around the room like someone was playing Frisbee."

INSURANCE CLAIM FOR WHAT?

Can one claim insurance for poltergeist damage?

The Resches asked their insurance company, Midwestern Indemnity of Cincinnati, for coverage of broken paintings, glasses, and lamps. Agents said they considered the family trustworthy, but they did not know who to blame for the damage, except to put it under the category of malicious mischief and vandalism.

One agent told the family they could probably win the claim because they had an all-risk policy, but the company was reluctant to put it through because it might open itself up to unusual or fraudulent claims in the future.

In the end, the Resches decided not to press for the insurance money.

CHAPTER 9

THE CIRCUS COMES TO COLUMBUS

"The Resch case boils down to simply a matter of faith."

–COLUMNIST JOE DIRCK IN THE **COLUMBUS CITIZEN-JOURNAL**

On Thursday, March 8, the circus came to Columbus in the form of a media conference in the Resch home. Until then, the family had granted few interviews and had been given pseudonyms to protect their identities. However, because they and the *Columbus Dispatch* had been besieged for interview requests, the Resches consented to a news conference.

The Resches seemed tense as reporters gathered in the house, following a heavy snowfall the night before. Tina said she was worried the journalists would judge her and blame her for everything that had transpired over the preceding week.

But before the reporters arrived, another incident occurred while family friend Barbara Hughes was making lunch. As she served Tina at a table, two kitchen chairs reportedly moved and hit Barbara in the stomach, and she doubled over in pain. Tina had been sitting across from her at the time. Then a baby chair slid into Hughes's knee. A witness was Peggy Covert, Joan Resch's married daughter, who was a nurse. Covert said that Tina had been in no position to move the baby chair.

By 1 p.m., about forty journalists had assembled in the Resch's 20-by-20-foot living room and television lights were making things hot. "I didn't want to do this," Tina said in her opening remarks. "If I say anything, people are going to think I'm crazy."

But the reporters, some of whom had cast her in their stories as a cross between characters in the movies *Carrie* and *Poltergeist*, were easy on her and they asked her to relax.

The first question was if she was afraid when objects moved in the house. "No," Tina said. "But it's scary when they're flying. I wish they would stop. I still don't believe things like this can happen."

Her father John agreed. "I see it and I still don't believe it. How a glass can fly at a 90-degree angle through a doorway and around a corner, or the television run with no electricity? I just try to clean up, to turn my head away when it happens."

Joan Resch explained that she had packed away her valuables "so they wouldn't get broken or hurt someone."

The media conference was supposed to last for just one hour, but the journalists wanted to stay, hoping to see paranormal activity for themselves. Two, three, and then four hours passed and the house was still full of reporters and cameramen walking through the rooms and peaking around corners, mostly following Tina. Video cameras were set up at various locations, but no phenomena were seen.

Finally, at about 9 p.m., the family's nerves were getting frayed. Joan got Tina aside and suggested she do something to get rid of the reporters. The mild-mannered Joan didn't have the courage to tell them to leave. "Something has got to happen," Joan reportedly said to her daughter.

Finally, at about 9:30 p.m., a large table lamp fell to the floor. Drew Hadwal of the Columbus station WTVN-TV believed he had caught the action on camera and he hurried to his station to check. What he discovered was that Tina had apparently intentionally knocked the lamp down with her hand. The videotape revealed that Tina had been unaware she was on camera when she knocked the lamp to the floor and then looked surprised, as though it had crashed on its own. The footage was shown on television and suddenly, sympathy for the poltergeist family plummeted. Had Tina been pulling stunts all along?

When faced with the facts, Tina admitted that she pulled the lamp, but she said she did it to give the reporters something so they would finally leave the house. "To me, what happened was understandable," parapsychologist William Roll would later say. "Nothing paranormal was happening that afternoon and she wanted to get rid of the reporters."

Meanwhile, unusual events continued to be reported in the home. The day after the press conference, Hughes said that a heavy kitchen table kept moving on its own near Tina. "This is a heavy table — it just went right out from under me," Hughes said. The same day, Hughes and Joan said a chair flipped Tina off of it, dumping her onto the floor with such force that her glasses fell off.

By this time, though, Tina's credibility had fallen in some people's eyes, although not in the eyes of her mother and father, Barbara Hughes, and others who had seen what they called amazing occurrences.

ENTER THE PARAPSYCHOLOGIST AND THE SKEPTIC

William Roll, director of the Psychical Research Foundation in Durham, North Carolina, and considered one of the leading authorities on the paranormal and poltergeists, still believed that the case was worth investigating. He had been following the story in the newspapers and he arrived, along with his assistant Kelly Powers, on Sunday, March 11, three days after the media conference.

Although Roll wondered if Tina had been playing tricks all along, especially after finding a book on magic in her room, he tried to keep an open mind.

Roll said the first thing he noticed about Tina was her clumsiness, her habit of bumping into walls and furniture, like many growing teenagers. If she was a sleight-of-hand magician, as some critics claimed, she didn't show it, Roll said. Tina even had spells of dizziness and her clumsiness and lack of balance had led to many falls in recent years and broken bones in her arm and nose. (After the occurrences had begun, Tina was taken to the Department of Neurology at Ohio State University for testing. She was found to be relatively normal, although she showed a tendency to have tantrums and a problem with controlling her temper.)

In Roll's first two days in Columbus, there were no reported incidents and he was a little discouraged. That was not unusual in poltergeist cases, he said, because the action often subsides when an investigator shows up, then it picks up again after he has been in the presence of the poltergeist agent for a while.

But Roll was able to interview many witnesses, including Tina. She seemed to bond to the fatherly Roll almost immediately and she told him that she wished there were fewer children in the Resch house. She also said that she had first believed that the paranormal incidents were related to the death of her friend, Tina Scott, in 1983, which had made her sad and angry, particularly because she had not been allowed to go to her funeral. Not long after her death, Tina Resch said she saw an apparition of Scott in her room.

Roll also investigated the theory that Tina might have psychokinetic powers, partly due to sexual issues. In many other poltergeist cases he had investigated, the adolescent or youth suspected of being the poltergeist agent was going through puberty at the time of paranormal occurrences.

Roll discovered that Tina had already entered puberty, but there was the possibility that there was sexual tension; she told him that she had been raped by an adoptive brother (who is not named in this book).

On March 13, the circus stepped up a notch with the spectacular entrance of James (The Amazing) Randi, a professional magician who had become known for debunking claims of the paranormal throughout the world. As much as Tina Resch had been at center stage, Randi now attracted some big headlines. And, in a way, he would turn out to be Roll's arch-rival.

When interviewed by the *Columbus Dispatch* about the case over the phone before he came to the Resch home, Randi had been quoted as saying, "I don't believe in things that go bump in the night. It's the same reason I don't believe in Santa Claus and the tooth fairy."

Wearing a cape and a beard, Randi came to Columbus as part of a scientific team sent by Paul Kurtz, a philosophy professor at the University of Buffalo and the founder of the Committee for the Scientific Investigation of Claims of the Paranormal (CSICOP), which has become known for debunking claims of paranormal occurrences. The team also included astronomer/professors Steven Shore and Nicholas Sanduleak of the Case Western Reserve University in Cleveland.

Despite Randi's telephone interview, Kurtz said his team was open-minded. "We think the public deserves an explanation," he said, but then he added, "Offhand, it seems to me there's a hoax being perpetrated and the whole country is being bamboozled."

And now Randi was standing in front of the Resch home and giving an interview for reporters and TV cameras. "I've never seen a bona fide paranormal event, but that doesn't mean I won't," Randi said. "When you've sat by the chimney on Christmas Eve for thirty-five years and have never seen Santa Claus, you don't say he doesn't exist. I'm always ready for a soot-covered fat man in a red suit to bounce down the chimney."

Randi, buoyed by the videotape that had shown Tina pulling down the lamp, held up from under his cape a check for $10,000, which he would present to the Resches if they could show him one paranormal event.

However, Randi was not allowed into their house. He claimed that the media and John and Joan Resch had invited him to come to their home, but that it was Roll who stopped him from entering. Roll had already taken up residence at the Resch home and "was having a grand time hyperbolizing the events for the media," Randi said.

However, Joan took responsibility for keeping Randi out on the sidewalk. "It's been rough on us; we've had a circus," she said. "Now we have a magic show. No, not here." She said she was offended by Randi's cheap jokes and offer of money, which she refused.

Some of the witnesses to events in the Resch home, such as Barbara Hughes, refused to speak to CSICOP investigators because they suspected they did not have open minds and might misinterpret things they told them.

Meanwhile, The Force in the Resch house continued. Also on March 13, Joan reported that an unknown, unseen force pushed her against a refrigerator while Tina was with her.

Over the next few days, Roll said he witnessed six different objects move while Tina was near him — a roll of lipstick, a book, a teacup, candy, his Sony tape recorder, and pliers. "She clearly did not touch them," Roll said. "I was persuaded this was for real...I had handled three of the objects immediately before they moved, precluding the further possibility that they were attached to the trick devices. Now I knew it wasn't all chicanery. Things were actually flying by themselves."

Roll was coming to the conclusion that Tina was wired differently than other people and that she was somehow suspending gravity at a short distance with her tension and unusual energy.

OFF TO THE LABORATORY

As noted in earlier chapters, Roll calls the suspending of gravity zero point energy. Hoping to prove his theory, Roll then convinced Tina to come to his home in Durham, North Carolina, from March 17 to April 12, so that she could be tested at the nearby institutes where Roll had worked — the Institute of Parapsychology and the Spring Creek Institute.

According to Roll, a number of paranormal incidents took place with Tina at the institutes and at his home, but nothing spectacular or conclusive. "I had a lot of Danish porcelain in my home and I asked her not to have anything crash to the floor," Roll mused. "My wife was very nervous."

On March 31, while borrowing a three-wheel motorbike in Durham, Tina crashed and broke her leg. There were no further incidents until she returned home to Columbus.

In August 1984, with the incidents in Columbus becoming less frequent,

Roll became chairman for a panel on the case, which also included James Randi, photographer Fred Shannon, reporter Mike Harden, Dr. Rebecca Zinn, a psychotherapist who counseled Tina in North Carolina, and electrician Bruce Claggett.

In October 1984, Tina returned to the Spring Creek Institute, where Dr. Stephen Baumann was setting up tests for psychokinesis. By this time, Tina's alleged powers were apparently subsiding. And yet one day, Roll, Baumann, and psychotherapist Jeannie Stewart set up a table with a 12-inch socket wrench on it, which they hoped Tina could move with her mind. According to Roll, Tina was not allowed near the table, but while Stewart and Baumann were standing between Tina and the table, there was a loud noise behind them and they saw that the wrench had moved off the table and about 18 feet along the floor, finally hitting a door.

Also in North Carolina, Zinn said she saw a number of paranormal incidents involving Tina. In one case, Zinn said she took Tina by the hand as they walked down a hallway leading to her office when a telephone suddenly came from behind them and struck the girl in the back. "There was no way anyone could have touched it," Zinn said.

Zinn was so shaken about being around Tina, she called it "a lesson in fear…there was a greyness around me. My skin felt clammy, my stomach slightly nauseous. I felt a thick, heavy energy in the air."

As well in North Carolina, there were reportedly four movements of objects in Roll's house and ten incidents at Spring Creek after Tina was hypnotized to try to recapture her mindset and emotions back in Columbus.

Meanwhile, Randi and Kurtz wrote reports about the case in the *Skeptical Inquirer*, the bible of the CSICOP. Randi said that if the phenomena surrounding Tina were genuine, it would be "a repeal of the basic laws of physics." Roll countered that by saying that physics does not say that objects cannot be affected without tangible contact: "The moon revolves around the earth and magnets attract pieces of iron — recurrent spontaneous psychokinesis (RSPK) requires an extension of the laws of physics, not their repeal."

In his 1985 book, *A Skeptic's Handbook of Parapsychology*, Kurtz wrote, "Our investigators came up with the following explanation: Tina Resch is a disturbed 14-year-old who has dropped out of school and is being tutored at home. She had seen [the movie] *Poltergeist* and had learned how to hurl objects into the air unobserved…if a person is once caught cheating, then the further display of his or her powers should be highly suspect. Tina Resch and [spoon-bending psychic] Uri Geller are like [psychics] Eusapia Palladino and D.D. Home of earlier generations." Kurtz believes that those three people also cheated.

Randi declared the Resch case "essentially dead...the parapsychologists [he didn't name them] I have spoken to have accepted the probable scenario that Tina Resch was a publicity-seeking teenager who used simple deception and considerable guile to create a story that an incautious and rather uncaring newspaper staff snapped up and used for as much mileage as they could get."

Randi and Kurtz added that they thought other incidents in the Resch home were orchestrated by Tina. "Carefully observe the people nearby," they wrote in their report on the case. "As soon as they are not looking, quickly shoot an object into the air. If you tell them it is a poltergeist, and they can't easily see how it could have taken off, then they may accept the claim as genuine. If there is a predisposition to believe and the situation is charged with drama and emotion, it is more likely to arouse an affirmative response." However, Randi admitted the scientists had not interviewed many witnesses, partly because, like Barbara Hughes, they would not cooperate.

Meanwhile, the *Columbus Dispatch* didn't buy the skeptics' claims. Reporter Mike Harden, who had described himself as "the ultimate skeptic of the paranormal" before he first set foot in the Resch house, stood fast to his story. "I was reporting what I saw and could not explain," he said in 1985. "I saw a phone move and didn't see anyone move it. But only a fool would think that human vision is absolutely infallible. The opinion should be left up to the experts. They're going to be debating this for a long time."

Fred Shannon stood behind what he saw and what he photographed, and he added that the case changed his life. "On my mother's grave, it wasn't a hoax," he said in 1994. "I was scared to death. Lots of things were flying. Things didn't just levitate, they became projectiles."

After interviewing all of the witnesses and reviewing the case, William Roll said, "There is no doubt that Tina used trickery. The incident when she was filmed by WTVN-TV pulling down a lamp makes that clear...it shows her willingness to deceive when she thought it was to her advantage, to get the reporters off her back."

But Roll denied that many of the other incidents were chicanery. "The careful preparation and clumsy execution of the lamp trick is very different from the 34 occurrences when Tina was reported to be in a different room or the 125 occurrences when she was observed at the time the object moved. There were 16 events where people said they were looking at an object when it took off."

Roll added that in order to pull off these feats, Tina would require advanced skills in sleight of hand and devices enabling her to reach or move the objects. "There was no evidence of such," Roll said. "If we suppose that she was assisted by an accomplice, the fraud theory obviously would accommodate more occurrences, but still a large residue remains, including many at her home and all of those that took place when she was in North Carolina. This was an extremely rich and exciting case."

In the celebrated Princess telephone incident, which led to a photograph shown around the world, Randi reviewed a series of photos taken by Shannon and proposed that Tina had thrown the phone each time from left to right while sitting on the reclining chair. But Roll countered that Tina was right-handed and that, in order to conceal her trick in front of several witnesses, she would need to be as fast and inconspicuous as she could. That would mean that if she was being deceitful, she would have set herself up at the other side of the table to take advantage of her right hand.

Overall, Randi basically dismissed Roll as a credible researcher and called him "a myopic [nearsighted] and wears thick glasses; he is a poor observer." Roll countered that he was not myopic, but actually farsighted.

Roll said that Tina Resch was not a publicity seeker, as perhaps some of the other youths involved in poltergeist cases had been. "She never felt pleased that all this was going on," he said.

Some people felt that John Resch, Tina's adoptive father, was a good witness. They say he had more motivation to catch Tina cheating than anyone because he was proud of their possessions, much of which had been destroyed or damaged by The Force. And he was deeply hurt that the four young foster children had to leave the home. And yet, after suspecting Tina of trickery early on, he said he never caught her cheating.

Skeptic Sammy: I think I'm in love—this chap Randy is a man after my own heart. They should have let him into the Resch house. Where do I get his books again? Actually, I really feel for the family, doing all that work for foster children and this is the thanks they get in the end, a broken house and the wrath of a community. And, hey, this Tina girl had a book on magic—doesn't that tell you something?

Rebutt Al: See Chapter 11 for more on (correct spelling) Randi. You had to know there was an "I" in his persona. It's unfortunate, for the sake of research and serious investigators, that there are fraudulent cases, or at least cases that have some fraud in them. I think we should step back and not be blinded either by sudden "miracles" or "tricks." Once we do that, we oversimplify a complex subject, as this appears to be. By the way, if Tina Resch can read one book on magic and become as good overnight as The Amazing Randi, what is she doing with an off-Broadway act in Columbus?

CHAPTER 10

TRAGEDY

"They're never good dreams... and I always find myself thinking—when I wake up—that I wish I could go and bulldoze that house to the ground. Like somehow, that would make me feel better."

—TINA RESCH IN 2004, SERVING A PRISON SENTENCE

This story ends badly.

The Resches sold their house on Blue Ash Road in early 1986 and their relationship with Tina was not good. They wanted to put her into foster care, but there was a backlog of cases and she would have had to stay in a detention center. Instead, she married a young man she had met at a convenience store.

That marriage lasted just seventeen months amid Tina's accusations that her husband had beaten her. In 1987, John Resch suffered another heart attack and died. Soon after that, Tina dated a man she had met at church. The relationship did not last long, but it produced a baby girl, Amber, on September 29, 1988. Still living in Columbus, Tina then married — partly for the baby's sake, she said — Larry Boyer and she changed her name to Tina Boyer. But there were problems in that relationship, as well, and they drifted apart.

Parapsychologist William Roll had been keeping in touch with Tina and he suggested that she and Amber move close to him in Carrollton, Georgia, where he was living since moving from North Carolina. He was professor of psychology and psychical research at the State University of West Georgia. Tina trusted Roll and his friends and she took up his offer.

Tina said her daughter, Amber, was much like she herself had been as a child, bubbly and high-strung. "She was smart for her age," Tina said. "She'd say her ABCs and sing 'Jesus Loves Me' in sign language."

But Roll said there was tension between mother and daughter and that Tina had problems raising Amber, so he enrolled her in a parenting class at Carrollton Tech. "Tina was starting to turn her life around," Roll said.

Then Tina met another divorcé, David Herrin, a twenty-nine-year-old truck driver, who had a three-year-old daughter. They lived together for about six weeks.

On April 13, 1992, Amber Bennett Boyer died at age three. Police said that Amber died of bleeding in the brain and swelling of the brain. Tina and her boyfriend David Herrin were charged with murder and cruelty to children.

Prosecutors in the Carroll County murder case filed a list of what they say were thirty-three alleged transgressions against the child, which were used to show an alleged pattern of abuse by Tina. Prosecutors say the girl was repeatedly struck, severely scolded, locked in a closet, and burned with a cigarette.

Assistant District Attorney Anne Allen called it "the worst case of child abuse I have ever seen."

"A couple of things are true," Tina said. "But they're not the way they seem."

Through her attorney, Tina denied beating Amber and she said that the child had been in Herrin's care when the injuries occurred. She said if she was guilty of anything, it was of not taking her injured child to the hospital in time to save her life. But Herrin blamed Tina.

Tina pleaded guilty to felony murder and cruelty to children in order to avoid the electric chair and, at age twenty-five, she was sentenced to life plus twenty years. Herrin was not prosecuted for murder, but he was found guilty of cruelty to children and received a twenty-year sentence.

Tina is serving her sentence at Pulaski State Prison in Hawkinsville, Georgia. She was denied parole in 2002 and has reported bouts of depression in prison. Prisoner No. 810071 is up for parole again in 2007.

Paul Kurtz, the psychology professor at the New York University at Buffalo and chairman of the Committee for the Scientific Investigation of Claims of the Paranormal, followed the Tina Resch case through the years, beginning in 1984 when he sent a team of investigators to the Columbus case.

Kurtz believes that the way people had pampered Tina and believed her poltergeist story helped lead to her downfall in Georgia. "There's no question in our minds the girl was cheating," Kurtz said in 1994. "She was so good at it that she deceived people constantly. She was seeking attention and everybody fell for it. I think all this was a factor in a destructive course later on."

One of his team members in 1984, magician James Randi, agreed. "We must ask ourselves whether a proper investigation of the claims that brought this woman to world attention, which might have deprived her of the celebrity status that she attained through support by scientists [Roll and others] and media who encouraged her, might have brought her to a healthier state of mind and adult lifestyle. Such an unhappy child, discovering that she could so easily manipulate the media, becomes an adult who is not in a position to make appropriate choices in life."

Randi said the parapsychologists and the media used Tina as well for their own purposes.

These days, Roll occasionally visits Resch in jail and believes she got a harsh sentence. Roll said there was no direct link between the poltergeist activity of 1984 and Amber's death, but "Tina's damaged psyche prevented her from making good choices for herself and her child."

Meanwhile, Tina said in 2004 that she still dreams about her house on Blue Ash Road in Columbus. "They're never good dreams... and I always find myself thinking — when I wake up — that I wish I could go and bulldoze that house to the ground. Like somehow, that would make me feel better."

Roll wishes people like Tina could be studied better scientifically. "I think the abilities she had were a natural endowment of the human mind," he said. "She's already made quite a contribution to science... but to understand ourselves fully, and to better understand our brains and their capabilities, we need to know more about people like Tina. She is a sort of natural treasure."

In 2004, Roll wrote a detailed book about the case with writer Valerie Storey, *Unleashed: Of Poltergeist and Murder, the Curious Story of Tina Resch.*

One of Tina's former neighbors in Columbus, Jim Kress, bought the book and was saddened by the way things turned out. "I lived next door to John and Joan Resch when I was a teenager," he said. "I remember when they adopted Tina. She was a cute little one. Too bad things turned out the way they did."

CHAPTER 11

THE GHOSTBUSTER (WILLIAM ROLL) AND THE MYTHBUSTER (JAMES RANDI)

"The most important sense to investigate the psychic sense is common sense."

—WILLIAM ROLL

In this chapter, we will discover more about two of the prominent characters in this book who have been involved on opposite sides of many poltergeist controversies over the years, parapsychologist William Roll and magician/skeptic James (The Amazing) Randi.

The dry, soft-spoken Roll feels uncomfortable with the term "ghostbusters." "I think we're called parapsychologists," he says, without ego. For nearly fifty years, Roll has been the face and the voice of poltergeist research, having reviewed hundreds of cases around the world and investigated dozens of his own.

The general area of PSI, and whether it even exists, is hotly contested these days among scientists, parapsychologists, and psychics, but it is hard for anyone to get angry at Roll. He goes about his business, gathering painstaking details in highly charged family cases, and he does not seem to take things personally if skeptics dismiss his theories.

Roll is a respected Ph.D. academic with an undergraduate degree from the University of California, Berkeley; a master's from Oxford University in England; and a doctorate from Lund University in Sweden.

For two decades, he worked under the leadership of another parapsychologist, J.B. Rhine, the founder of modern parapsychology, at the Institute for Parapsychology at Duke University in Durham, North Carolina.

William George Roll was born in 1926 in Germany where his father was a counsel, but his father and mother divorced when he was three and he and his mother moved to her native Denmark.

Roll grew up in Birkerod, near Copenhagen, and had a traumatic childhood. In 1940, the Nazis occupied Denmark and his mother died suddenly two years later. Roll, who became a ward of a guardian who didn't like him, did poorly at school.

A determined Roll joined the Danish resistance movement from September 1944 to the country's liberation on May 5, 1945, and was a courier between the leader of the resistance and the group leaders. "They were the best times of my life... it was exciting and I was working for a good cause, freedom from the barbarians," he says today. "My confidence was restored."

During his teens, Roll said he had out-of-body experiences. "I wondered if I was having some sort of hallucination, or a serious case of absent-mindedness, or whether my soul had detached itself from the body."

A curious Roll began reading up on the subject and discovered "there was a field that explored experiences like this medically."

In 1947, he moved to California to be close to his father and to attend the University of California, Berkeley, then he married Muriel, a girl he had met in New York.

After joining Rhine at Duke in 1957, Roll got his first poltergeist case the following year at the home of James and Lucille Herrmann on Long Island, New York. (See Chapter 19.) Tops were mysteriously popping off bottles of soda and holy water and porcelain figures were flying into walls. The Herrmanns thought that a spirit had invaded their home.

But after investigating with Gaither Pratt, assistant director at the Duke institute, Roll suspected that the couple's twelve-year-old son, Jimmy, was unconsciously using his mind to cause the occurrences. It was a rare and complex phenomena, Roll and Pratt said, and they termed it "recurrent spontaneous psychokinesis." Until then, the general public and even researchers had believed that poltergeists were actually a type of ghost.

Since 1958, Roll has investigated numerous aspects of the paranormal, including ESP and its relationship to memory, the way magnetic fields affect people's perceptions of psychic occurrences, and the possibility of ghosts and life after death.

But he is most known for his work on poltergeists. "I found the poltergeist work more interesting than conducting ESP tests," he said.

Starting in the 1960s, Roll studied 116 written reports of poltergeist cases spanning over four centuries in more than 100 countries. Roll identified patterns that he labeled RSPK. Generally, he discovered, the most common agent was a child or teenager whose unwitting RSPK was a way of expressing hostility without the fear of punishment, he said. The subjects or poltergeist agents were usually girls entering puberty. The individual was not aware of being the cause of such disturbances, but was, at the same time, secretly or openly pleased that they occurred.

The mild-mannered, soft-speaking Roll believes that psychic events and poltergeist cases occur more often around magnetic fields, which are often near geological faults. It is a complex subject and he does not claim to have all the answers, only unproven theories.

Other major cases Roll has investigated besides Long Island include the following:

- *Portsmouth, Virginia, 1962:* Cups and vases crash in a house, making a newspaper reporter jump aside. By the time Roll arrives on the scene, the incidents have died down, but he suspects that a young, unhappy boy is causing them through RSPK.
- *Miami, 1967:* Police officers and Roll watch as a nineteen-year-old worker reportedly uses his mind to make objects fall. (See Chapter 21.)
- *Olive Hill, Kentucky, 1969:* Roll and another researcher say they see objects move, but the family, who are Jehovah's Witnesses, asks them to leave and believe that an evil spirit is involved. (See Chapter 20.)
- *Columbus, Ohio, 1984:* Many events revolve around a troubled fourteen-year-old girl, and a photograph of a telephone jumping across her lap is circulated around the world. (See Chapters 8 through 10.)

In retrospect, Roll considers Columbus and Miami his most convincing cases because they both had "so many reliable witnesses."

After working with Rhine in North Carolina, Roll became a professor of psychology and psychical research at the State University of West Georgia in Carrollton, Georgia.

Over the years, Roll has been contacted by many people having problems with poltergeists or ghosts and in many cases he has alleviated their fears somewhat with his calm demeanor and the facts as he sees them. He is a trusting figure, but sometimes stressed-out families do not allow him into their homes (see the Mulvey case, Chapters 5 and 6) or they kick him out because they believe he has brought evil spirits with him (the Olive Hill case).

Although he is sympathetic, Roll says he's not easily hoodwinked and tries to go into cases with a skeptical yet open mind. He says he has caught some people trying to fake paranormal occurrences. "The most important sense to investigate the psychic sense is common sense," he said.

Such an occurrence happened in Mexico when he was in a room with a medium, who was conducting a séance. Roll was skeptical about the validity of the séance, so he used what he calls "the toothpaste test for ghosts." He hid some toothpaste in his shoe and when an apparition came close to him while everybody held hands in the dark room, he used his stockinged feet to mark the ghost's foot. Later, when the lights came on, Roll found a white smudge of toothpaste on the foot of a woman who owned the apartment. She had masqueraded as the spook.

Roll has appeared on six segments of the television show *Unsolved Mysteries* and has also been on the Discovery Channel and other television programs. He has written three books and more than 200 scientific articles. He speaks at conventions and is a regular contributor to the *Journal of Parapsychology* (www.parapsych.org).

In 1996, Roll received the outstanding career award from the Parapsychological Association and in 2002 he received the Tim Dinsdale Memorial Award from the Society for Scientific Exploration.

Roll has never seen a ghost, but he says he has seen things move in several poltergeist cases "without any familiar physical causes."

Roll retired in 1990, but he continues to write about his experiences and also investigates occasional cases of the paranormal while living with his second wife in Carrollton. He has three children who are in more conventional jobs: Lise, teaches children with learning disabilities at the University of Stockholm in Sweden; William Tertius, a financial adviser; and Lies, vice-president for an insurance firm.

At age seventy-nine in 2005, Roll is saddened that there doesn't seem to be anyone ready to take up his torch as a dedicated poltergeist investigator. "I wish there were."

THE AMAZINGLY CYNICAL RANDI

"We may disagree with Randi on certain points, but we ignore him at our peril."

—LATE ASTRONOMER/AUTHOR CARL SAGAN

If I can prove in this book that poltergeists exist, then James (The Amazing) Randi owes me a million bucks American (here in Canada, that's a lot of dough).

Randi seems to be the enemy of poltergeists, a disbeliever in the strongest sense. He goes by the nickname "The Amazing," but really, his theory about life is that nothing is amazing, except for science and things that can be proven without a doubt.

In Randi's world, if you didn't see it happen, it likely didn't happen. And even if you saw it happen, someone could have duped you.

There is nothing wrong with this premise, his many fans declare. They say there are far too many charlatans in the world, too many things we unquestioningly accept.

For decades, Randi has proudly worn the crown as the world's No. 1 skeptic and he looks the part with his bald head, white beard, and suspicious eyes glaring at you over the top of his glasses. Sometimes he sounds as though you just got him out of bed.

In 2004 when I asked him if it was possible that a particular poltergeist case could be real, he cracked, "I dunno. I wasn't there, and neither were you."

Randi's skepticism seemed to develop in his native Toronto when he was a fifteen-year-old amateur magician. While visiting a Spiritualist church, he was irritated at seeing what he called "common tricks" being passed off as divine intervention.

But when he tried to convey this to the churchgoers, they called the police and Randi was dragged down to the police station for four hours of questioning.

Years later he would comment, "We have fought long and hard to escape from medieval superstition. I, for one, do not wish to go back."

Randi developed a career as a professional magician and staged spectacular acts such as Houdini-style escapes from chains.

In 1976, Randi was one of the founding members of the Committee for the Scientific Investigation of Claims of the Paranormal (CSICOP), which publishes a journal, the *Skeptical Inquirer*, for about 50,000 subscribers.

He has boundless energy for promoting science and critical thinking and has an eagle eye for frauds.

Randi tries to expose everything from faith healers to water dowsing to superstition to the existence of the Bermuda Triangle and UFOs to astrology. Two of Randi's main targets over the years have been spoon-bending psychic Uri Geller and televangelist Peter Popoff.

"If Geller [bends spoons] by divine power, he does it the hard way," Randi muses.

"Acceptance of nonsense as a harmless aberration can be dangerous to all of us," he says. "We live in a society that is enlarging the boundaries of knowledge at an unprecedented rate, and we cannot keep up with much more than a small portion of what is made available to us. To mix that knowledge with childish notions of magic and fantasy is to cripple our perception of the world around us. We must reach for the truth, not for the ghosts of dead absurdities."

Randi is particularly worried about the growing popularity of exotic cures and therapies for people who may be sidetracked from effective treatments. "For me, it's a mission and also an obsession."

He feels sympathy for people who put their money into things beyond their control such as faith healing, astrology, and psychics. "It's a very dangerous thing to believe in nonsense," he says. "You're giving away your money to the charlatans; you're giving away your emotional security, and sometimes your life."

In 1996, Randi established his own foundation, The James Randi Educational Foundation (JREF), a non-profit organization founded in 1996, which is funded through member contributions, grants, sales of books and videos, seminars, and conferences. Its aim is "to promote critical thinking by reaching out to the public and media with reliable information about paranormal and supernatural ideas so widespread in our society today."

The foundation holds lectures and seminars, and supports and conducts research into paranormal claims using experiments. It has a comprehensive library of books, videos, and archival resources that is open to the public.

On its Web site (http://www.randi.org), the foundation's goals are the following:

- Creating a new generation of critical thinkers through lively classroom demonstrations and by reaching out to the next generation in the form of scholarships and awards.

- Demonstrating to the public and the media, through educational seminars, the consequences of accepting paranormal and supernatural claims without questioning.
- Supporting and conducting research into paranormal claims through well-designed experiments utilizing "the scientific method" and by publishing the findings in the JREF official newsletter (*Swift*) and other periodicals. Also providing reliable information on paranormal and pseudoscientific claims by maintaining a comprehensive library of books, videos, journals, and archival resources open to the public.
- Offering scholarships and awards to students and educators.
- Assisting those who are being attacked as a result of their investigations and criticism of people who make paranormal claims by maintaining a legal defense fund available to assist these individuals.

One of the things that makes Randi effective is his delivery — his cutting sarcasm, deft skills, and stage presence as a magician. He often duplicates tricks that are passed off as supernatural events. "As a magician, I know two things — how to deceive people and how people deceive themselves."

With his Project Alpha, he put magicians in a university parapsychology lab to determine whether fakes could be debunked.

Randi is also an accomplished lecturer and television personality, who has appeared on *Larry King Live* and at the White House in 1974.

THE $1 MILLION PARANORMAL CHALLENGE

Now back to the really important stuff — the money. To raise public awareness on the issues of poltergeists and other supernatural goings-on, Randi's foundation offers a US $1 million prize to any person or persons who can demonstrate any psychic, supernatural, or paranormal ability of any kind under mutually agreed-upon scientific conditions. The money is held in a special account that cannot be accessed for any purpose other than the awarding of the prize.

Over the years, Randi and his colleagues have tested hundreds of applicants, but no one has claimed the $1 Million Paranormal Challenge.

He says that, faced with solid evidence, he would be glad to hand over the prize.

"That would be such an advance for our knowledge of the universe that it would be well worth a million dollars," he says. "The possibility is very, very small, but it's there."

Critics of the challenge say that Randi is unfair to applicants. "[Randi] has obsessive concentration on minor or unimportant matters in order to divert attention from the major issues," said Australian lawyer and parapsychology writer Victor Zammit. He added that Randi shows "contemptuous dismissal of evidence inconsistent with his conviction that all evidence for the paranormal is bunk, and all who contend otherwise are deluded fools."

Other Randi critics say that many people with paranormal abilities are scared to get into the ring with him because of the chance for bad publicity if they cannot perform their unusual, and perhaps unpredictable and fleeting, gifts under pressure and the bright lights of a camera.

Says Scott Teresi, a Web programmer and essayist, "Unfortunately, in his zealousness to combat psychic charlatans, he has sometimes generalized instances of fraudulent phenomena as being representative of the whole of parapsychology. Indeed, most serious parapsychologists would just as quickly dismiss the same outlandish phenomena as he does. Randi is more concerned with diminished unwarranted public deception than with advancing research into subtler psi anomalies."

Randi is well aware of his critics, and even afraid of some of them. "I get threats all the time," he says. "I don't answer the door unless I know who's there."

But over the years, he has some big backers, including the late scientist/author Isaac Asimov, who said, "Perhaps nobody in the world understands both the virtues and the failings of the paranormal as well as Randi does. His qualifications as a rational human being are unparalleled."

Of course, Randi does not believe in poltergeists or psychokinesis. He says there are many frauds, particularly teenagers seeking attention.

He says that some poltergeist phenomena have rational explanations. For example, in 2004, in Rome, some people and media speculated that a poltergeist was at work when a new knife suddenly exploded while a woman was slicing a piece of cheese.

"Local police were able to ascertain that the woman had sliced the cheese while it was on top of an electrical cable," Randi said. "The knife cut through the cheese and the cable at the same time and shocked the woman. Case closed."

According to his Web site, Randi was born in Toronto in 1928, became a naturalized United States citizen in 1987, and now lives in Florida "with an old red cat named Charles, several untalented parrots, numerous other unnamed creatures and the occasional visiting magus. He is understandably single."

For more information, contact:
The James Randi Foundation
201 S.E. 12th St. (E. Davie Blvd.)
Fort Lauderdale, Florida 33316-1815

Web site: http://www.randi.org
Phone: 954-467-1112
FAX: 954-467-1660
e-mail: jref@randi.org

HELP FOR THE VICTIMS

How do you get rid of a poltergeist? Most cases seem to die a natural death after a few weeks or months and sometimes it eases with the reduction of stress in a household.

Sometimes the occurrences end when the agent realizes he or she is the cause. At other times, psychotherapy seems to help.

Exorcisms don't seem to work, but parapsychologists report some relief when they counsel the family victims.

"If the stress is addressed, paranormal activity will often disappear," said Alan Murdie, chairman of (England's) Ghost Club Society (www.ghostclub.org.uk), which bills itself as the oldest organization in the world devoted to psychical research. "What we deal with is often haunted people, not haunted homes."

"People who call up are often very upset about what's happening," says parapsychologist Maurice Grosse, chairman of the spontaneous cases committee for the Society of Psychical Research in England, who has been investigating phenomena for more than sixty years. "I reassure them that they won't be damaged by it, and sometimes this helps. Our role is partly being a social worker."

Stephen Mera says that his organization, Manchester's Association of Paranormal Investigators and Training (MAPIT), does not claim to get rid of poltergeists. "Most of all, our investigations help the family through the crisis, giving them information, support and assistance and we try to identify what is causing the occurrences."

Grosse advises people not to move out of their homes, otherwise the paranormal activity will likely be dragged along with them. Rather, they should try to work out their problems and issues, he says.

In a case in Baltimore, parapsychologist Nathan Fodor suggested that suspected poltergeist agent and frustrated writer Ted Pauls receive encouragement for his writing talent. The family agreed and gave Ted praise and credit for his work. Not long after, the disturbances ended, Fodor said.

Some of the youthful poltergeist agents recover from their problems, while others do not.

"Some of them go on to normal lives," parapsychologist William Roll said. "Some have psychological problems to begin with. When the phenomena stops, the problems continue."

PK in the UK

Chapters 12 through 15 are about the most celebrated poltergeist case in modern times in the United Kingdom—the Hodgson family case in Enfield, north of London, in 1977. It is described in detail with everyone from parapsychologists to police officers to skeptics giving their opinions about it.

Chapter 16 tells of a lonely Irish girl, who moves to Scotland and becomes the agent of moving sideboards at home and levitating desks at her school. In Chapter 17, we see that skeptics go to great lengths to try to prove that a young man in Runcorn was physically moving drawers to simulate poltergeist activity, but the drawers reportedly continued to shake as they sat on him. Other UK cases are mentioned in thumbnail sketches.

CHAPTER 12

ENFIELD: WATCH OUT FOR THE LEGO BRICKS

"Poltergeist activity is so inherently improbable that most rational people simply cannot believe it. And when they see it and have to believe it, they find it very hard to convince anybody else that it really happens."

—GUY LYON PLAYFAIR, AUTHOR OF **THIS HOUSE IS HAUNTED**

From across the road, 284 Green Street looked like so many other semidetached council houses in the north London borough of Enfield. The neighborhood, which had sprung up in the 1920s, had lots of alleyways and small gardens in front of the homes and a school across the way. There seemed nothing foreboding about the area.

But inside the three-bedroom home, all was not well with Peggy Hodgson and her four children. The events in 1977 would live on for decades in British lore.

Mrs. Hodgson, a recently divorced single parent in her mid-forties, struggling to get by on welfare and support payments from her ex-husband in the working-class neighborhood, was a short, plump woman with small eyes that at times could be piercing. But, overall, she was friendly toward visitors and known as down-to-earth and trustworthy by those who knew her. The family was reportedly a close-knit group, starting with Peggy's daughter Janet (eleven), who looked like her mom, but was more outgoing, energetic, and large for her age. Janet talked fast and had a somewhat mischievous look about her.

Another child, Margaret, was tall, pleasant, and looked older than thirteen. She did not have Janet's bubbly qualities. Their seven-year-old brother, Billy, wore a large pair of spectacles, and had a speech defect. Another brother, ten-year-old Johnny, was away at a hospice for sick children during most of the events in the Hodgson house. He was suffering from brain cancer.

But Johnny was involved when the incidents began on August 30, 1977. On that evening, Johnny and Janet informed their mother that frightening things were happening in their room — their bed was shaking and furniture was moving about on its own accord, and there were shuffling noises and loud "raps" on the walls.

"The bed was going all funny," Janet said. But nothing out of the ordinary occurred after Peggy walked into the room. The mother was not too upset and believed it was just the children's antics. A second bedroom, where Margaret and Billy had been sleeping with their mother, was quiet.

On the next night at about 9:30, Peggy was summoned to Janet and Johnny's room once again by the sound of their excited or nervous laughter. Unusual noises were coming from the floor of the bedroom, they said. Janet said it like sounded like a chair moving, so Peggy removed the only chair from the bedroom and took it downstairs with her. Later in the evening, Peggy heard the same shuffling noise that her daughter had described coming from Janet's bedroom. When she went to check on them, the children were apparently asleep. From their room, Mrs. Hodgson said she heard four loud knocks coming from a wall that adjoined the neighboring house. Curious, Peggy turned on the lights. What happened next was hard to explain: A heavy chest of drawers moved about 18 inches away from the wall, she said.

Surprised but not alarmed, Peggy pushed the dresser back against the wall, but it would not cooperate, allegedly moving right back to its position away from the wall. When Peggy tried to push it back again, it would not budge. At this point, she began to panic, shaking like a leaf as she awakened her children. "As many people probably do when they suddenly realize they are in the presence of something totally strange, Mrs. Hodgson began, literally, to shake with fear," writer/researcher Guy Lyon Playfair later wrote in his book on the case, *This House Is Haunted*.

That was quite enough for Peggy, who hustled all four of her children — still in their nightclothes — out of the house — and they went to their next door neighbors, Vic and Peggy Nottingham, for help. Vic and a relative went into the Hodgson home and said that they, too, heard knocking coming from the walls. They searched the home and could find no explanation.

Police were summoned and Constable Carolyn Keeps searched the Hodgson house. While she was investigating, the officer saw a chair move 3 or

4 feet toward the kitchen door, apparently without the help of human hands. Constable Keeps did not know what to think, but she was so convinced she had seen something unnatural, she was not afraid to record it in her official report that night.

Years later, Constable Keeps signed this written report to authenticate her findings:

> On Thursday, September 1, 1977, at approximately 1 a.m., I was on duty in my capacity as a policewoman, when I received a radio message to 284 Green Street, Enfield. I went to this address where I found a number of people standing in the living room. I was told by the occupier of this house that strange things had been happening during the last few nights and that they believed that the house was haunted. Myself and another PC entered the living room of the house and the occupier switched off the lights. Almost immediately, I heard the sound of knocking on the wall that backs onto the next door neighbor's house. There were four distinct taps on the wall and then silence. About two minutes later, I heard more tapping, but this time, it was coming from a different wall, and again it was a distinctive peal of four taps. [The officer and the neighbors then checked the walls, attic, and pipes, but found nothing unusual. The other officer and the neighbors then went into the kitchen to check the refrigerator, leaving the family and Keeps in the living room.] The lights in the living room were switched off again and within a few minutes, the eldest son [Johnny] pointed to a chair which was standing next to the sofa. I looked at the chair and noticed that it was wobbling slightly from side to side. I then saw the chair slide across the floor towards the kitchen wall. It moved approximately 3 to 4 feet and then came to rest. At no time did it appear to leave the floor. I checked the chair but could find nothing to explain how it had moved. The lights were switched back on. Nothing else happened that night, although we have later reports of disturbances at this address.

From that night on, the Hodgson family would have the attention of the police department. On the third night of the occurrences, Sergeant Brian Hyams was on duty at the local police station when a neighbor of the

Hodgsons came to the station asking for help, for someone with authority to come back to Green Street to witness the events. Hyams took another officer with him and they went to the Hodgson home, where they heard loud thumping, even though apparently no one was in the home except Peggy Hodgson, who remained in a hallway where she was in plain view of the officers.

In a downstairs room, Hyams and the other officer, who was not named, reported that toys began flying about the house. "Lego bricks just started to levitate, or move about I should say, jump about like jumping beans," Hyams said. "There was a bird in a cage that started squawking. And suddenly, one or two Lego bricks starten to fly towards us." Hyams and the other officer became afraid and ran out of the house. Years later, he would say, "I'm no hero. I went straight out of the door and I think there was a rush between us who got out the swiftest."

Outside the house, the officers met with two journalists from the *Daily Mirror* newspaper, reporter Douglas Bence and photographer Graham Morris. The journalists had been in the house earlier, but there were no incidents, but after talking with the police, all four decided to go back into the house.

Inside, Morris set up his camera to record the events. "While we were talking, the Lego bricks started to vibrate again and started pinging towards us," Hyams said. Morris was reportedly smacked in the face by a flying toy brick while taking a photograph. "I saw the Lego pieces flying about and I was hit on the head by a piece while I was attempting to photograph it in flight," Morris said. "I had a bump on my forehead after the incident." (When the film was developed, the picture strangely showed nothing but a hole where the flying toy should have been.) When picked up, the small plastic bricks felt hot.

As the days went by, weird occurrences continued in the Hodgson home, even after clergy and mediums were brought in. On September 4, seventy-two-year-old Bob Richardson, Mrs. Nottingham's father, said he was in the kitchen of the Hodgson home when "two marbles passed me at terrific speed and hit the bathroom floor. When I picked them up, they were hot."

Another newspaper, the *Daily Mail*, joined in the coverage. Meanwhile, the *Daily Mirror* sent senior reporter George Fallowes to investigate. He became so impressed that he suggested that the family contact the Society for Psychical Research (SPR), which was founded in 1882 by a group of Victorian enthusiasts who wanted to apply rigorous scientific method to the study of the supernatural.

THE LEAD INVESTIGATOR ARRIVES

Maurice Grosse, an investigator with the SPR, arrived on the scene on September 5, 1977, one week after the events had begun. Grosse was a middle-aged businessman and inventor, who had just made a lot of money by designing a dispenser box for newspapers. "That money allowed me to focus on paranormal investigations," he said. Just two years earlier, Grosse had lost his own daughter, aged twenty-two and ironically named Janet, in an automobile accident. With his glasses, shirt, tie, heavy moustache, and trustworthy appearance, Grosse looked like an investigator, perhaps Sherlock Holmes.

After reading newspaper accounts and talking with those close to the case, Grosse had decided it was worth investigating. When he arrived at the home, he assured the family that there had been many similar poltergeist cases in the past, and that they usually subsided after six to eight weeks. Grosse admitted to those close to him that neither he, nor anyone else in the world, actually knew for certain what a poltergeist was, but he did not reveal this to the family. By presenting himself as an authority, he thought they would trust him and relax in his presence.

Indeed, Peggy Nottingham later noted that most of the people in the house seemed to calm down with Grosse on the scene, explaining the events. Grosse further calmed Mrs. Hodgson by asking her to help him with the case. She agreed to write daily notes about things she saw.

Grosse was disappointed when nothing happened for a few days after his arrival. The only incident of note was reported by a teenaged friend of the Hodgsons, who said she had been in Janet's bedroom when two books jumped off the shelf and flew at her.

By this time, the management at the *Mirror* was sending more journalists to cover what it considered an important story. The knocking on the walls was becoming a nightly event. On September 7, reporter George Fallowes heard knocking on a wall at the side of Janet's bed and he later reported that he did not consider it possible for Janet to be responsible for the knocking. And there were reportedly more flying Lego bricks, one of which struck journalist Bence.

In the wee hours of September 8, Grosse and three journalists from the *Daily Mirror* assembled on the upstairs landing, which led to the three bedrooms. They were joined by photographers Graham Morris and David Thorpe and Bence. At about 1:15 a.m., they heard a crash in Janet's bedroom and rushed in to find her bedside chair had moved about 4 feet across the room and was lying on its side. David Thorpe saw the chair topple. Janet, who was alone in the room, appeared to be fast asleep. A short time later, she awoke and started crying before falling asleep once more.

About an hour after the first chair incident, photographer Thorpe said he saw the chair move and fall to the floor on its side. He snapped a photo of the chair on the floor, but he was unable to get a shot of it falling. The four men looked at Janet, who still appeared to be fast asleep. Fallowes said it was almost as though she were in a trance. Grosse lifted her eyelid to find the eyeball up in its socket.

All of this was beginning to impress Grosse, who left the house before dawn, suspecting that there was legitimate poltergeist phenomena going on at 284 Green Street. He returned that night to hear that the Hodgsons had seen marbles flying through the air and a sideboard drawer had opened by itself. They were so scared that they went next door to stay briefly with the Nottingham family. Then, at about 10 p.m. on September 8, Grosse said he saw a marble fly past him out of nowhere. It seemed to move over the heads of the children, although the investigator believed that none of them had thrown it. A short time later, door chimes hanging on a wall started swinging to and fro, even though no one was activating the front door bell. Then Grosse was called to a bathroom, where he saw a door allegedly open and close on its own, not once, but three or four times. Grosse felt a cold draft, even though no windows were open. Nearby in the kitchen, Grosse said he saw a T-shirt move off the top of a pile of clothes, down to the table, and finally to the floor. He said that no one could have touched the T-shirt without him seeing them do it.

And there was more action soon after — three airborne marbles apparently just missed Janet. Grosse noticed something unusual about the marbles — rather than bounce a little or roll when they fell to the floor, they simply came to an immediate halt. There were also unexplained electrical disturbances and mechanical failures in the house.

Of course, through all of this, the family seemed nervous and at times downright scared, but they were comforted by Grosse's presence. (In all of his poltergeist cases, Grosse made himself available to counsel families "because there is a social services side to our job. Most poltergeist cases are caused by high stress — marriage problems, drinking problems, and illness.") As well, Mrs. Hodgson was able to keep relatively relaxed and focused by keeping a logbook of the occurrences.

After a cardboard box "jumped" off a table as Janet walked past, Grosse came to the conclusion that the eleven-year-old girl was the "epicenter" for all or most of the activity, that she was not faking the incidents but was somehow causing them through highly unusual emotional or mental forces. Most parapsychologists call this a poltergeist agent.

According to her mother, Janet had been acting rather strangely in the past few weeks, perhaps partly because she was entering puberty. Otherwise, Janet seemed like many other girls her age, wearing braces and a hairstyle like famous singer Olivia Newton-John. Janet watched John Travolta movies and listened to the rock group Bay City Rollers. It hardly seemed she could be such a prankster. To be safe, however, Grosse asked members of the house and the investigators and journalists to carefully watch Janet. What they did notice was that, from time to time, there was tension among the family members, particularly between Peggy and her children. They put that down to the fact that she was a recently divorced single mother. Peggy sometimes became irritated with Janet to the point when her eyes would become piercing, especially when objects started flying around the house. The girl thought her mother often blamed her for the occurrences. "Mum winds up shouting at me a bit," Janet said. "'Cause it's happening around me. That's what I say—'It comes to me.' I've got a lot of energy, people say."

On the afternoon of September 9, Bob Richardson said he found a chair in Janet's bedroom precariously balanced on top of an open door. When he touched it gently, it fell off the door. He accused Janet of putting the chair up there, but she denied it as she had denied pulling any previous "pranks." A few minutes later, Richardson said he saw the lid of a goldfish tank "jump off" and land 4 feet away while Janet was in another room. "Well, I didn't do that, did I?" Janet reportedly said to him, a little sarcastically.

On September 10, the case made the front page of the *Daily Mirror* with the headline "The House of Strange Happenings." In the story, Fallowes wrote: "Because of the emotional atmosphere at the house and in the neighbourhood, ranging from hysteria through terror to excitement and tension, it has been difficult to record satisfactory data. Nevertheless, I am satisfied the overall impression of our investigation is reasonably accurate. To the best of our ability, we have eliminated the possibility of total trickery."

More media became involved and the story was picked up by the London television show *Night Line* and some of the principle characters, including Grosse, Peggy Hodgson, and a neighbor, appeared on the show. Other media followed, including the BBC Radio 4 news show *The World This Weekend*. That show's reporter, Rosalind Morris, said that in the early hours of September 11, 1977, she saw Janet's chair fly across the room and her bed shake up and down on its own.

Morris put her account on the airwaves and author/paranormal researcher Guy Lyon Playfair listened to it while eating lunch. Earlier, Playfair had considered joining Grosse in the investigation, but he had just finished a lengthy project in Brazil and was hoping for a vacation in Portugal. In the end, though, Playfair recalled the words of psychical researcher Hernani Guimaraes Andrade, who had told him, "When spontaneous cases come up, we drop everything and go after them. They will not wait for us." And so, Playfair joined the Enfield investigation.

CHAPTER 13

ENFIELD: STRANGE TWISTS AND TURNS

"I was bloody petrified."

—JOHN BURCOMBE

On September 12, 1977, Guy Lyon Playfair joined Grosse at the Hodgson house in Enfield. The first thing he noticed was that the house resembled a photographer's studio with cameras and tripods everywhere. Graham Morris showed him a bruise on his forehead where a piece of Lego had reportedly hit him. "It was a nasty looking mark and the speed of the little toy brick must have been tremendous," Playfair said. Playfair established that over the previous twelve days and nights, at least ten witnesses outside the family, including the police, Grosse, and journalists, had seen phenomena. "I wanted to convince myself beyond reasonable doubt," Playfair said. "In spite of everything, I was suspicious. Perhaps it was that mischievous glint in Janet's eyes."

For the next few evenings, Playfair, Graham, and others kept a vigil outside Janet's room, but there were few major occurrences, except for marbles that fell off her bed and seemed oddly to land on the floor immediately without rolling. The bed shook, drawers opened, and chairs fell over. When Playfair and Grosse tried to repeat the strange antics of the marbles, they could not get them to stop dead. They always rolled when dropped. "This seemed to be an unusually active poltergeist case," Playfair noted.

On the night of September 20, Playfair said that a book did some bizarre things in the air, flying off a mantelpiece before going through a door, then slammed into a closed door of a front bedroom, although no one actually saw its entire flight. "It must have hit the door at a 30-degree angle and bounced off at right angles, defying the laws of physics," he said. The book, which came to rest open and upright on the floor, was entitled *Fun and Games for Children.*

"We've got a little girl playing games with us," Playfair said, referring to what he believed were Janet's paranormal powers.

On that same night, family members were near hysteria after a loud crash in Janet's bedroom. A heavy chest of drawers — reportedly too big for a child to maneuver — had tipped forward, falling onto an armchair with its drawers spilling out.

"Oh my God, what strength it has!" Margaret shouted. "Whatever it is, it's bloody powerful!"

"It's getting more powerful every day," Janet said. "I saw that. I was looking there. I saw it move, I saw it tilt over. I heard creaks on the floor." When queried, Janet said she did not know what force was at work, only that she was not trying to hoodwink anyone.

The following night, Maurice Grosse saw another thing he couldn't explain. He was alone in the kitchen when a teapot next to the stove started to rock back and forth for about seven seconds, "doing a little dance right in front of my eyes." When he examined the pot, it was empty and quite cold. "There was just no way it could do that normally." Janet was nowhere near the kitchen at the time, Grosse said.

Also that night, Grosse and Playfair were looking for ways to document the goings-on, so they brought in the production manager and chief demonstrator of Pye Business Communications. PBC officials set up cameras in various locations, including Janet's bedroom, but soon discovered to their dismay that their equipment was malfunctioning for no apparent reason. The buttons on the video recorders would all come on at the same time and the tape would not rewind. Some of their equipment inexplicably jammed, which cameraman Ron Denney said had never happened before.

It was the second time in a week that cameras had failed to operate in the Hodgson house. On September 13, photographer Graham Morris said that three of his expensive electronic flashguns developed faults simultaneously after being recharged in the Hodgson home. "As soon as they were set up, they started to drain themselves of power," he said. They had never given him trouble in the past and were considered foolproof, he said. As soon as he took them out of the house, they worked normally.

When Denney got the video equipment to work, there was no unusual activity for several days, which made Grosse and Playfair suspect two things: either Janet did not want to be caught cheating or her poltergeist entity was mischievous and did not want to be discovered.

MOVING NEXT DOOR

The strange incidents were not exclusively confined to the semidetached Hodgson home at 284 Green Street. From time to time, the Hodgsons were too tense or frightened to stay in their house, and so they went to their neighbors.

For instance, on Sunday, September 25, Peggy Hodgson awoke at about 6:45 a.m. to hear what she said sounded like footsteps. A small chair by the bed jumped, Peggy said, "then as I got out of bed, it jumped again." Five minutes later, a large chest of drawers inexplicably moved and fell onto its side, Peggy said. She believed that Janet and no one else had physically caused it to happened.

Peggy then decided to take Janet and two of her other children, Margaret and Billy, to visit her brother John Burcombe and his wife, Silvie, at neighboring 272 Green Street. That afternoon, John Burcombe reported "paranormal phenomena" in his house. He said that while he was in an upstairs bedroom, an old television set, likely too heavy for a child to move, moved to an angle of 45 degrees and two skirts placed upon a bed suddenly became crumpled. The only person in the room with Burcombe was his daughter Denise.

(At one time, John Burcombe had been skeptical when his sister Peggy Hodgson had told him of the goings-on in her home. He believed things had moved because of vibrations, but he said he was convinced after he saw a number of incidents in his home and his sister's home, including a drawer open by itself; a lamp slowly slide across a table and fall to the floor; and a strange, bright, fluorescent-type light, about 12 inches long, suddenly appear in the air, then fade away. Months later he would say, "I know I saw these things. That's a bit hard to explain... I was bloody petrified." His sixteen-year-old daughter, Brenda, also said she saw objects move in her bedroom.)

Also on September 25 at about 5:30 p.m. at the Burcombe home, John's wife, Sylvia, was making tea and chatting with several people, including her daughter, Denise, and her sister-in-law Dianne Hyde. As she was pouring water from the kettle, Sylvia said that a plastic rod, which had been part of a toy set, suddenly appeared in front of her face. She screamed and dropped the boiling kettle onto the floor. The piece of plastic, which was about 6 inches long, then jumped in front of her again, she said, and finally dropped onto the kitchen countertop. It had not been thrown by anyone, she insisted.

Dianne and Denise said they both saw the plastic rod, but had no idea where it had come from. Dianne's husband, David, said he had been sitting in a chair at the kitchen door, watching the children, when the plastic rod appeared, and that none of them had thrown it.

Back in the Hodgson home over the next few months, crazy things were reported around Janet, such as spoons and other small metal objects bending and snapping. And then things went one step further — Janet said that a curtain beside her twisted several times into a tight rope and attempted to wrap itself around her neck. Her mother said she tended to believe her. Automatic cameras set up by investigators caught some strange movements of curtains and bedsheets in Janet's bedroom in mid-December 1977. Two cameras were set up in the bedroom and were controlled by a button outside the room. Whenever investigators heard something, or suspected something was going in inside the room, they activated the cameras, which were set to flash at half-second intervals.

Grosse said that the still cameras took a series of photos that showed bed covers moving up a wall while Janet and her sister Margaret were asleep. The windows were closed and there were no drafts in the room, Grosse said. In the final photo, the curtains had twisted and the bedclothes had also mysteriously twisted. (These photos are available on the Internet at http://www.tcpstudios.com/zurichmansion/ghosts/video1.html.) In contrast to what were supposedly paranormal events, the walls of the Hodgson bedroom seemed typical for those of young people at the time, and were decorated with posters of movie and television stars, including David Soul and Paul Michael Glasser of the TV police series *Starsky and Hutch*. Besides these mundane images, the cameras reportedly also snapped pictures of a pillow moving in a zigzag fashion.

And then, incredibly, Janet claimed to have been levitated in her room. She said she was picked up and tossed about the room by an unseen entity, which was witnessed only by neighbors passing by who looked up through a window into the girl's bedroom, but their testimony was inconclusive and they could have seen the girl simply jumping. Janet claimed she had been moved many times by the unseen force, which often threw her off her bed.

On one occasion, the same automatic cameras caught her airborne off her bed as her mother and Margaret watched in the bedroom. The set of pictures (also available on the same Internet site) show her literally soaring like Peter Pan, with her body upright and both her legs tucked under her. She is high off the bed and about to land hard onto the floor. She either jumped off the bed or was tossed. (Critics say she could have jumped because she was a good athlete, although the bed was reportedly hard with stiff springs and hardly a trampoline.) It's doubtful that her sister Margaret, shown tucked in her own bed nearby, and her mother Peggy, in the foreground, could have done it. Her mother told investigators that Janet did not jump off the bed. "Janet was lying in bed and I was talking to Janet... Janet was suddenly flying through the air," Mrs. Hodgson said. As well, her mother said that on several previous occasions, she had seen Janet come off the bed in a similar fashion.

Meanwhile, Maurice Grosse was becoming a little skeptical of some of Janet's claims, but he tended to believe that she had levitated at least once. While reviewing the case years later, Grosse said that Janet's levitation had been possible because in 1982, four years after the occurrences ended at the Hodgson home, Professor John Hasted, head of the physics department at Birbeck College in the University of London, put Janet through some tests to see if she had some paranormal ability. He had her sit on an electronic weighing machine. Over a thirty-second period, her weight briefly dropped by nearly 1 kilogram, Hasted said. The professor could not explain this, unless Janet had some ability that allowed her to levitate or to mentally affect the machine's recording mechanism.

Grosse and other investigators believed that some of the activity involving Janet occurred while she was in a trance. Some of the episodes turned violent as Janet became hysterical. "At one point, I thought she was going to kill herself," Grosse said. "She would rush against a wall and smash her head, cursing and swearing. It was dreadful." At those times, doctors gave her 10-milligram injections of Valium to calm her. One of the photos shows Grosse holding a grimacing Janet, as if to protect her from herself.

The possibility that the occurrences had a spiritual cause was not overlooked — mediums Annie and George Shaw prayed for Janet and held a type of séance for her. Their visit, which was done free of charge, was not that eventful, although Annie believed that Janet was possessed by several spirits.

THE POLTERGEIST AS A CURE

As strange as it sounds, a poltergeist case can be good for relieving tension in an unusual family situation, said British psychologist Dr. John Layard. "Poltergeists are not chance phenomena, but have a definite purpose . . . it is a curative one, having for its object the resolution of a psychological conflict," he said. Often, the poltergeist agent has no other way to relieve the unusual buildup of frustration or tension, whether it is psychological or sexual, he said.

THINGS GET DANGEROUS

Although some people still suspected Janet was a trickster, on October 15, Playfair said he witnessed phenomena first-hand. He said he was getting off a chair in the Hodgson kitchen when a table suddenly turned upside down with a thud. Janet was with him, he said, but she did not cause the table to flip because he was watching her at the time and she was not within its reach. He seemed gleeful and exclaimed to Janet: "I saw you standing there the minute that thing went over. Well, you didn't do that one!" Later, Playfair said that he and Grosse discovered the table was too wide and heavy for one person to flip over.

The following week, things got dangerous. An iron grille, which had been under a fireplace in the children's bedroom, somehow came flying across the room and landed on little Billy's pillow, narrowly missing him. Two days later, someone or something ripped a heavy iron frame weighing about 50 pounds out of the fireplace and severely bent it. "This was a major demolition job, for the thing was cemented into the brickwork," Playfair said.

Meanwhile, Janet was having problems adjusting to her new school, which may have had some impact on the unexplained occurrences. And, perhaps partly because of the nightly events, it was affecting her schoolwork and she often fell asleep, exhausted, in class. Teachers said they would give her the benefit of the doubt and didn't penalize her. As well, Janet claimed that some phenomena occurred at school, and that her chair jumped from time to time. Grosse said he and Playfair interviewed Janet's teachers and they believed something paranormal was at work with Janet.

Other incidents were reported outside the Hodgson home. According to Playfair, there were many occurrences at local stores, on buses, and on the street. At an optician's store, a box of lenses allegedly began shaking as Janet went near it and a door opened and closed on its own. At the supermarket, vegetables often rolled onto the floor, Playfair said. Grosse and Playfair did not document many of these cases because they said they did not want to draw too much outside attention to the Hodgsons, who had been given anonymous names in the *Daily Mirror* and on BBC TV. Their true identities as the poltergeist family were known only to their close relatives and neighbors.

However, some people discovered their real identities, which caused problems. There were some threats from annoyed neighbors and a group of Jehovah's Witnesses, who warned the Hodgsons to be wary of devils and demons. At one point, a letter was sent to the family, reportedly from some residents of nearby Beachcroft Way: "Get off this estate. We don't want to live with witches and devils like you. You made your flat [home] catch fire and when you let your cat and dogs out, you had better watch where they are. We smashed your car light in the other night. Next time we will smash you in."

Also in the fall of 1977, Janet and Margaret were sent for a rest at a council care home, operated by nuns, several miles from their house. There, Margaret said, a wardrobe shook in their presence, a cupboard fell over, and bedclothes mysteriously moved on their beds.

All of this, of course, was very stressful for the whole Hodgson family, but Janet told Grosse it was actually starting to feel commonplace for her. "I'm getting used to it," she said. Janet seemed confused about whether she was psychically causing the events or whether an entity was doing it in her presence, or working through her. She reported, however, that she often got a funny feeling in her tummy about the time the incidents were taking place.

Curiously, her mother Peggy said she was also feeling poltergeist symptoms. Just prior to some of the events, Peggy reported feeling an unusual pain in the front of her head. Right after the events occurred, it would subside. During her youth, Peggy had had numerous bouts of epilepsy, although she had not suffered an attack in many years. (Some paranormal researchers report a high incidence of epilepsy among poltergeist agents.) However, few people ever suspected that Peggy was the poltergeist agent in this case. A social worker, who had known Peggy for a long time, described her as a down-to-earth woman, a respected member of the community, and "not prone to hysteria." She added that the Hodgsons were a close family, well liked by family and friends.

On October 29, the emotionally and physically tired family left for a vacation at Clacton-on-Sea. Few incidents were reported while they were away.

CHAPTER 14

ENFIELD: THE VOICE

"Everyone thinks it's all in my little mind, but it isn't."

—JANET HODGSON

The circus came to Enfield for November and December 1977. That seems the only way to describe the series of events in the Hodgson neighborhood. Either some children were as good as Cirque de Soleil performers, or poltergeists really do exist, or both.

On November 5, after returning from the relatively uneventful week's holiday in Clacton-on-Sea, the Hodgson family were joined in their home by their investigators, Maurice Grosse and Guy Lyon Playfair.

It was Guy Fawkes night in England, with people setting off fireworks and lighting big bonfires in celebration of a rogue, Guy Fawkes, who had attempted to blow up the Houses of Parliament and its ruling monarch, King James I, in 1605.

Ironically, there were no fires or sparklers in the yards and alleys of Green Street on this night. But inside number 284, that was a different story. As everyone was going to bed, knocking and rapping began in the house and appeared to come from the second floor. Grosse rounded up Janet, Margaret, and Billy and kept them together to establish that they were not producing the noises. He confirmed that they were not because the noises continued while he was watching them. It was hard to pinpoint where the banging was coming from — perhaps the skirting boards or in the walls — but it seemed to have a rhythm or pattern to it: Rat tat-a tat-tat... tat tat.

If someone or something intelligent was making these noises, Grosse thought he would try to make contact. He did so while in the presence of

Playfair, Mrs. Hodgson, Janet, Margaret, and Billy, along with neighbors John Burcombe and Peggy Nottingham.

Grosse asked the knocker what five and five added up to. The reply was fast: ten quick knocks. Later, everyone in the room would attest to the fact that they heard the answer, and no one admitted making the knocks. In fact, it seemed as though everyone was watching everyone else.

Then Grosse developed a system for the knocker to answer: one knock for no and two for yes. But for the next while, he could get no replies to follow-up questions. "Are you having games with me?" Grosse said. The answer hit Grosse in the head. According to the other witnesses, a cardboard box containing small cushions jumped off the floor next to the fireplace, flew 8 feet over a bed, and hit Grosse in the forehead.

"Oh crumbs!" Grosse laughed. "It hit me in the face!"

The people in the room did not believe anyone could have tossed the box, certainly not Janet, who was in her bed at the time.

But the strange movement of objects was soon to be replaced by another mystery. In December, the Enfield case took on its own voice — literally. Janet, who had turned twelve on November 10, started talking in the voice of a gruff, old man. The case would never be the same.

The new twist began on December 10, when two psychologists from the Society for Psychical Research, Dr. John Beloff, head of the Edinburgh University psychology department, and Anita Gregory, of North London Polytechnic, joined Grosse and Playfair to observe the case. When Beloff and Gregory visited the Hodgson house, they heard strange barking noises and loud, piercing whistling, which seemed to come from Janet's (who else's?) direction, but they could not be directly traced to her. Janet denied making them.

Grosse believed that if Janet did indeed have a poltergeist entity or spirit that was trying to communicate, it might be productive to try and get it to talk, as Professor John Hasted of Birbeck College had suggested. Grosse started the bizarre proceedings in the upstairs bedroom, which Janet shared with her sister Margaret and her mother Peggy.

Grosse decided to call the poltergeist entity Charlie and he challenged it to call out his name, Maurice Grosse. At first, there was no clear answer, except for more barking and whistling noises, so he asked Charlie to call out Doctor Beloff's name. When Grosse left the room and shut the bedroom door behind him, a voice apparently coming from Janet said in a raspy tone, "Doctor." And then, "Grosse, Grosse." Grosse did not hear it properly on the other side of the door, but a tape recorder left in the room picked up the conversation and he was later able to decipher it.

"It was loud and harsh, unquestionably the voice of an old man," said Playfair after reviewing the tape. (Some of the conversations between Grosse and Janet/poltergeist have been available on the Internet. I have listened to them and found them startling. In nearly four decades of journalism, I have heard some creepy things, but this pretty much takes the cake. If you want to listen yourself, check: http://www.pixeldeviant.com/experiment_enfield.shtml.)

Shortly into the Grosse/entity questioning, The Voice told Grosse that his name was Joe Watson, and he had lived in the Hodgson house at one time. Joe became irritated and sometimes angry at Grosse's questions and several times told him to "Shut up!" or "F —- off!"

Occasionally, Janet's natural voice could be heard during the question period, but only while speaking for herself. Janet had been known for talking a lot; now she was talking for two people! At one point after the deep voice spoke, she said in her natural voice to Grosse, "Did you hear what he said?"

Margaret was also in the bedroom and she said at times The Voice seemed to be coming from under the bed, rather than from Janet.

Much of Grosse's conversation with The Voice took place when his back was turned to Janet or when he was behind a closed door. In fact, much of the early questioning of the entity came outside the bedroom because Joe wanted it that way, which made Grosse suspicious that Janet was faking The Voice and did not want to be found out.

When Dr. Beloff tried to interview Joe, there was no response. When Anita Gregory asked a question, the deep voice told her to "Bugger off!"

After Dr. Beloff left for the night, he said it was possible that Janet was a ventriloquist, throwing her voice or altering it significantly. In fact, after just a brief visit with Janet, Beloff and Gregory would later say they thought Janet and Margaret were playing tricks on the investigators, but Janet denied her own involvement: "Everyone thinks it's all in my little mind, but it isn't," she said.

When Grosse replayed the tapes at home, he noted that Joe's voice was gruff and guttural, significantly unlike Janet's normal voice. He found it hard to believe that she had faked it.

On December 12, The Voice was back, louder and bolder than before, but he was still shy. From behind the bedroom door, Grosse managed to carry on a long conversation with The Voice, which now called itself Bill, who described himself an old man who had died in the house. Bill said that Janet's bed sometimes shook or moved because he was sleeping in it, apparently as an entity. "Get out, Janet!" the gruff Bill said.

Grosse's conversation with Bill went on for about an hour. At one point, Grosse got the voice to sing along with him in a humorous skit to the tune "Daisy, Daisy." At times, Janet's higher natural voice would chime in, and so it became a singing trio comprised of Grosse, Bill, and Janet. Grosse stressed that there was a distinct difference between the old man's voice and the girl's giggle.

Under questioning, Janet said she had no control over The Voice, and Grosse was beginning to believe her. "You bring me a girl who can imitate that voice for three hours and I'll give you £500," he said.

On December 13, a new investigator entered the picture — Maurice Grosse's son Richard, who had started work with a law firm in London. He had been skeptical of his father's assertions that there was a poltergeist in the Hodgson house, so he came, with an open mind, to see for himself.

As Guy Lyon Playfair noted, it was the first time that a poltergeist has ever been submitted to cross-examination by a lawyer!

At first, Bill's voice would not talk directly to Richard Grosse, but answered questions from him relayed through two other people. Bill said he died when "I went blind and had a hemorrhage and fell asleep and died on a chair in the corner downstairs." Once again, Janet sometimes talked in her normal voice with the questioners, then Bill would interject with his old man's grunts.

In 1978, Richard Grosse wrote of the incident:

> In my opinion, the voice could not have been produced by Janet under normal circumstances. I was also satisfied that the voice was not being produced by any electrical or other apparatus concealed in, or near, the room. Whilst I admit that Janet may be able for an interval of a few seconds only to produce something similar to the voice by herself, I am absolutely certain that it was not possible for her to produce such sounds for approximately two hours. At the end of the proceedings, Janet's voice was sweet and clear as at the beginning, and if anyone were to hypothesize that she alone could produce such a noise, then if nothing else, she would have had at the very least a sore throat. More likely still, she would have severely damaged her vocal chords. Since my first visit, other investigators, so my father informs me, have been able to sit in the room and watch Janet whilst also listening to the voice. At the time

> of my visit, I was not able to identify the physical source of the voice. In any event, in my humble opinion, there is no physical explanation for such a voice being produced by an 11-year-old girl [actually, she had just turned twelve].

The next step was for local doctors and psychiatrists to examine Janet. Grosse even brought in speech therapists, who concluded that the girl was not speaking with her normal voice, but through a second set of "false" vocal chords, which everyone has but which few people ever use or even know exist. Actors are sometimes trained to use this second voice, but it can be painful for both sets of vocal chords. But Janet's normal voice did not seem to be affected or weakened, even though she often talked for hours in the "gruff" voice.

Janet's "second" voice was recorded and run through a larynograph, which registers patterns produced by frequency waves as they move through the larynx. The machine was designed by Professor A.J. Fourcin of University College in London and the tests were carried out by Professor John Hasted, head of the physics department at Birbeck College, who said that the false vocal chords are a type of auxiliary chords that protect the trachea from damage. The speech carried out through these rare vocal chords was called *plica ventricularis*. When someone uses them, he or she will get a sore throat within two minutes, since there is not enough liquid to lubricate these auxiliary chords and they become inflamed. Hasted showed Playfair and Grosse the wave patterns of Janet's normal voice and her other voice and they were completely different.

December 15, 1977, was a perhaps a milestone in the case. Janet had her period for the first time. Bill seemed to know this because during questioning from Grosse, Playfair, and Richard Robertson of Birbeck College, he went into great detail about girls' menstruation. Many paranormal researchers believe there is a link between poltergeist activity and girls or boys near the age of puberty. (Margaret had recently gone through puberty.) For his theory, Playfair believed that one of the possible sources of poltergeist energy may be from a youth's pineal gland, which is located in the center of the brain and controls the release of sexual hormones. "When a child suddenly acquires this new force, there is a need for an outlet," he said. Playfair added that if there is no outlet, the energy could result in poltergeist activity.

Discounting the circus atmosphere and the mysterious voices, the Hodgson home looked like any other London home at Christmas with bright lights and colored streamers all over the walls and gifts under the tree, including a box of chocolates for Bill, The Voice (that was the family's British humor at work).

The Voice was still a part of the nightly ritual, but it was becoming more relaxed and allowed Grosse, Playfair, and others to be in the room when it spoke, which sometimes lasted for up to three hours. They observed that Janet's mouth seemed to be moving, but that her lips did not move in the way they would with normal speech patterns.

Meanwhile, physical incidents continued in the home, several just before and just after Christmas, in which Janet wound up with things around her throat. On one occasion, with Peggy Hodgson watching, Janet was sitting in the living room, next to the window, when curtains tightened around her neck.

Playfair told the family that violence in poltergeist cases was rare, and yet a few days later, the curtains were wrapped around Janet's neck again like a lasso and she seemed terrified as her sister Margaret and neighbor Peggy Nottingham watched and her mother Peggy Hodgson swore for one of the first times in public.

On other occasions, the investigators had caught, with their automatic cameras, bedsheets doing strange things in Janet's bedroom, billowing about on their own, even though the windows were shut tight. On New Year's Eve, Peggy Hodgson reported more incidents: She said she saw a cupboard jump to and fro for about ten minutes, making such a racket that she sent Margaret next door to Peggy Nottingham's home to apologize for the noise. Then Mrs. Hodgson said she saw her small Christmas tree attacked by an unseen force; she said it actually rose off a table and moved across the living room. "It went halfway across the room," she said. "Then [the unseen force] started chucking books about and they shot everywhere... in the end, it literally turned the place upside down." And the Christmas decorations had been unceremoniously torn down.

THE LIGHT SHINES ON MARGARET

Also on New Year's Eve, there was a stunning development — The Voice spoke through Janet's thirteen-year-old sister Margaret. It didn't say much dramatic, but it sounded like the old man's voice that had been coming out of Janet, albeit somewhat more fluent and communicative, Playfair noted. Grosse and Playfair certainly did not need any more complications in this case!

Could the poltergeist, if there was one, also involve Margaret? Could it be a separate entity that attaches itself to more than one person? Or did Margaret, like her sister, have the same abilities and stresses?

The investigators now had to look at Margaret's history in this case. Indeed, she had been in the room or nearby during many of the occurrences when objects moved or Janet talked with The Voice. When The Voice first vocalized through Janet, Margaret had been involved in the conversations (in her natural voice) with Janet, Bill, and the researchers.

Margaret often had been alone in the bedroom with Janet, which they now shared with their mother, when something happened. On one occasion, Margaret reported her own bed shook up and down a number of times. "Things have happened when Margaret is around, as well," her mother said. "It looks as if [the poltergeist] is using all of our energy."

Grosse queried Margaret about her new voice. How did it feel?

"I could feel a vibration in my neck, as though it was right behind me," she said.

The involvement of Margaret in the case seemed to alert some critics. Early in 1978, the *Daily Mirror*, which had already extensively covered the case, returned with a team of journalists and others to do a feature article. They brought along a local ventriloquist, Ray Alan, to check out Janet's mysterious voice, although the Hodgson family members claim that Alan talked to Margaret and not to Janet.

After a few days of research, feature writer Bryan Rimmer called Maurice Grosse to report that Margaret told him she and Janet had been faking voices all along to keep the case in the limelight. She apparently confessed that they had been creating The Voice with their diaphragm.

"It's very sad," Ray Alan said in an article in the *Daily Mirror*. "But these little girls obviously loved all the attention they got when objects were mysteriously moved round the house, and they decided to keep the whole thing going by inventing the voice."

Alan wasn't the only one to cry foul. Anita Gregory, of the Society for Psychical Research, who had spent just a short time at the Hodgson home, said the mysterious men's voices were simply the result of Janet and Margaret putting bedsheets to their mouths. In addition, Gregory said that a video camera had caught Janet attempting to bend spoons and an iron bar by force and "practising" levitation by bouncing up and down on her bed. When faced with this evidence, Janet admitting to faking some instances, but not all of them because she "wanted to see if the investigators would catch [her]. They always did," she said. (Later, in June 1978, Janet's mother said she was worried about the stress buildup in her daughter. "I now believe she's doing some of these things and she doesn't know she's doing them," Mrs. Hodgson said.)

If indeed Janet had faked some or all of the occurrences, it may have been related to the syndrome I refer to throughout this book as the When the Circus Comes to Town Syndrome. In that syndrome, a case might have some genuine paranormal activity, but one or more of the people involved with the case, usually a child or youth, resort to trickery. The theory is that a child may bask in the attention of investigators or the media and may start throwing things around (or, in this case, putting on a pretend voice) to keep the case going.

Circus? The Enfield case had certainly attracted a lot of attention, beyond the many friends and family and investigators who were now trampling through the house. Media were starting to have a field day with it. By now, the Enfield case had become known across Britain and was catching on abroad. After the *Daily Mirror*, *The Observer*, and BBC television and radio had publicized the event, the *National Enquirer*, America's sensational tabloid, arrived upon the scene. (In most instances, Grosse, Playfair, and other investigators had convinced the media not to use the family's real name or address.)

Another newspaper, the *Daily Express*, had run its own story accompanied with a photograph of actress Linda Blair from the popular movie *The Exorcist*. Some people noted the resemblance between Blair and Janet Hodgson. And *The News of the World* had a large story about the case with the headline: "Ghost Hunters Clash over Mystery of Spook or Spoof Kids."

But Grosse and Playfair didn't necessarily buy The Circus Comes to Town Syndrome in this case. For one thing, they were skeptical about Margaret's confession to the *Mirror* because apparently she did not even know what a diaphragm was, never mind being able to use it to deceive investigators.

When Grosse went to see Margaret, she was in tears, claiming that ventriloquist Ray Alan saw her only briefly and that the *Mirror* writers had bullied her. She had not confessed anything, she said, but had simply nodded her head from time to time under intense questioning and pressure. Janet denied trickery as well, telling Grosse, "I haven't faked The Voice."

Their mother, Peggy, was angry with the *Daily Mirror* and claimed that the ventriloquist could not learn anything in such a short visit.

The police also did not believe that Janet, Margaret, or anyone else had been cheating, at least not earlier in the case. "Well, to be honest, I didn't know what to make of it," Sergeant Brian Hyams said in 1996. "In 28 years in the police service, that's the only time I've consciously become aware of something like that, and I think that it is so rare and few and far between. When I tell the story, people still look at me as much as to say, 'Is he or isn't he telling the truth?' and I say, 'Look, this is really what happened and what I saw.' I don't think I would like to see it again. If I did, I don't think I'd react in any other way."

Peggy Nottingham said that one mainstream media publication had offered her £1,000 to say that what happened in the Hodgson home had been faked. She said she refused the offer.

However, Playfair said that Janet and Margaret likely played a few tricks during the case, but none of them involved the major events of moving objects or The Voice. "All children play tricks in their own house, but you can't fake the real thing," Playfair said in 2005. "I am sick of answering questions about their cheating. This case was legitimate."

After The Voice controversy died down, the case got back to normal as the physical movements and knockings continued.

On May 30, 1978, there was a disturbing incident in the middle of the day when the Hodgson children had a spat with neighboring children across the garden wall. Showers of stones, milk bottles, and bricks were thrown by children or unseen forces. Gardens of at least five homes were damaged, and yet none of the neighbors reported seeing anyone throw anything. The incidents reportedly continued even after Peggy Hodgson had brought Janet and her other children inside their home. The children denied throwing anything. One area resident, Bob Richardson, the brother of Peggy Nottingham, said a clod of earth had moved through the air on its own and he didn't see anyone throw it.

MEETING OF THE UNUSUAL

It was the most unusual meeting—two people who had both been so-called poltergeist entities. On December 17, 1977, Matthew Manning visited Janet Hodgson in Janet's home at the request of investigators. By this time, Manning was a famous psychic, who helped people deal with their paranormal abilities and experiences. But when he had been a boy, Matthew had allegedly caused things to move in his home and at his school.

With Janet, Manning shared his feelings and got The Voice to talk, although it did not make much sense and answered "dunno" to many of his questions. He said that, during his boyhood poltergeist experiences, he had headaches similar to those that Janet was having.

He tried to convince Janet to develop what he termed psychic abilities, as he said he had done himself since becoming an adult. During his eight-hour stay in the house, there were several loud crashes, but no paranormal events were witnessed. For more on Manning, see the chapter on psychokinesis.

CHAPTER 15

ENFIELD: EPILOGUE

Janet Hodgson spent three months in hospital from June to September 1978. Doctors found her to be normal physically with no indication of epilepsy, which her mother had suffered from as a young woman. Upon her return, Janet looked well and more mature. Few incidents were reported after that.

But the case continued to receive much publicity and controversy in the coming years and decades.

In 1984, Playfair published a book on the case, *This House Is Haunted*, and the Enfield case was one of several used for a 1998 British film, *Urban Ghost Story*. According to Playfair, another film company was interested, but was turned off by a Christian fundamentalist group, which convinced the filmmakers that the Enfield case was the work of the devil. He also believes that the 1982 movie *Poltergeist*, directed by Steven Spielberg, was partly based on the Enfield case, although he cannot prove it.

Not everyone was prepared to accept the facts in the Enfield case, even some people at the Society for Psychical Research. Tony Cornell, a one-time Cambridgeshire County councilor, author, and one of Britain's leading paranormal investigators, had some misgivings while reviewing the case, although he did not investigate it first-hand. Cornell felt that Grosse was too inexperienced to do a good job. Cornell said, "One had the impression that [Janet and Margaret Hodgson] were listening to him talking about what he expected to see, and then doing it. But there were indications that right at the beginning, some of [the phenomena] were genuine."

Dono Gmelig-Meyling, a Dutch psychic, had a theory that Maurice Grosse's stake in the case was related to the death of his own daughter, ironically named Janet, two years before he started the Enfield investigation. The psychic believed that his dead daughter's spirit drew him to the case in order for him to be distracted from his grief.

Grosse admitted that some of the incidents turned out to be what he termed childish pranks, but that it would be too easy and wrong to dismiss the entire case because of them. "When I look back now, I realize how transparent most of their tricks were compared to the real phenomena," he said years later.

But overall, Grosse remains steadfast that the case had strong paranormal elements. "I'm 100 percent, no, 150 percent satisfied that this case was genuine poltergeist activity," Grosse said in 2005.

It was the sheer volume of events that most impressed Grosse. In only a few months, his investigators counted more than 1,500 unexplained incidents, he said. In fact, Grosse believed it was the most thoroughly investigated poltergeist case of all time, partly through the researchers' patience and hard work and partly through improved equipment. "Thanks to the tape recorder and other instruments, we were able to review events immediately after they had taken place," he said. "Without this capacity to recall, the phenomena could have been called into question and possibly held up to ridicule."

Grosse noted that the case had many "reliable, independent witnesses, who have given great weight to our evidence." He said that at least thirty people had seen phenomena, including police, journalists, tradesmen, council workers, and the Hodgsons, Nottinghams, and Burcombes, "three perfectly ordinary families who would satisfy any jury that they were telling the truth." Grosse was so sure that The Voice that emanated from Janet was not her own voice, he offered £500 to anyone who could duplicate it. He had no takers. "I'm sure she didn't cheat [on the voice]," he said.

Margaret Hodgson signed a letter, witnessed by Maurice Grosse, on November 26, 1987: "I, Mrs. Hodgson, would like to say that everything that happened in the pologist [*sic*] case was perfectly true. Nothing was faked... this is my honest statement."

John Zaffis, an international paranormal investigator for nearly thirty years, reviewed articles and transcripts in the case and speculated that it contained both real phenomena and also fraud. "It is believed that this case began with genuine phenomena, but soon turned to trickery," Zaffis said. "For paranormal researchers, this case is a rare find, and some spend a lot of time looking for this type of poltergeist case."

Guy Lyon Playfair, who investigated other poltergeist cases and went on to write many other books about the paranormal, believes the Hodgson case was very complex, perhaps involving a spirit of a dead person as well as Janet's unconscious paranormal ability. He found the Enfield case exhausting. "I don't want to go through another case like that again," he said in 2005. "One was enough. It was always action."

As for Janet Hodgson, she apparently went on to live "an ordinary life, like most folk," Grosse said. She married and had four children, one of whom died young.

Janet does not give interviews about the case and lives in central England with her husband, who works in child care. In one of only a few interviews since 1978, she told a British television show, *Jane Goldman Investigates*, in 2004 that she did not fake any of the major occurrences. "She doesn't speak eloquently in her East London accent, but I believe her," Playfair said.

Her brother, Johnny, died of a brain tumor at age fourteen, not long after the disturbances at Enfield ended. "I don't think the family was ever told by doctors how serious Johnny's illness was," Playfair said. "That family has had more disasters than any family I can think of."

Janet's sister, Margaret, also married. Their mother, Peggy, died in 2002. (*Note:* In some books and media reports, the Hodgson family members have pseudonyms that protected their identities while the case was transpiring. In many reports, they are referred to as the Harper family.)

INVESTIGATORS' EVIDENCE

After the Enfield investigation was complete, Maurice Grosse logged what he said were the key events he witnessed throughout the case, "all in good lighting conditions." Grosse claimed he had seen the following in the Hodgson house:

- Glass marbles and plastic pieces, which appeared to come from walls and windows, were in unusual trajectory at high speed and always fell to the floor without bouncing.
- An aluminum teapot vibrated and bounced up and down while Grosse was alone in the kitchen.
- A table lamp that was out of reach of anyone tilted its shade at a 45-degree angle and then moved back to its original position.
- A bathroom door opened and closed on its own power several times even though there was no one in the area and no drafts.
- A cardboard box was thrown at him while he was trying to communicate with the poltergeist by knocking.

- A couch rose up vertically to a height of about 4 feet, flipped backwards, and fell to the floor. Eight or nine people were in the room, but nobody was sitting on the settee.
- John Burcombe was pulled out of a chair and whirled around 180 degrees before he fell to the floor.

Skeptic Sammy: Old men's voices? Ghosts singing "Daisy, Daisy"? And look out for the dangerous Lego bricks. I don't believe in psychics, but that Dutch psychic had a point when he said Maurice Grosse may have been looking for answers "from beyond" because he had recently lost his own young daughter in an automobile accident. As well, there was probably tension in the house because Peggy had recently divorced her husband and four young children were vying for a single parent's attention. And so, Janet does the Peter Pan thing off her bed.

Rebutt Al: Peggy Hodgson didn't seem the type to allow a whole nation to come into her home unless there was something to this case. If young Janet staged everything, she should have been up for the 1977 Oscar in the Leading Lady category. I think the best circumstance evidence came from the police.

CHAPTER 16

THE IRISH GAL AND WEE HUGHIE

"It is, however, beyond all possibility that five responsible persons should be so deceived at various occasions over a period of two weeks."

—DR. A.R.G. OWEN, FELLOW AT TRINITY COLLEGE

Virginia Campbell was an attractive eleven-year-old Irish girl, large for her age, with blonde hair and blue eyes. By all accounts, she wore her beauty quietly and was a shy lass.

Virginia was raised by her parents on a farm in the hamlet of Moville in County Donegal, Ireland. She was said to have a lonely life in the country and two of her very favorite companions were her dog, Toby, and another little girl, Anna.

But in the autumn of 1960, a traumatic thing occurred in Virginia's life — her father sold their farm and she moved to Scotland with her mother Annie to live with Virginia's married older brother, Thomas Campbell, a miner, in a council house at 19 Park Crescent in the small village of Sauchie in the central part of the rugged country.

Also living in the house were Thomas's wife and their two children. Virginia apparently did not like sharing a room with her nine-year-old niece, Margaret. It was not ideal for Margaret, either, who gave up her privacy and had to share her bed with Virginia.

In mid-October 1960, Virginia began attending Craigbank Primary School in Sauchie, where she made friends and seemed normal. According to her teacher, Miss Margaret Stewart, Virginia was placid, "with above average intelligence and a very honest disposition."

The first sign of things amiss came on the evening of Tuesday, November 22, 1960, when people in the Thomas Campbell house heard a mysterious "thunking" noise, similar to the sound of a bouncing ball, in Virginia's bedroom, on the stairs, and in the living room. They thought it was probably just Virginia, who was fond of games.

It seemed no game at teatime the very next day, however, when Thomas and his wife said they saw a heavy sideboard move out from a wall approximately 5 inches, then returned to its original position without anyone's assistance. Virginia had been sitting in the living room, near the sideboard, but she did not touch it, the Campbells reported.

Later that night, while Virginia was lying awake in her double bed, along with her niece Margaret, loud knocks were heard coming from their bedroom.

The puzzled and frightened family didn't know what to do, but a neighbor called in Rev. T.W. Lund of the Church of Scotland. The minister did some investigating and believed that the noises were coming from the headboard. He moved Virginia down in the bed, where she was sleeping alone, so that she was not near the headboard. But the loud knocks continued, the minister and family members reported.

That same evening, Rev. Lund said he saw the impossible — a large linen chest, located near the bed, rocked sideways, raised itself off the floor, and moved in a jerking motion parallel to the bed for a distance of about 18 inches. And then the full chest (which measured 27 by 17 by 14 inches and weighed 50 pounds) moved itself back to its original position. The stunned minister and a neighbor, who shall remain unnamed, lifted the chest, their fingers understandably shaking a little, out onto the landing. When they suggested that Margaret join Virginia in the double bed, an even louder knocking reportedly came from the headboard. The minister and the neighbor said no one — certainly not the two girls — had caused the noise.

On the following evening, Thursday, November 26, Rev. Lund came back to the home and family members reported that there had been a new occurrence — Virginia's pillow had reportedly rotated about 60 degrees while beneath her head. The family's physician, Dr. W.H. Nisbet, of nearby Tillicoultry, also came to the home, along with another minister and another doctor, both of whom shall remain unnamed. (As in many poltergeist cases, many people do not want to be identified, sometimes for themselves and sometimes out of respect for the family.)

And then Rev. Lund and Dr. Nisbet said they saw a curious rippling movement on Virginia's pillow, but they could not explain it and did not believe that Virginia had caused it. Meanwhile, on that same evening, Rev. Lund said he heard more rapping noises and more movement of the linen chest. What was going on here?

Another witness to some of the events was Malcolm Robinson, an investigator for Strange Phenomena Investigations and its magazine *Enigma*. He reported:

> I was in Virginia's bedroom with a number of other individuals. I was standing close to the bed in which Virginia was lying; she had the covers up to her chin... seconds later, I observed the pillow next to Virginia, which had been plumped up, suddenly take what appeared to be the shape of a person's head. A clear indentation of the pillow was seen by myself and others in the room. Now during this time, strange knockings, bangings and scratchings and what sounded like sawing noises were coming from all over the room. You couldn't really pinpoint the exact source of the noise; it was coming from everywhere! Most unusual was the sound... like a ping-pong ball constantly being bounced.

The local newspaper, the *Alloa Journal*, reported some violence: "Sitting on the edge of Virginia's bed, Mrs. Campbell was roughly pushed off as she watched... she saw the blankets and sheets rising and falling above Virginia whilst the child made little moaning noises like someone in pain."

Another witness to the pillow incident was a close friend of the family, who asked not to be named. He described what he saw:

> I was standing close to the bed and Virginia had the bedclothes pulled up to her chin. Suddenly I observed the covers making a rippling motion from the bottom of the bed right up to her chin. I am convinced that Virginia did not do this by herself. There was no movement from below the covers, i.e., from her legs, just this peculiar rippling movement running up and down the top sheet.

The man said he then saw the pillow next to the girl take the impression of a person's head. "Others and myself saw a clear indentation in the pillow." He also reported strange knockings, scratching sounds, and what sounded like sawing noises. "There was also the noise sounding like a ping-pong ball bouncing... Virginia was very upset during all this and we could not settle her."

Rev. Lund and several other ministers and church officials believed that something paranormal, if not spiritual, was happening. "People scoff about stories of ghosts and spooks, but they have not studied the subject," said Rev. Thomas Jeffrey of the Church of Scotland. "In the case of this little girl, we have examples of well-known phenomena."

Apparently no official exorcism was attempted and little discussion was given to the possibility that the girl had been possessed by a spirit or demon.

Although the case received much national publicity, the Church of Scotland did not take an official stance or even offer much comment beyond the individual ministers. However, one evening, a prayer service was held in the Campbell home. While several members of the Church of Scotland recited The Lord's Prayer, the banging and loud noises reportedly became even louder than before. Virginia was watched closely while all this was going on. No one else in the home was suspected.

"Happenings such as are taking place with this little girl are not nearly so unusual as many people think," said James McNee, an official of the Spiritualist National Church. "And contrary to much popular opinion, they are not necessarily evil in nature. Children are much more alive physically than are adults and are often, although unconsciously, real mediums."

Lots of other people had unusual advice. An African shaman wrote Virginia a letter, advising her to "pound down some bones and dance over them." A woman wanted to touch Virginia because she was "one of God's chosen ones."

INCIDENTS AT SCHOOL

The incidents, of course, were having a terrifying effect on family life at 19 Park Crescent, not to mention "the effect which gossip and publicity are having upon them," the *Alloa Journal* said. For the next two days, November 23 and 24, Virginia was kept home from school. When she returned to school on Friday, November 25, her teacher witnessed something she later called "unnerving."

Miss Margaret Stewart was fond of Virginia. She said of her student, "Virginia was a shy, withdrawn girl, but very pleasant. She wasn't really forthcoming, but was normal in every other way, and she was good at her lessons...I had never really heard the word poltergeist before; indeed, I thought it was a name for some form of medicine!"

But during a session of silent reading and essay writing, Miss Stewart said she observed Virginia trying to hold down her desk lid, which several times raised itself to an angle of 45 to 50 degrees. Miss Stewart recalled: "The class was quiet, and writing away. We still had the old school desks which had a lid top. Anyway, I looked over at Virginia and noticed she was sitting with both hands pressed firmly down on top of her desk lid. I saw the desk lid rise and fall, with Virginia trying her best to keep the lid shut with her hands." Miss Stewart said she could plainly see Virginia's hands flat on the lid of the desk and her legs were underneath the desk.

A short time later, when another student got up to bring a jotter to the teacher, Miss Stewart said that the unnamed student's unoccupied desk (which was behind Virginia) slowly rose off the floor, perhaps about an inch or two, and then settled down again, coming to rest a slight distance from its original position. Still suspicious of a prank, Miss Stewart immediately went to the desk to check it for strings or wires, but there were none. That was one day when the teacher became the student!

On that same day, when Virginia left the classroom, Miss Stewart discovered she could not shut the door behind her student. "I had to summon help from three of the children to help me push the door shut," she said.

That night, Dr. Nisbet stayed with Virginia in her bedroom. While the girl was lying motionless on the bed without bedclothes over her, the physician said he heard unexplained knocks in the room. And the linen chest started moving again — about a foot. He moved the chest away from the bed and suddenly its lid reportedly opened and shut several times in succession. The surprised Dr. Nisbet said he also saw the pillow under Virginia's head rotate about 90 degrees and a curious rippling passed across the bedclothes.

On Saturday, November 26, Dr. Nisbet's medical (unnamed) partner tried his luck in the bedroom. He said he saw a puckering of the bedcover and pillow rotations similar to those reported by Dr. Nisbet.

On the following day, Dr. Logan was back with Virginia. This time, he brought along his pet dog. She liked it, saying it reminded her of her beloved dog Toby back in Ireland. Later, Virginia seemed to go into a trance and called out for Toby. At about 11:30 p.m., Rev. Lund arrived and then the girl cried out loudly, striking the air with her fists. When they left the room, she fell into a quiet sleep.

Dr. Nisbet recalled: "Virginia is not responsible for what has happened. The child is innocent. The child herself did not conjure up what has taken place — an outside agent is responsible. Believe me, something unfortunate has been going on in that house. The girl was hysterical all the time the phenomena were appearing. We decided to try sedation; Virginia was given mild tranquilizers to quiet her. If the phenomena were being conjured by her own imagination, they would no longer appear if her brain were dulled. Even though her brain was not working normally, the phenomena still appeared."

Virginia returned to Craigbank Primary School on Monday, November 28, for more events. While Virginia stood, hands clasped behind her back, next to Miss Stewart's large oak table, the teacher said she saw a blackboard pointer lying on a table suddenly start to vibrate and move across the table until it fell to the floor. While the pointer was moving, Miss Stewart put her hand on the heavy table and discovered that the table was vibrating. Then the whole table reportedly started to swing away from the teacher in a counterclockwise motion. Virginia started to cry and said she was not causing the disturbance. Worried about spooking the rest of the class, the teacher told Virginia to help her straighten the table back to its normal position.

In 1994, Miss Stewart told researcher Malcolm Robinson that the table incident was unnerving. "At first, it was vibrating slowly, then increased as the seconds wore on. I sat transfixed looking at this. Then the table, which was quite a heavy one, started to rise up very slowly into the air and also vibrate. I put my hands on the table and tried to push it back down, but with no success. I was quite horrified, but it did not stop there. The table continued to vibrate as it hovered a few inches off the floor. Then the table rotated 90 degrees so that, where I had moments before I sat behind the long edge of the table, the table had rotated so that its narrow edge was now directly in front of my stomach. I looked up at Virginia and saw she was quite distressed, and I remember her saying, 'Please, Miss, I'm not doing that, honest I'm not.' Then I calmed her down."

Keeping the other children calm with Virginia in the eye of a storm was a concern, but the teacher managed. "I explained to the children that sometimes people are ill and don't know what's wrong with them. That doesn't necessarily mean there is anything really odd or strange. And I explained that something like that was happening to Virginia. They had heard stories about ghosts, but I assured them that I wouldn't be staying in a room if there was a ghost in it, but if I stay in it you are all right. And they accepted that quite happily."

Miss Stewart reported that other strange occurrences followed Virginia—schoolbooks and jotters would levitate and then fall.

THE POLTERGEIST GETS A NAME: WEE HUGHIE

Also on November 28, a relative drove Virginia to the village of Dollar, several miles away. Dr. Nisbet visited her there at a home and again said he heard knockings that were louder than they had been at 19 Park Crescent in Sauchie.

The following day, there were more occurrences at Dollar. Another physician, Dr. William Logan, and his wife heard several bursts of knocks, which seemed to be coming from Virginia's vicinity. Mrs. Logan, who had previously been skeptical, did not believe that Virginia was causing the noises, at least not in a normal physical sense.

That night, Virginia reportedly went into a ten-minute trance, talking loudly in a strange voice and calling out for her dog Toby and for Anna, her friend back in Ireland. She tossed around on the bed and answered questions while apparently still in the trance. Her replies to questions seemed to indicate a lack of normal inhibition, as if repressed thoughts were emerging.

No incidents were reported on the following day, Wednesday, November 30, when Virginia returned to the Campbell residence in Sauchie. But by now, the so-called poltergeist had become such a fixture that some people in the house nicknamed it Wee Hughie. It was a sign that Virginia and her niece Margaret and others were trying to see some humor in the situation, and that the occurrences were not violent or even threatening in nature. Wee Hughie was more of a prankster than a mugger.

At about this time, the *Alloa Journal* reported: "Just over a week ago, strange things began to happen to Virginia. Heavy pieces of furniture were seen to move when she entered a room, doors opened and when she approached them and then were found difficult to shut." Then national media took an interest in the story and the Campbells, who did not want publicity, became prisoners in their own home. Frustrated journalists wound up interviewing their friends and neighbors.

On the evening of Thursday, December 1, Dr. Nisbet and Dr. Logan went to 19 Park Crescent with a tape recorder and a movie camera. A number of loud knockings and loud sawing noises were captured on the tape recorder. At times, Virginia talked hysterically. At 11 p.m., Rev. Lund and two other ministers conducted prayers, during which there were several knocks.

Some observers noticed that the loud noises and furniture movements never seemed to occur while Virginia was in a trance-like state. One theory was that the trances were an alternative outlet for her stress and suppressed emotions.

Finally, the bizarre occurrences seemed to dissipate after December 1. There were a few minor incidents — Virginia and her niece Margaret reported that they were pinched several times.

One of the last incidents was on Monday, January 23, 1961, at school when Miss Stewart said that Virginia put a bowl of flower bulbs, which Virginia had attended to over the Christmas holidays, on her table and they moved unaided across the top of the table.

At about this time, Miss Stewart noted that the disturbances in Virginia's life seemed to peak in twenty-eight-day cycles; the bowl incident occurred fifty-six days after one of the major incidents at the school. The disturbances, the teacher said, "started off fairly violently, then leveled off and disappeared, and then came back again."

Dr. A.R.G. Owen, a fellow at Trinity College in Cambridge, England, tended to agree with the cycle theory and went further — it could have had something to do with Virginia's menstrual cycle. Dr. Owen had heard of the Sauchie case and visited Virginia at her home. He interviewed witnesses Rev. Lund, Dr. Nisbet, Dr. Logan, Dr. Logan's wife, Miss Stewart, and others.

The twenty-eight-day cycle, Owen said, "is a very suggestive figure, if the phenomena are related to physiological happenings associated with a quasi-menstrual cycle occurring as a result of exceptionally rapid pubescence."

In the end, teachers and students at the school seemed glad when the events began to wane because journalists had been hounding them for interviews. At one point, headmaster Peter Hill had the school gates locked to keep reporters at bay.

In his investigation and interviews of witnesses, Dr. Owen reported that there were other phenomena that were alleged to have occurred, but not always corroborated: An apple levitated above a fruit bowl and a shaving brush, a small vase, and a china dog moved on their own. In bed, the two girls were said to have had their legs pinched or poked, their pajamas pulled off or rolled up their bodies.

Eventually, the disturbances ended altogether as Wee Hughie seemed to die a natural death. Virginia was finally reunited with her dog, Toby, and her Irish eyes were smiling again.

Overall, Dr. Owen concluded that there were too many reliable witnesses to dismiss this case as fraud or accident. "The five main witnesses believed themselves to have heard certain sounds and seen certain movements of objects," he said. "It is just possible in principle to suppose that one person could be the victim of illusion or hallucination. It is, however, beyond all possibility that five responsible persons should be so deceived at various occasions over a period of two weeks. Thus we must conclude that they heard actual noises and saw actual motions of real objects."

At no time was Virginia or anyone else in the Campbell home caught cheating.

THE THEORIES

If the occurrences were indeed paranormal, what could have possibly caused them?

According to Dr. Owen, during the time of the disturbances, Virginia was going through "a burst of extremely rapid physical development and maturation. Puberty in the full sense had not arrived, but she was going through a very rapid pubescence." Dr. Owen added that Virginia was probably upset during the "poltergeist activity," but it was not evidence that she was mentally ill.

Dr. Logan and others suspected that having to leave her dog and best friend in Ireland was partly responsible for stress in Virginia's life and thus the paranormal occurrences. "It was almost certainly due to some suppressed emotional state over which she had absolutely no control," Dr. Logan said.

Rev. T.W. Young, who saw Virginia in the house one night, suggested that being away from her dog was an important factor in the occurrences. "The family told me she'd been rolling about in bed, her eyes wide open as if in a trance," he said. "She had been calling for her dog Toby and her friend Annie. Intermittently, she had been barking like a dog."

It is possible that Virginia caused the events subconsciously through a type of psychokinesis or recurrent spontaneous psychokinesis, several observers noted. At one point, Dr. Logan made a curious finding when he checked Virginia while she was in an agitated state "both physically and emotionally." Despite the agitation, her pulse rate remained normal and quite slow. "I thought this rather unusual, but I can't explain it," Dr. Logan said. "It was as if the subconscious part of her brain was aware that the phenomena was emanating from her and there was nothing to fear, and the irrational side was producing a standard fear response."

Others brought forward additional theories. At the same time as the incidents occurred in the Thomas Campbell house, there were minor earth tremors in the vicinity of Sauchie, but probably not enough to cause the incidents. However, some people felt that strong magnetic fields created by these seismic disturbances could have had some effect.

Not many details are known of Virginia's life after Wee Hughie, although she got married and went to live in Sheffield, England. She remains silent about the case and refuses to discuss what happened in 1960–1961 in Scotland.

Skeptic Sammy: This is one motivated student at school! As they say, Virginia was fond of games. Wee bit hard to digest, all of this. Fruit bowl across the table—could it be that ants were inside it? Making the teacher's desk levitate? If I had done that, I would have been sitting in the vice-principal's office, my head between my legs.

Rebutt Al: Let's see—a little girl, or "The Force" made believers of the police, the doctors, the parapsychologist, the ministers, and the teacher. Anybody else left?

CHAPTER 17

LIVELY CASE IN CHESHIRE

"I was amazed at the destruction of such a solidly-built piece of furniture. It would have taken two strong men to lift it upside down and a large ax to dismember what happened to it, all in the course of about 30 seconds."

–THOMAS BARROW ON WHAT HE SAID WAS DESTRUCTION CAUSED BY A POLTERGEIST

There are a number of ways to expose a teenager you suspect of faking a poltergeist case. You can put a video camera on him twenty-four hours a day, truss him up with packing tape, or sit on him.

Friends of John Glynn Jones chose the third option to eliminate the possibility that he was using tricks to scare them in 1952 in Runcorn, England. Four of them sat on top of him on a bed, and yet they said drawers in a dressing table continued to rattle under their own power.

This lively case began in mid-August 1952, in the town of Runcorn, located on the Manchester ship canal on the Mersey River in the northwest of England, a town known for its shipbuilding, production of chemicals, and an old castle.

It was almost exclusively confined to a small house at 1 Byron Street, where John lived with his sister, Eileen Glynn; their grandfather Sam Jones, a sixty-eight-year-old widower; Sam's sister-in-law, Lucy Jones; and an unidentified woman in her mid-fifties, a spinster who was lodging at the home.

The story revolves around young John, who was an apprentice draftsman at the Imperial Chemical Industries, West Point Power Station.

By all accounts, John was a well-behaved, slightly built youth with a quiet disposition. In fact, his personality was described as shy and even retiring. He was serious about studying to become a full-fledged draftsman and there was nothing to suggest he might be the focus of a paranormal event.

The first disturbances began when Lucy Jones's son and his wife, who lived in North Wales, visited the family for a week. That made the house crowded and John had to share a double bed with his grandfather Sam. Meanwhile, Lucy Jones and John's sister, Eileen, had to share another bed in the same room.

When they had all climbed into bed and were trying to fall asleep, a dressing table in the room reportedly started to make noises. The mysterious sounds gradually grew louder and the frightened occupants eventually left the bedroom. When they returned a short time later, the noises reportedly started up again. The family checked the dressing table, but could not find the source of the noise.

On the following night, the situation repeated itself with one new wrinkle — the dressing table was said to move about a foot away from the wall under its own power.

By this time, John had become the main suspect and other family members grilled him and checked him for strings or magic contrivances, but they found none.

To remove any doubt, four of John's relatives and friends sat on him as he lay on the bed, but the noises and rattlings of the dressing table continued.

Sam Jones had lived in the house for thirty-five years without any such problems and the dressing table had remained quiet for forty-two years until now.

When sitting atop John did not stop the rattling, the family sealed the drawers of the dressing table with adhesive tape, but it reportedly continued to rattle and its mirror swung back and forth on its pivots.

Local police officers could not solve the riddle. They set a trap for John, but they could not prove he had faked the occurrences. In fact, the police became victims of what they believed was an unseen force. According to the local newspaper, the *Runcorn Guardian*, three burly bobbies were thrown off an empty chest in the hallway of the house "and soon realized that the disorderly conduct at No. 1 [Byron Street] was something outside their knowledge and control."

On one evening, it was estimated that fourteen people saw what they believed to be paranormal activity in the movement of furniture and the smashing of china. A woman who was visiting from Sutton said that her husband's spectacle case was tossed across a room.

As similar occurrences of noises and furniture movements continued for ten weeks, the *Runcorn Guardian* followed the case closely with articles, and the case eventually made it onto the wire services around the world. Sympathetic people wrote letters with offers of advice to get rid of what they thought was a poltergeist or a case of demonic possession. Many of the writers recommended exorcism, and other well wishers, along with curiosity seekers, showed up at the Jones' house.

When nothing seemed to work, the family called a Spiritualist medium for a séance, but that only seemed to provoke more problems as many objects — a picture book, a tin of ointment, a table cover, and two Bibles — starting flying about the bedroom, according to several witnesses. However, sometimes nothing would happen for days, allowing people to catch up on their sleep.

In September, things heated up again as a clock and other objects reportedly moved 5 feet across the bedroom, then witnesses reported seeing John lifted out of his bed and thrown to the floor.

A member of the Society for Psychical Research in London, Rev. W.H. Rev. Stevens, a Methodist minister, came to the Jones' home to investigate.

Rev. Stevens said that one night, while the lights were off in the bedroom, the dressing table creaked loudly and moved out from the wall and began to shake and rock. "When the light was turned on, the movement ceased," Rev. Stevens said. Also sleeping in the bedroom at the time were John Glynn and a neighboring friend, John Berry.

When the light was turned on, Rev. Stevens said he saw the two boys in the bed, wrapped in the bedclothes, and the table was rocking back and forth with no one near it "for about three seconds... I went to see if the table would rock on its own accord, but it was firm on the floor." Earlier, Rev. Stevens shone a flashlight, but could see no one trying to rock the table.

On another night with the lights off, books and a box containing a jigsaw puzzle reportedly flew around the room. Rev. Stevens said he shone his flashlight to see the boys still under the covers "in the exact position as they had been when the light was switched off" and the puzzle box flying about 7 feet in the air.

Another visitor in the room, J.C. Davies, said that the box was "almost in suspension above a bed, almost as if it was being carried with directional intent."

Many parapsychologists believe that a youth with RSPK powers may unleash them when he or she thinks no one is paying attention, or cannot see what is about to happen. He or she may not want to be observed, hence acting when the lights were out. Or perhaps someone just threw the items physically under the cover of darkness, although Rev. Stevens said he monitored the situation closely with his flashlight.

Although he was a Methodist minister, Rev. Stevens concluded that the issue revolving around John Jones was not so much spiritual or demonic, but one of RSPK. Rev. Stevens believed that John suffered from a buildup of repressed energy, which manifested itself in a very unusual way. When it did, there was a decrease in energy and a recuperation period before the disturbances started up again, Rev. Stevens said. The minister said there was no way that John was at the center of a hoax.

Just like the police, Rev. Stevens was treated with disrespect by the "force." At one point during his investigation, he said he was hit on the head by a flying dictionary.

On another occasion, another visitor, Mrs. E. Dowd, claimed she was hit in the face by a flying book.

Two other Methodist ministers came to the house and said they believed the happenings were paranormal.

As the case dragged into the fall of 1952, it became more complex and some occurrences raised suspicions that it had deteriorated into some trickery.

John Glynn and several friends, including Thomas Barrow, a longtime friend of the Jones family, wondered if the disturbances were somehow related to a spirit or ghost.

They conducted an informal séance and tried to communicate with the spirit by asking questions. They claim it answered through a series of knocks and identified itself as a witch doctor.

If this sounds suspicious, Barrow said he wondered if further disturbances in the bedroom were the result of tomfoolery.

Barrow spent four nights in John's home. Most of the time, the goings-on occurred only after the lights were turned off.

Barrow slept in a single bed while John Glynn and another friend who lived nearby, John Berry, slept in a double bed. As soon as the light was turned off, Barrow said he was hit between the eyes by a book. Several times during the night, objects were airborne when the light was off, Barrow said.

On the following night, two police officers sat on the single bed. As soon as the light was turned off, an old chest in the room rose a few feet in the air and dropped to the floor, Barrow said. A short time later, when the lights were off again, the single bed on which the police were sitting rose several feet off the floor with the officers on it and crashed to the floor, Barrow said.

"It lifted a couple of feet in the air and then dropped them down, after which they promptly departed," said Barrow, who was eighteen at the time and on leave from the British Army. The officers did not charge anyone with a crime, Barrow said.

"Whenever we'd shut the light off, the thing would go berserk," Barrow said in 2005. "It upturned a huge, old-fashioned chest and it got ripped into small pieces. I was amazed at the destruction of such a solidly built piece of furniture. It would have taken two strong men to lift it upside down and a large ax to dismember what happened to it, all in the course of about 30 seconds...I got smacked on the arm and leg by flying pieces and I received a piece of timber in the middle of the back, which almost knocked me down the stairs, much to the two Johns' delight...It was amazing no one broke an arm or leg."

At no time did he see anyone throw anything, Barrow said, but he was surprised that John Glynn and John Berry seemed to treat the incidents in a lighthearted way, at least near the end of the case.

Barrow said he couldn't believe that John Glynn would deliberately damage his grandfather's home. "John had lived with his grandfather since an early age and it appeared to me that he did not seem the type to upset his grandfather, of whom he was very fond."

In an editorial, the *Runcorn Guardian* said it believed the incidents were of a paranormal nature:

> The manifestations...have reached proportions that settle any dispute as their reality. Too many independent witnesses have been present on too many occasions, apart from our own representative [a reporter]. Two psychic researchers from a body of investigators, well known for their logic, not to say skeptical approach, three Methodist ministers and at least two police officers are among the witnesses. Phenomena have occurred in the presence of all these witnesses under conditions precluding the possibility of fraud without their connivance.

Over the ten weeks, damage was estimated at about £20,000 with all the broken items and a crack in the kitchen ceiling. Although most of the damage occurred at Sam Jones's house, there were reportedly minor incidents at the home of one of John's friends in the nearby village of Frodsham, in which a glass smashed near John, and at a pig farm where he did some work.

The farmer said that while John was working at the farm in the late summer of 1952, at about the time of the occurrences at Sam Jones's house, fifty-three of his pigs died, and veterinarians could not explain why. Shortly after the pigs died, the farmer said he saw a mysterious black cloud or apparition near John Glynn Jones. Apparitions are rare in poltergeist cases, but they have been reported.

In the book *Real Ghosts, Restless Spirits and Haunted Places* by Brad Steiger (Detroit: Visible Ink Press, 2003), there is a photograph of John Glynn Jones surveying some of the damage (on page 75) in his grandfather's house. It shows a rather bewildered-looking John, small shouldered and clean cut, wearing a cardigan and tie, looking at the complete destruction of his bedroom with mattress springs and pillow fluff everywhere and broken furniture flung upside-down. The story was published in the prestigious *Life Magazine* on December 8, 1952, nearly two months after the occurrences subsided.

"In the end, there was no satisfactory explanation as to the cause of all the trouble," said Mark Bevan, editor of the *Cheshire Magazine*, which has published stories about the case (www.cheshiremagazine.com/issue28/runghost.html). "The SPR investigator, a local spiritualist organization and several independent psychic detectives could not agree on the origin of the phenomena, or on what an ordinary, quiet living family could have done to invite the attentions of some evil force to wreak its vengeance on their household and disturb their lives this way."

After the disturbances at 1 Byron Street, John Glynn Jones reportedly settled into a normal life in northwest England, married, and had two children. He died about 1994.

The middle-aged female spinster, who had been living in the Jones home at the time of the occurrences, met an untimely death — she fell off a cliff known as Frog's Mouth near the home in October 1952 at about the time the disturbances were ending. It was another strange aspect of an unusual story.

Skeptic Sammy: Boy, these young adults were juvenile with their lights-out scenarios. Did they just come back from summer camp? And when there is £20,000 of damage and fifty-three dead pigs, shouldn't the bobbies conduct more of an investigation?

Rebutt Al: I think the police tried. If getting tossed about on a bed didn't motivate them to lay charges, then material damage would not.

IRISH FAMILY ON THE MOVE

An Irish family said they were forced from their home by a poltergeist or ghost.

In 1997, Jackie Fahy and his wife, Esther, their two grown children, Michael and Martha, and their infant granddaughter, Sarah, lived in a home in Corrib Park, Galway. They complained of pictures flying off the mantelpiece, toys being tossed around, a toilet flushing on its own, a coffee table flipping over, and a porcelain dog exploding.

Many of the incidents were said to have been witnesses by family and neighbors.

"I get the impression that all of this is genuine, that strange things are really happening here," said Father Conan Garvey, a philosophy lecturer at University College in Galway, who visited the family. "I am sure there are no tricks involved. The porcelain dog was sitting only a foot off the floor and if it had just fallen, it would have broken into a few large parts — but it was in smithereens, almost as if it had exploded from inside."

Galway believed one of the family members was a poltergeist agent and he prayed for them. However, the Fahy family believed a ghost was at work and summoned a well-known Irish psychic, Sandra Ramdhanie, who performed a special ritual with herbs and salts.

At one point, the family moved out of the house, but it is not known what became of them.

SOME OTHER CASES IN THE UNITED KINGDOM

- *A Normal Poltergeist:* It's nice to have a normal poltergeist for a change. That's how Professor S. Ward of Wokingham described disturbances in 1926 in a thatched cottage in Finchampstead, England, occupied by a wheelwright/carpenter, George Goswell, and his two daughters, fourteen and sixteen. For fifteen years, things had been quiet, then a small bath reportedly overturned, chairs did somersaults, and pictures fell from walls — all in the daytime. Wokingham called it a mild case, sparked by the unconscious influence of one of the teenagers. However, he termed the force one "unknown to any science of which we are possessed."

- *Driven Out:* A thirty-four-year-old woman said she was driven out of her house on Mount Pleasant Road in Carlisle, England, in 2004. Carol Tuttle and her nine-year-old daughter went to stay with Carol's mother. "I won't live there again," Carol said. Her neighbor, Kevin Blythe, thirty-seven, was skeptical until he went into her house to retrieve her cats. "Two glasses flew right in front of me and smashed against the wall," he said. "There was a pepper pot flying in one direction and a wire basket flying in the other direction. It was really powerful. You couldn't have caught it." Another neighbor said a perfume bottle flew toward her and a light bulb from a lamp shot into the ceiling. Tuttle had the house blessed by a priest, but she would not return.
- *Seafaring Spook:* The widow Murphy and her family lived in a mountain cottage in 1913 near Brookborough, County Fermanagh, Ireland, where they were said to be plagued by flying pots and pans and clothes rising off a bed. A member of Parliament, Cahir Healy, and a minister reportedly saw some of the events. The family had to leave, partly after being ostracized by superstitious neighbors. It was said that the poltergeist activity followed them in their sea voyage to America. Some people refer to it as the Coonian Ghost.
- *London, 2000:* A seven-year-old boy was said to unconsciously cause loud knocking nightly in a London home in 2000. Researchers Maurice Grosse and Mary Rose Barrington were confident the boy was not cheating. Some of the psychic tension building around the boy had to do with his mother's divorce and her alcoholism, Grosse said. "He was quite disturbed about the divorce," Grosse said. The knockings lasted about three months. Grosse and Barrington counseled the family and, after the activity subsided, Grosse received a telephone call from the estranged father, thanking him. The names were not released because the family was upset about others finding out about their problems.
- *Woman Blames Poltergeist for Fire:* A forty-year-old woman was jailed for fifteen months in 2001 for setting fire to her own home in Barry, south Wales. Adele Gallivan blamed a poltergeist or ghost for strange occurrences, including an apparition in her curtains. Gallivan admitted setting fire to the house, causing about £2,000 damage, and she told police, "I'm not going back into that house — there's a poltergeist in there. It's my house and I can do what I like." Apparently not.
- *Water Everywhere in Rochdale:* In August 1995, paranormal investigators Stephen Mera and Peter Hough say they saw weird outpourings of water

in a home in Rochdale, which plagued Jim and Vera Gardner's family for months as water at times reportedly shot from one room to another. "At times, it was coming down like rain," Gardner said. The water occurrences, along with movements of objects, seemed to follow the Gardners' granddaughter, Jeanette. No leaks were found in the bungalow, but the water was tested and for some reason showed a higher electrical content than tap water.

Around the World

Poltergeists are reported around the globe, as we see in this section. In Chapter 18, there are interesting tales of a "super-static" girl in Bavaria, who wreaked havoc in a lawyer's office; water weirdness in Jacksonville, Florida; and a thirteen-year-old Polish girl, who made a mustard jar take flight, reportedly from the electric charge in her mind and/or body.

Subsequent chapters describe incredible claims and controversies in Long Island, New York, a poltergeist who allegedly moved around in Kentucky, and souvenirs that reportedly smashed all over a Miami warehouse.

CHAPTER 18

THE SUPER-STATIC GIRL AND MORE ELECTRICITY

"Achtung! Die Lampe!" (Watch out for the lamp!)

We probably all know coworkers who change the atmosphere of an office when they walk through the door, but this is ridiculous!

When nineteen-year-old secretary Annemarie Schneider walked into a lawyer's office in the Bavarian town of Rosenheim, Germany, at 7:30 a.m. daily, it was said that any one, or all, of a number of things could occur — light bulbs exploding; pictures rotating, then falling to the floor; light fittings swinging as she walked beneath them; and telephones supposedly dialing on their own.

It was autumn of 1967 at the office of Sigmund Adam. A typical incident is described in Richard S. Broughton's 1991 book *Parapsychology*:

> [Annemarie] walked down the entrance hall, taking off her coat as she went. As she passed under the hanging lamp, it began swinging, but she did not notice it. As she continued toward the cloakroom, the lamp began to swing more animatedly... a lamp began swinging, too. An employee shouted: "Achtung! Die Lampe!" Annemarie ducked for protection. Seconds later, a bulb in the hall lamp exploded. She got a broom and swept up.

Talk about making a lasting impression in your first few days at the office! To all of those in attendance, this commotion was puzzling, even frightening, during the first day or so, a little funny the next day, and exasperating from then on. The damage alone was concerning Mr. Adam. There had been considerable electrical malfunctions since Annemarie joined the company, and fluorescent lights high on the ceiling kept popping, sometimes preceded by a loud bang and sparks.

An electrician was summoned, but that created more questions than answers. On one occasion, he scurried up a ladder to discover that each of the fluorescent tubes had been twisted 90 degrees in their sockets, snapping their connection. He fixed them, but suddenly — bang!!!— the same thing reportedly happened all over again. Electrical fuses also blew and the cartridge fuses were ejected from the sockets.

All four office telephones would sometimes ring at once — and no one was at the other end of the line. When lawyers and secretaries were on the lines, sometimes they were suddenly cut off. And the telephone bills skyrocketed, including for some calls that had never been made. Across the room, the photocopiers would act up, or their fluid would spill out.

Not to worry — engineers from the municipal power station and the post office (operators of the phone system) were on their way. They were prepared to get at the root of the problem, installing monitoring equipment on the power lines to detect unusual surges. Immediately, the monitors revealed large and unexplained power surges.

To isolate the situation, the office was disconnected from its main power sources. An emergency power unit was put in, yet the disturbances continued. Whatever was happening electrically was happening in the confines of the office building.

A similar system was set up for the wonky telephone lines. All calls made from the office were recorded. Strangely, calls were registered even though no one was in the office! Some lines were dialed up to six times a minute. On October 20, forty-six calls were "made" in fifteen minutes. Strangely, there were many calls, up to four a minute, that connected with a line giving the local time. Was someone in a hurry to get work over for the day? Annemarie?

Technicians had no answers, even after they had ripped up the road outside to access underground wires. One postal official stuck to his guns, claiming that someone inside the office must have been making some of the calls, but all of the employees denied it. Somebody please get a lawyer! Mr. Adam, who, of course, *was* an attorney, filed formal charges with the police. If the person responsible was ever caught, he or she would be prosecuted for mischief. And so, the Rosenheim Police criminal investigation division took over the case.

As well, paranormal investigators got involved, including Professor Hans Bender of the Parapsychology Department at the University of Freiburg, a veteran of paranormal cases, who came on December 1 with some of his colleagues. A week later, two physicists from the Max Planck Institute for Plasma Physics arrived, G. Zicha and F. Karger, to take another look at the telephones and the power system.

After all of this snooping around, it was established that:

- The disturbances took place only during office hours (how about calling it the nine-to-five poltergeist?).
- Ruled out as causes of the disturbances were variations in the power supply, electrostatic charges, loose contacts, manual interference, and other physical explanations.
- Annemarie had something to do with the problems. The power-monitoring system would kick in whenever she walked through the door.

Dr. Karger said the phenomena seemed to be the result of "non-periodic, short-duration forces," but he did not know what these forces were, except that they seemed to be intelligently controlled.

Could Annemarie unconsciously or consciously be controlling these events with her mind? "It seems that the girl was the focus of RSPK," Bender said.

After studying many poltergeist cases, Bender developed a theory that in some or many instances, poltergeist agents tap into alternate sources of energy, such as electrical supplies. He said it doesn't seem possible for such agents to generate the power they need to move heavy furniture, so they somehow, perhaps without realizing that they are doing it, "organize energy sources rather than project their own energy."

He speculated that Annemarie was tapping into the electric supply of her office to cause lights to swing and objects to move, and meanwhile the lights and telephones went haywire.

By this time, Annemarie was becoming very self-conscious and tense with everyone scrutinizing her and suspecting that she was the problem. It was not uncommon for workers to find her shouting or crying. "I never had influence over anything," she said. "I was very hurt indeed."

According to Bender, Annemarie had emotional problems — she was insecure and had difficulty handling frustration. "She seemed to instigate psychokinesis in response to her emotional problems," Bender said. He wanted to hypnotize her to try to learn more about her issues, but her parents refused to allow it.

Becoming more and more nervous, Annemarie developed hysterical contractions in her arms and legs. In the publication *Skeptical Occultist*, writer Terry White said: "She reacted to the disturbances around her with hysteria and muscular spasms which temporarily paralysed one of her arms." When she was sent on leave, nothing happened.

As long as Annemarie was around, the disturbances in the office did not dissipate with the arrival of all the technicians and investigators, who said they saw paintings swing off the walls, heard many loud, mysterious bangs, and jumped back from sparks. Some of the action was caught on videotape, including a picture rotating 320 degrees on its own power.

The Freiburg researchers say they saw papers move mysteriously and drawers open without help or were ejected. All the while, the police suspected Annemarie until an oak cabinet, estimated to weigh 400 pounds, moved away from a wall twice. It took two burly cops to push it back.

Investigators were able to get a video recording of a lamp swinging unaided and they also got an audio recording of loud bangs that sounded like electrical discharges. At no point did police or anyone else see Annemarie or others in the office cheating or playing tricks.

In all, there were forty witnesses to the incidents, including police, journalists, and clients of the lawyer (and they thought they'd seen everything in court!).

The office was quiet over the Christmas holidays that year, although things got back to "normal" when Annemarie returned to work on January 9. The intensity increased and on January 17, Annemarie, along with several coworkers, was said to have received electric shocks.

Meanwhile, the media had a field day. Some journalists started referring to Annemarie as the "Super-Static Girl." Two German television firms made documentaries and one of them appeared in Britain.

Finally, in early 1968, the damage was becoming too expensive and Annemarie was dismissed and — surprise — the incidents abruptly ended. The final bill for the damage was about 15,000 deutschmarks.

After leaving the firm, Annemarie got a job at another office. The peculiarities followed here there, but they were not as pronounced and eventually subsided.

When she was taken to laboratory settings, researchers tested her and she was said to have strong ESP abilities, but she did not score well on psychokinetic tests. The latter was not unusual, however, since psychokinesis and recurrent spontaneous psychokinesis are said to dissipate in poltergeist agents as time goes by.

Bender said the Rosenheim case was the most impressive of his more than thirty-five previous investigations.

The widely publicized Rosenheim case changed the German public's view of poltergeists; before the Annemarie case, 18 percent of the people polled believed in poltergeist and after the case it was 28 percent.

FEELING OTHERS' PAIN

After experiencing what he felt were paranormal incidents in his office in Rosenheim in 1967, lawyer Sigmund Adam sympathized with another so-called poltergeist case in Nicklheim, Germany, in 1968. Adam visited a laborer and his wife, who reportedly were victimized by loud knocks and flying objects and stones in their home. Apparently, the activity was centered around their thirteen-year-old daughter. Adam told them of his experiences with Annemarie Schneider and it seemed to make them feel less alone in their troubles.

Skeptic Sammy: Boy, they must be tolerant of their workers. Did they have unions in 1967? Why couldn't they just let her work from home? And, hey, nineteen-year-old girls usually make a lot of phone calls, don't they? And they like to get attention when they walk into an office.

Rebutt Al: Don't get sexist, now.

ELECTRICAL BRAIN BURSTS?

Before he considered paying out such an outlandish claim, James Holland, a senior loss analyst for a major insurance company, wanted to make sure that water damage at a Florida home in 1996–1997 was indeed from a paranormal source. He knew who to call — Andy Nichols, a parapsychologist with the American Institute of Parapsychology and City College in Gainesville, Florida.

Nichols and a colleague, Russell McCarty, showed up at the seven-year-old, single-storey house in an affluent suburb of Jacksonville.

The occupants were Mary Barton, a sixty-two-year-old financial consultant, who also owned a pet-grooming business; her son Keith, twenty-eight; her granddaughter Krista, eleven; and her mother Lillian, eighty-seven.

Mary Barton told Nichols that the occurrences, which were "episodic and unpredictable," began on November 7, 1996 when a series of unexplained rapping noises was heard from several interior walls. Lillian Barton said that light sprinkles of liquid or water fell on her head while she was sleeping and occasionally during the day as she walked through the house.

The sprinklings became more frequent — falling on other occupants of the house — until puddles of water accumulated on the floor.

One day, Mary said she was standing in the kitchen when a small paper cup filled with water, which had been 8 feet behind her on a counter, became airborne and lodged itself in the handle of a lower cabinet. No one else was in the area and Mary was surprised to find that the cup still contained most of its water.

Lillian Barton became the most popular victim of liquid attacks and sprinklings over the next few weeks; sometimes she got soaked and no one could establish where the water was coming from.

A heating contractor checked the heating/air conditioning system and found there was nothing wrong and a plumbing contractor could find no leaky pipes, even though they both got wet from the mysterious liquid. A plumbing assistant, Mike Thigpin, was so alarmed from getting soaked in the living room that he left the house, believing it had to be haunted.

The Bartons themselves started to think that something supernatural was at work when a large, gilt-framed mirror, which had been securely mounted on a wall for years, suddenly collapsed and narrowly missed Lillian, who was lying on a couch. "Upon examining the mirror, it was found that the wire which secured it to the wall was unbroken and the heavy mounting screws which protruded from the wall were also intact," Nichols said.

At one point, Mary, Krista, and Lillian all fled the house after getting soaked by the unidentified liquid, but the liquid reportedly drenched a van in which they tried to leave. The incidents lasted more than one month.

Nichols said that they occurred only in the presence of eleven-year-old Krista, but Mary Barton doubted her granddaughter could have faked the disturbances because she was closely watched by the others.

Nichols and McCarty interviewed witnesses and conducted many psychological and electromagnetic tests. It turned out there were high magnetic fields in the area, perhaps from high-voltage transmission towers within one-quarter mile of the house, and the Jacksonville Naval Air Station, 5 miles away, with its numerous radar transmitters and other sophisticated equipment.

When conducting psychological tests on the family members, Nichols was wary of criticism of other cases, in which psychologists knew the people being tested were suspected poltergeist agents and therefore may have been biased in their interpretations of the test results. And so, after interviewing the Bartons, he sent their results to Dr. David Bortnick, a clinical psychologist, without telling him who the test subjects were.

Dr. Bortnick said that the answers suggested that both Krista and Lillian had what he called "high temporal lobe lability," meaning that they may have had an increased number of minor symptoms associated with temporal lobe epilepsy, but without having a seizure, and they were subject to bursts of electricity in their brains.

He said that Krista reported having repetitive dreams, hearing unexplained buzzing or sizzling sounds, and having a strong sense of *déja vu*.

Lillian reported repetitive dreams, unusual sensations of cold, the smell of burning rubber, and a sense of presence in the house.

Both said that these sensations were more common when family stress levels were high.

Mary Barton was also tested and she, along with her mother and granddaughter, showed a high degree of aggression in their interpersonal relationships, Nichols said.

"All show unhappiness, insecurity and a recourse to an unrealistic fantasy life," he said. He added that Krista showed aggression toward others and an inability to handle even minor frustrations.

"Krista was also typified as harboring a potential for physical violence, which is kept in check by her reliance on repression... she displayed the typical profile of the poltergeist personality," Nichols said. "Her relationship with her great-grandmother, Lillian, seemed particularly strained. It is significant that Lillian was most frequently the target of the RSPK activity."

Nichols added that the Bartons, "while outwardly displaying the façade of a happy home, were a deeply troubled family."

The source of the mysterious liquid or water was never identified, since the occurrences had reached their peak by the time the researchers arrived at the home and they were not able to get sufficient quantities of the liquid for testing.

After Krista began psychotherapy in January 1997, the occurrences stopped. However, she continued to have emotional problems and a short time later, she was arrested for shoplifting. "Like the poltergeist, the incidents of theft may represent another outlet for displacement of her inner turmoil," Nichols said.

In another case in San Francisco, reported by parapsychologist Lloyd Auerbach in 1996, water manifestations appeared to represent a symbolic retaliation, stemming from an adolescent's resentment of being forced to participate in swimming activities against his will.

"Although no specific symbolic correlations were apparent in the Barton case, such metaphorical expressions of unconscious processes — so often seen in dreams — cannot be discounted," Nichols said.

"Cases of this kind emphasize the need for researchers to be aware that poltergeists, like hauntings, may take a variety of forms reflecting the interpersonal dynamics, psychopathologies and emotional needs of the witnesses."

Meanwhile, Nichols never found out if the insurance company paid the claim for "paranormal" damage. (*Note:* Names of the Barton family members are pseudonyms.)

Skeptic Sammy: If I alerted anyone to a water poltergeist in my home, I wouldn't want people knowing my real name either. This case sounds familiar... hey, did this family happen to move here from Rochdale, England? And can you get an insurance payout for being off your rocker?

Rebutt Al: It's a good thing you are not an insurance agent—you don't seem to believe anything or anybody.

THE POLISH PHENOM

Joasia Gajewski was thirteen years old when things began happening in her apartment in Sosnowiec, a mining town in Poland. Her mother was a telephone operator and her father was a plumber.

Just after the death of her beloved grandmother, Joasia was about to enter puberty when her family and friends noticed she seemed highly charged with static electricity. They said she crackled with it to the extent it sounded like someone snapping their fingers. And she was suffering from headaches and fever.

On April 4, 1983, while Joasia was in bed with her grandfather, plates and glassware reportedly started flying about the room, windows rattled, furniture shook, and some shattered glass struck the girl, cutting her.

The frightened family fled the apartment. Later, several police officers, including Sergeant Tadeusz Slowik, said they saw glasses, screws, and other small objects fly at unusual trajectories. While city engineers were checking for abnormalities, they said they saw a mustard jar fly through the air.

In all cases, Joasia was nearby, but witnesses said she did not throw anything.

Dr. Eustachiusz Gadula, a respected surgeon and vocational rehabilitation specialist, put together a team of scientists and psychologists to test Joasia under laboratory conditions. They said that the girl had unusual thermal spots or warm areas around her fingers, toes, head, and just above her solar plexus. She also had rapid changes in body temperature and very high static electrical charges on her body, which did not dissipate when she was grounded.

During tests, a number of scientists say they saw incredible phenomena — an armchair moved with Joasia sitting cross-legged in it. When she got out of the chair, it continued to move, they said, and then it rose in the air and rotated. Three men reportedly tried to hold the chair down, but they could not. On another day, a blanket, which had been rolled up on a couch, allegedly levitated, moved across the room, and covered Dr. Gadula.

Joasia turned down offers to try to perform her unusual skills on tour and reportedly went into the health-care profession.

CHAPTER 19

THE DETECTIVE PUZZLER ON LONG ISLAND

"When the statuettes struck objects, they did so with an almost explosive sound. It's unlikely that [a twelve-year-old boy] could have thrown them with such force."

—*NEWSDAY* REPORTER DAVID KAHN

Nearly twenty years before the Amityville Horror, the big paranormal news on Long Island was Popper the Poltergeist.

The 1950s heralded the birth, or perhaps the rise, of the middle class in America. The Nice People were taking over in the suburbs. More and more of them had a home and a car, and even a television set. And in many areas of the United States, people were starting to blend in behind the rows of bungalows, pretty public parks, and tree-lined avenues.

James Herrmann and his family, who lived in the suburbs in Seaford on Long Island, New York, seemed to fit this middle-class standard while living in their six-room, green and white, ranch-style home.

James was an "interlines" representative for Air France in New York City. His wife, Lucille, was a registered nurse. Their two children, Lucille, thirteen, and James Junior (Jimmy), twelve, seemed normal. They were each named after one of their parents.

The extraordinary, however, started to become the norm on the afternoon of February 3, 1958. Mrs. Hermann, who was home with her two children, said she heard popping noises at about 4 p.m. A quick check revealed that a small bottle of holy water on her bedroom dresser had its top off and had fallen onto its side, spilling its contents. In her son's adjacent bedroom, she found that a plastic ship model and a ceramic doll were broken. In a bathroom cabinet, two bottles had their caps unscrewed and their contents spilled. In addition, a bottle of starch in the kitchen and a gallon bottle of bleach in the cellar were spilled.

The children denied having done this and Mrs. Hermann was at a loss for what was responsible.

Over the next two days, other bottles had their caps popped off while the children were at home alone.

While no one in the family saw what happened with any of the bottles, they heard unusual popping noises. That was puzzling because most of the bottles were fitted with twist-off caps, which needed to be turned three or four times to get them off. If someone had simply taken them off in the usual manner, it could not create a popping sound. Did it have anything to do with air pressure or chemicals in the bottles or too much carbonation?

The occurrences continued for nearly a week and involved bottles of rubbing alcohol, nail polish, and detergent.

Mr. Herrmann's first and most obvious theory was that his son, Jimmy, who liked science, was behind it all, perhaps with a liquid mix that was setting off belated mini-explosions. And so, even though Jimmy, a seventh grade honor student, denied any involvement, his father closely watched him without making it obvious. But on Sunday, February 9, three bottles popped and rocked back and forth on shelves in various rooms while James was keeping his son under observation. The father said it was impossible for the boy to have sneaked away and rigged the bottles to pop at different times because he had been monitoring him closely.

Also that day, Mr. Herrmann claimed he saw other phenomena right in front of him. In a bathroom, with Jimmy standing nearby brushing his teeth, Mr. Herrmann said he saw a bottle of medicine move across the top of the basin and drop into the sink. A few seconds later, a bottle of shampoo also moved on its own power across the sink and crashed to the floor, Mr. Herrmann said. "One moved straight ahead, slowly, while the other spun to the right for a 45-degree angle."

The perplexed man went throughout the bathroom, looking for strings or wires that could have tripped the bottles, but he found nothing. People who knew Mr. Herrmann tended to believe his account because they described him as a straightforward man who did not embellish things.

Convinced that no one in the house was doing pranks, Mrs. Herrmann called the cops on February 9. At first, Patrolman James Hughes of the Nassau County Police Department, Seventh Precinct, was skeptical, and suspected Mrs. Herrmann of heavy drinking, but the family had a good reputation in the community.

And Hughes got an immediate sample of the action on his first visit when he heard several bottles in the bathroom pop their lids. He found that medicine and shampoo bottles in the bathroom had spilled. "The complainant said there were no tremors in the house, and no high frequency equipment," Hughes said in his report.

Five of the bottles were sent to a police laboratory in Mineola, NY, and found to have no unusual chemicals or components that could have caused the bottles to unscrew themselves.

ENTER THE GUMSHOE

The case became serious enough for the police department to assign it full time to Detective Joseph Tozzi, thirty-two. He was one of the force's best, having come out of the US Navy in 1949, and if anyone could get to the bottom of this case, it was Tozzi, described as having a "sharp and pleasantly cynical mind."

The first entry in Tozzi's police log was made on February 11 when he noted that a bottle of perfume opened in twelve-year-old Lucille's bedroom and spilled. No one was in the bedroom at the time, Tozzi said.

Then the bottle of holy water took center stage for a few days, popping its lid on several occasions. Once, when James Herrmann picked it up, the bottle felt warm. This was upsetting for the family, who were devout Catholics, and particularly for Mrs. Herrmann, who had put out the holy water to keep away potential evil spirits.

During Tozzi's second day at the house, the detective and Jimmy were walking down the basement steps when a bronze figurine of a horse, weighing nearly 100 pounds, reportedly flew across the basement and hit Tozzi in the back of the legs. Suddenly, Tozzi feared for the safety of the people in the house and decided to step up his questioning.

Tozzi let his police instincts take over and accused Jimmy of throwing the horse, even though the officer had not seen him do it. Tozzi intensely questioned the thirteen-year-old boy, but Jimmy denied wrongdoing in any of the occurrences. Even the sight of Tozzi's police badge didn't break him.

Without any other theories, Mr. Herrmann also suspected Jimmy at first, but his son begged for his father to believe him. "Dad, I had nothing to do with any of it," he cried.

The family was in such hysteria that they went to a friend's home for the night, as they did several times during the nightmare.

On February 15, a visitor to the house reported a different type of disturbance. Marie Murtha, a middle-aged cousin of James Herrmann, said she was watching the black-and-white television in the living room with the two Herrmann children when she saw a porcelain figurine rise off a coffee table and hover in the air. It reportedly moved several inches and dropped to the carpet. Murtha said, "I saw the figurine wiggle like a worm cut in pieces as it went in the air, then it crashed to the rug, unbroken."

When the police were unable to stop the strange events, the Herrmanns reached out to the church for help. Next to enter the home was Father William McLeod, of the Church of Saint William the Abbott, who sprinkled holy water in all six of the rooms and blessed the house, yet the disturbances continued when he left.

By this time, the family was making the news. "When I came to work on February 10, I saw a story headlined BALMY BOUNCING BOTTLES JAR LONG ISLANDERS' HOME," said *Newsday* reporter David Kahn.

Other newspapers, along with radio and television stations, began contacting the Herrmanns or coming to their home. Television was a novelty in 1958 and news and updates of Popper the Poltergeist, as "he" was known, became popular on nightly newscasts across America and was featured on the series *Armstrong Circle Theatre*. No paranormal phenomena were recorded by the camera, only the aftermath of things like a figurine denting a wall.

But reporter Kahn said he saw something on February 24 at 8:10 p.m. He was sitting on a living room couch, facing Jimmy's bedroom when, "suddenly, a 10-inch cardboard globe of the world flipped silently out of the room in my direction and bounced into the opposite corner of the living room. I jumped up, ran into Jimmy's room and snapped on the light. He was sitting up in bed, the covers on his legs. Could he have thrown it? I thought it was possible, but improbable."

To have done some of the things suspected of Jimmy, Kahn said, "he would have had to have been extraordinarily strong and agile. When the statuettes struck objects, they did so with an almost explosive sound. It's unlikely that he could have thrown them with such force."

In fact, Kahn did not suspect anyone in the family, especially not Jimmy's sister Lucille, who "didn't seem the type."

Meanwhile, about 250 phone calls and letters poured in from a fascinated public. Everybody, it seemed, had a theory about what was going on in Seaford or advice for solving the problems. It was the Martians who had landed, or Satan, or perhaps just simply boring electromagnetic fields or sun spots. In fact, some people theorized that, as a Cold War tactic, the Russians had sent a submarine offshore and it was causing magnetic field disruption.

Many, if not most, people believed the Herrmanns to be innocent, since they were well liked by their neighbors and because police could not find a prankster.

Some people believed that spirits were responsible, due to the damage to the holy water and a figurine of the Virgin Mary. Religious groups tried to help and some people thought the Herrmanns need to repent for something they had done, whatever that was. Some ministers conducted rituals on their front lawn.

Robert Zider, a physicist from Brookhaven National Laboratory, examined the property with dowsing rods. He believed that underground streams below the property were causing strange things to happen in the house, perhaps creating an unusual magnetic field, which is sometimes a theory in poltergeist cases. But a geological survey found nothing unusual. Neither did visits to the house by a structural engineer, a professor of engineering from Cooper Union College in New York, a civil engineer, and an electrical engineer from the Nassau Country Society of Professional Engineers.

During his eight-week investigation, Detective Tozzi did not rule out any theory. Were sonic booms from airplanes causing vibrations in the house? Tozzi checked with the Air Force, who said their flight plans did not correspond with the area. And officials at the local Mitchell Air Field said none of their equipment could produce the effects erupting in the home. Well, how about disturbances from radio waves? The Radio Corporation of America sent one of their test trucks and found nothing unusual. Tozzi also brought in the Long Island Lighting Company, which put an oscilloscope in the cellar to try to pick up underground vibrations. There were none. As well, all the wiring in the house, along with the fuse panels, were checked out.

The Seaford Fire Department and the Town of Hempstead Building Department checked the house and surrounding area, but found nothing unusual — no drafts or anything else.

And yet, the occurrences continued: Objects moved seemingly under their own power, a bottle of ink opened and made a mess on a wall, and a sugar bowl fell off a table as Tozzi watched. Young Jimmy was in the room, but Tozzi said he was not close enough to have touched the bowl.

Most of the time when the occurrences happened, Jimmy was in the house. When the family left home briefly, nothing occurred. Many of the incidents took place in Jimmy's room or other rooms when he was in them: A record player moved 15 feet, a large bookcase fell to the floor, and the Virgin Mary statue "flew" about 12 feet and banged into a mirror.

Sometimes Tozzi nearly got dinged; a globe of the world came down a hallway, he said, and just missed him. Other neutral observers reported unusual things; John Gold, a photographer from the *London Evening News*, said his flashbulbs moved by themselves off a table and flew into the air, hitting a wall.

MEET THE GHOSTBUSTERS

Was the five-year-old house haunted? After more than a month of the bizarre, members of the Parapsychology Laboratory at Duke University in Durham, North Carolina, came to the home on March 10. They were Dr. J. Gaither Pratt and William Roll, who had been studying the possibility that in rare situations, people, especially adolescents going through puberty, were able to move things unconsciously with their emotions or their minds.

By the time the investigators arrived, the disturbances were already beginning to wane. They grilled Detective Tozzi, who said he had been closely watching Jimmy for weeks and was sure the boy was not pulling pranks. Roll also ruled out young Jimmy, "who seemed a likeable boy, and intelligent."

However, Roll and Pratt suspected that Jimmy unconsciously caused the events through subconscious mind over matter, partly because he was going into puberty and partly because of his attitude toward his father. After interviewing family members, Roll concluded that Jimmy was angry with his father and vented this anger through his unusual mental powers at objects in the home, particularly those he associated with his parents. "Most of the disturbed things belonged to the parents and the events often happened in their living space," Roll concluded. Because many of the incidents involved bottles that might be associated with a woman, they may have reflected "unmet dependency needs" that Jimmy had with both his parents.

Roll also looked at the possibility that more than one person was involved in a prank, but he soon ruled it out because "the family was much too shaken for it to be a colossal hoax. And why would they fake things in front of all the people who came into their home?" Roll said that Mr. and Mrs. Herrmann had impeccable credentials — he was with the airlines and was also a volunteer member of the auxiliary police in Seaford, and Lucille was a former supervisor at a large hospital.

The unexplained activity in the Herrmann household finally ended with a whimper at about 10 p.m. on March 2, 1958, when a dish broke and a table and bookcase fell. Altogether, some sixty-seven incidents were recorded.

Duke University put together a forty-five-page report on the case entitled *The House of Flying Objects*. The investigators said they could not prove something paranormal had occurred, but they suspected it had because, despite all the attention given by neutral observers in the house, no one was caught faking anything.

Paranormal writer Troy Taylor would later note, "Unbelievably, the Herrmanns had been visited by detectives, building inspectors, electricians, plumbers, firemen, parapsychologists and half of the 'nutcases' on the east coast and yet none of them had been able to present a satisfactory explanation for what had occurred."

The family remained puzzled years after the events. Mrs. Herrmann told a reporter: "I don't think there is a definite solution. It was just one of those things with no rhyme or reason to it. But there was a definite physical force behind it."

Lucille also became sympathetic to reports of other families who had suspected paranormal activity in their homes. When she saw news reports of a poltergeist case in Newark, New Jersey, in 1961, Mrs. Herrmann telephoned the family to offer her emotional support and to tell them of her experiences.

In the years following the Popper case, the family fell out of the limelight and it is not known what became of them. Detective Tozzi went on to a successful career, arresting many Mafia members, and was police chief of Colleyville, Texas, from 1976 to 1984.

Newsday reporter David Kahn was still writing about the case in 2004. For lack of a better explanation, he still referred to it as a poltergeist. Wrote Kahn, "As Hamlet said, 'There are more things in heaven and earth, Horatio, / Than are dreamt of in your philosophy.'"

Skeptic Sammy: Where do we start? Until the mid-1960s, everybody in the school yearbooks looked like their parents! Hey, these two kids were both named after their Mom and Pop! A girl named after her mother! No wonder they wanted to rebel. And what's this about Jimmy's "unmet dependency needs?" Hey, we all had those . . . we fought through it and we lived our lives in quiet desperation, without throwing religious statues around.

Rebutt Al: Nice prose, but let me get a close look at you—yes, as suspected, you still look like your parents.

CHAPTER 20

KENTUCKY: THE POLTERGEIST WHO MOVED AROUND

"At one point, I was following Roger, walking right behind him into the kitchen, when the kitchen table jumped into the air, rotated 45 degrees and fell down on the backs of the chairs that stood around it, its four legs off the floor."

—PARAPSYCHOLOGIST WILLIAM ROLL

Even the paranormal world has its "good news, bad news" scenarios.

The good news in the Olive Hill, Kentucky, poltergeist investigation was that, for one of the few documented times, two paranormal researchers reportedly saw a full-fledged levitation of objects in a home. And the bad news was that they were not allowed to stay very long because the religious family thought the researchers had brought demons with them.

The story, which jumps from house to house in rural Kentucky, began in 1968 in Olive Hill at the home of an elderly couple, John and Ora Callihan. Living with them were their son, Tommy, and his wife, Helen, and their five children, Beverly, fourteen; Roger, twelve; and two younger brothers and a sister, Marcelene. Also in the home was a teenage girl, who had been unofficially adopted by the family and helped to take care of the small, frame house. After what happened, there was a lot of cleaning to do.

One day in late November, the family reported strange rumblings in the house. Glass shattered in a picture of Jesus Christ on a wall and furniture reportedly moved unaided. It was the beginning of mayhem. From then on, about 200 such incidents were reported in the home, leading to considerable damage, including the smashing of most of the Callihans' ceramic lamps and figurines. Their grandson, Roger, helped them to clean up the mess.

Believing that the occurrences had something to do with the house itself, on November 23 Tommy, Helen, and their children moved to another home nearby on Zimmerman Hill.

But something apparently moved along with them because furniture started "getting legs." In early December, after Helen said she saw an apparition in her bedroom, she began believe a ghost was responsible.

The local newspaper, the *Ashland Daily Independent*, published an article that intrigued John P. Stump, a psychology student at the University of North Carolina and a budding parapsychologist. Stump went to the home for some field research and was told by the Callihan family and friends that some ninety incidents had occurred in their new home, with the smashing of knickknacks and crockery and the movement of larger items, such as a coffee table, a refrigerator, and a kitchen table.

Many of the events had been witnessed by family and friends, Stump was told. But the activity was sporadic and sometimes days went by when nothing happened.

At this point, witnesses in the house were family and two friends of the Callihan family, Phyllis Cranks and her husband, Odis.

Mrs. Cranks said that on Sunday morning, December 8, while Roger was walking toward her in a bedroom, a bedside table rose in the air behind him, moved over his head, and crashed to the floor in front of him. It had traveled about 10 feet, she said. "That force scared me!" she added.

On other occasions, Mrs. Cranks said she saw knickknacks and pictures move 15 feet or more.

And Marcelene said she saw plastic flowers in a bowl move slowly on a table and fall to the floor.

Nothing out of the ordinary occurred on the day Stump arrived, December 12, but early the next morning, things heated up over at the grandparents' house. Over the next forty-eight hours, Stump said he witnessed dozens of strange incidents at the grandparents' home. In one instance, Stump said he was standing in the kitchen with John and Ora Callihan and twelve-year-old Roger when two bottles and a glass jar of canned berries "moved by themselves" from on top of the sink unit down into the sink. Roger and his grandparents had been standing next to a stove and had not touched the bottles or the jar, Stump wrote in his report.

On the same day, Stump reported another incident. He said that when John Callihan entered the living room, which was nearly filled with people, Stump pointed to a vacant chair where he might sit when suddenly the chair flipped upside down. The closest person to the chair was Roger (who was about 3 feet away), but Stump said he had been keeping the boy under close observation and that there was no way he could have grabbed the chair and turned it over without being seen.

Since Roger seemed to be present during most of the occurrences, Stump suspected him of trickery. But Stump found no strings or devices with which the boy could fool the older people.

On another occasion, Stump said he was watching Roger, sitting nearby on a chair in front of a television set in the living room, when he heard a loud crack from the TV set. Roger jumped away as a cloth doily and a large plastic bowl fell to the floor behind the set, Stump said. Strangely, plastic flowers that had been inside the bowl remained atop the TV. Then, the flowers slowly moved off the TV and fell to the floor, Stump added.

Then a clock fell in the other direction off the TV, said Stump, who quickly checked for strings, but found none.

An amazed Stump then contacted William Roll, a parapsychologist at Duke University. Roll arrived in Olive Hill on December 14. He went first to the grandparents' home, then over to the new home of Tommy and Helen on Zimmerman Hill.

Roll noted that the house was well kept and that Helen seemed a good mother. The children seemed well behaved, he said, and were not as frightened as the adults. Helen was particularly traumatized and Roll believed that was because she had been told by her fellow Jehovah's Witnesses that a demon was causing the events.

Roll explained his theory — that natural forces were at work and that "some people seem to function like a battery, giving emitting an unusual type of energy." But Helen didn't buy that. On December 16, while she was discussing the religious angle in the Zimmerman Hill home with Roll, Stump, and her husband, they heard a loud crash upstairs. A bowl of fruit had fallen off a dresser. It seemed an innocent event, but it turned out to be the beginning of a whole series of disturbances, from furniture moving to tables being flipped over to the kitchen stove reportedly moving 6 inches under its own power.

Roll recalls:

> At one point, I was following Roger, walking right behind him into the kitchen, when the kitchen table jumped into the air, rotated 45 degrees and fell down on the backs of the chairs that stood around it, its four legs off the floor. Roger and the table were in full view... [later] when I was standing in the door between the living room and a children's bedroom, I saw a bottle fly off the dresser and land about four feet away.

Roll added that the bottle did not slide or roll, but was clearly in the air. "Roger was in my peripheral vision on my right [in the living room] and walking away," Roll added. "His sister was standing behind me and there was no one else in the room. I could find no way the event could have been faked."

On another occasion, Roll said he saw a coffee table, weighing about 70 pounds, flip over while Roger had his back to it.

Altogether, Roll estimated there were ten incidents while he and/or Stump were watching. In all ten, he said, they were also watching Roger. "He had no tangible contacts with objects."

Roll wanted to document the case more closely with photographs and psychological tests of all the family members, perhaps after taking them to Duke University, but Helen Callihan was becoming more uncooperative.

The family brought in a minister from the Jehovah's Witnesses, but the incidents continued, Roll said. And then Helen delivered a bombshell — she told Roll and Stump that they had unintentionally brought demons with them from John and Ora's home nearby.

"Mrs. Callihan was convinced a demon was responsible and she asked me to leave. End of investigation... it was very disappointing," Roll said. "She hoped the demon would follow me back to Duke University."

But if the family believed that the disturbances would end when Roll and Stump left, they were wrong. Apparently, there were more incidents in the subsequent days and an exorcism failed to stop the "demon." The next step was for the family to take Roger's clothes out into the yard and burned them, but that did not work, either.

Then the family moved away from the house for some time and when they returned, there were no more incidents.

Roll was disappointed that he could not stay and document the case in more detail, but he still says that it is one of his favorites:

> Though our study of the Olive Hill poltergeist was cut short, it was unique in one respect; it is the only case I know of where two parapsychologists saw the beginning stages of movements of several objects. It was not easy for John [Stump] and me to believe that we were somehow fooled — or that we fooled ourselves. We saw these objects take off, with nobody near enough to push them, and we could find no evidence of strings or other gadgets.

Roll concluded that Roger Callihan was the agent for the poltergeist activity and that he exhibited subconscious mind over matter. He speculated that the boy was frustrated "at spending time with his grandparents and that was part of the explanation for the breakages in their home. The inclusion of Roger's own home when we were there, I thought, was due to the attention we paid to the boy. [As in some other cases], the presence of investigators seemed to change the incidents."

Skeptic Sammy: Hey, that's one snappy name for a gumshoe, John P. Stump. Does he have a TV mini-series now? Otherwise, maybe those people spoiled their grandson too much. Everybody does. Maybe the kid was moving things at first and then, because of their religious beliefs, they hallucinated the rest.

Rebutt Al: What about Roll and Stump? Either you believe William Roll or you don't.

Skeptic Sammy: Sometimes people see things they want to see. Your next book wouldn't happen to be coauthored with Mr. Roll, would it?

CHAPTER 21

MIAMI: FIRE SALE AT THE SOUVENIR PLACE

"From then on, everything seemed to happen—boxes came down, a box of about 100 back scratchers turned over and fell with a terrific clatter over on the other side of the room and then we realized that there was something definitely wrong around here. And for three days, we picked things up off the floor as fast as they would fall down."

—WAREHOUSE OWNER ALVIN LAUBHEIM

The winter of 1966–1967 was not a booming time for the souvenir business, at least not at Tropication Arts, Inc., a novelty warehouse on 54th Street in Miami, Florida.

Over the course of six weeks, novelties were being smashed at an alarming rate — back scratchers, mugs bearing Elvis Presley's likeness, alligator ashtrays, and imported cocktail glasses. No one knew who the culprit was, or perhaps who among the nine workers was incredibly sloppy. Or was the southern humidity getting to everyone?

The co-owners of the business, Alvin Laubheim and Glen Lewis, investigated and came to a stunning conclusion — a ghost was responsible. What else could it be, they thought? Earth tremors? A hurricane on the way? Laubheim had earlier suspected that his employees were clumsy and he had talked to them about it, but the breakage continued.

On January 12, Laubheim instructed nineteen-year-old shipping clerk Julio Vasquez to put mugs on the shelves with the handles facing out to prevent them from rolling, but almost immediately, a mug went flying onto the floor. Laubheim later recalled:

> From then on, everything seemed to happen — boxes came down, a box of about 100 back scratchers turned over and fell with a terrific clatter over on the other side of the room and then we realized that there was something definitely wrong around here. And for three days, we picked things up off the floor as fast as they would fall down. It was going on all day — quite violently — but not hurting anything, but things would fall to the floor. We tried to keep it quiet because we knew it would hurt our business, because we are right in the middle of a season — the beginning of a season — and it would draw a bunch of curiosity-seekers and the like, so we tried to keep it quiet for about four days. Then, finally, delivery men saw those things happen and people coming in and out would see it happen and word got out and there were more and more people coming in. And somebody suggested that with the glasses being thrown around and with the girls crying in the front from fright, we had better notify the police. So I did.

On the night of January 12, one of Tropication's employees, Bea Rambisz, was listening to a radio talk show on which a ghost researcher, Suzy Smith, was plugging her new book on the paranormal, *Prominent American Ghosts*. Rambisz phoned Smith to alert her about the goings-on at the warehouse. The next day, Friday the 13th, Smith was on the scene and claimed she saw strange movements of souvenirs. Insurance agent William Drucker checked all the warehouse shelves for vibrations, but found them all solid.

On January 14, the owners had had enough and called police. At first, Patrolman William Killin was wary of the call and thought it was a joke, but after checking with the police complaint's officer, Killin reluctantly got into his cruiser and drove to the warehouse. There, he found two employees, co-owner/manager Laubheim and shipping clerk Julio Vasquez. While Laubheim and Vasquez stood at the back of the 30-by-40-foot warehouse, the patrolman patrolled the aisles. At one point, he turned around just in time to see a highball glass from a nearby shelf mysteriously shatter on the floor.

A short time later, Killin said he saw two boxes flip over by themselves.

Vasquez was standing near the officer and not nearly close enough to affect the boxes, Killin said. The mystified officer said he would personally deliver an official report on the occurrence to his sergeant, William McLaughlin, because he feared the superior officer would think he was nuts if he heard about it secondhand. Killen then phoned McLaughlin, who came to the warehouse along with two patrolmen, Ronald Morse and David J. Sackett.

Joining the investigation that morning were newspaper reporters, a magician, television crews, and other investigators. Some of them reported seeing objects move mysteriously about the warehouse — ashtrays, a cowbell, glasses, mugs, key chains, rubber alligators, and rubber daggers. Some objects reportedly fell not straight down, but at unusual angles.

The magician was Howard Brooks, a friend of Laubheim's, who was working at a nearby ice show. Brooks brought along a friend. With at least eight men all keeping an eye out for spooks or vandals, and watching Vasquez, who was becoming a suspect in some people's eyes, two more events occurred, including a box of address books falling from a shelf. The cops said they were sure no one had been close to the box when it fell.

At first, magician Brooks had laughed it off as a cheap trick and he tossed an item across the room, just to show how easily it could be done. But then, after he and a police officer saw highball glasses and beer mugs levitate and several cartons drop to the floor, Brooks became dumbfounded and was unable to explain. "I can't buy this spook theory at this point," Brooks said. "But something did move tho"e things, and I couldn't figure it out." Brooks also checked the area for wires or secret mechanisms, but found none.

On January 16, Tropication employee Ruth May, an artist who decorated the souvenirs with flamingoes and Florida scenes, said she saw a plastic tray fly off a shelf, then take an unusual trajectory to another shelf before flying back to the original area. She said Vasquez was a considerable distance away from the tray.

The following day, a visitor to the warehouse, Eastern Airlines pilot Sinclair Buntin, said he was about 15 feet from a box and could clearly see it when it "fell at an angle which it could not have been at if it had just been pushed off — it came at about a 30-degree angle, out away from the shelf." A few minutes later, he said it moved again. No one was near the box in either case, Buntin said.

Another witness was Laubheim's sister, Joyce George, who was watching a mug when it reportedly moved. She said it "sort of scooted off" the shelf, levitated, then dropped straight down. Paranormal researchers say that said it is uncommon for "poltergeist projectiles" to move erratically.

On January 19, parapsychologist William Roll came to the warehouse. Meanwhile, Suzy Smith took notes. After interviewing the police and other witnesses, Roll suspected that something paranormal was at work.

Roll and other investigators quickly focused on Vasquez, who was a Cuban refugee. The events seemed to occur only when he was nearby.

As the days went by, Roll tried to make himself inconspicuous in the warehouse as the employees and investigators walked about. Whenever something fell, which happened often, Roll ordered everyone to hold their positions and he quickly got to the item to investigate. At no time did he find that anyone had deliberately smashed an item.

After seven days of intense research, Roll had to return to North Carolina for a few days. When he came back, he brought a fellow researcher, J. Gaither Pratt, of the University of Virginia. They investigated the warehouse from January 27 to January 30, keeping Vasquez under close surveillance.

Pratt and Roll continued to test Vasquez, at times hiding from him. At one point, they told Vasquez to put a tray on a shelf. Pratt recalled what happened when the tray tumbled to the floor:

> The point on the shelf where it was standing [in Aisle 2] was not visible from my observation point. I could, however, see Julio. He was working in the south part of Aisle 3 and was separated from the disturbance by the tier of double shelves. I could see both his hands. In one hand he held a clipboard and the other was by his side. At the time of the incident, he was walking toward my position. No one was in Aisle 2 where the tray fell and broke, and Julio was the nearest person. I was not able to conceive of any way in which the falling of the tray could have been caused to happen in a normal manner.

A few moments later, two ashtrays fell and broke.

Pratt and Roll set up other "experiments" in which objects broke mysteriously. In one incident, Roll placed a glass on a shelf with several small items in front of it, blocking its path to the floor. But the glass smashed on the floor, reportedly without disturbing the other objects.

Then Roll took a previously damaged beer mug and placed it on a shelf. The young Vasquez joked to Roll that the "ghost" might not like damaged goods. Roll went along with it and handed a new mug to Julio. Roll recounted what happened next:

> At 2:09 p.m., only a little more than a half hour after it had been put out, the new mug crashed to the floor in Aisle 4. This beer mug had been placed behind two small cartons and between a Fanta [pop] bottle and a cowbell. Like the glass, it too must have moved up into the air to have cleared the obstacles. At the time of this event, I was by the front desk, looking up Aisle 3, where Julio was walking toward me with a broom in his hand. [Author] Suzy Smith and a visiting psychologist were next to me near the front desk. No one else was present. The mug moved in a northwesterly direction, its place of origin being about four feet from Julio and the direction of movement away from him. Again, I was unable to explain the event normally.

Investigators noted that incidents seem to happen more frequently when Vasquez was irritated or tense, but the police and researchers cleared him of any tomfoolery and he was not charged with causing damage.

Roll and Pratt wrote down everything they saw or put their observations into a tape recorder. In all, they registered thirty-two incidents, none of which, they say, Vasquez could have caused through physical means. According to Roll, these were the number of incidents with the distance that Vasquez was from them when they occurred:

- 1–5 feet: 10
- 6–10 feet: 10
- 11–15 feet: eight
- 16–20 feet: two
- 21–25 feet: one
- 30–35 feet: one

(*Note:* The warehouse was 30 by 40 feet.)

Roll concluded that the closer Julio was to objects, the more they moved. One object moved mysteriously 22 feet. Roll called it a case of recurrent spontaneous psychokinesis (RSPK), or poltergeist activity. He felt that Vasquez was causing things to move with his mind, perhaps subconsciously.

A total of 222 "paranormal" incidents were recorded over about ninety days from mid-December 1966 to February 1, 1967 by a number of witnesses, including about seventy by Roll. He said that forty-four incidents took place when he or his coresearcher, Pratt, was present.

Probing further, Roll interviewed Vasquez about his emotional health and his family life. Roll discovered that his family life had been quite troubled and he yearned for his mother and grandfather, who were back in his native Cuba. He apparently had feelings of unworthiness and low self-esteem. In December 1966, just before all hell broke loose in the warehouse, his stepmother had asked him to move out of her house. He began having nightmares, which revealed, according to psychologists, a need to be punished and even suicidal tendencies. According to Roll, Vasquez also had feelings of hostility, particularly toward parental figures, but he could not express them openly.

Roll was open about the events with Vasquez and when an object moved, he asked him how he felt. He said that they often made him feel good, that they released some of the emotional tension and frustration he had been feeling about his family and situation.

While he was wrapping up his investigation, Roll concluded that the"force causing the warehouse damage posed a "curvilinear field," that RSPK energy was not bowling over the objects like a train, but carrying them along in a falling trajectory until it was closed off from the source (Vasquez) or became too weak to keep the object in motion. Roll consulted a mathematician, an engineer, and others, who charted the moving objects' rotations and the distances they moved" Roll concluded that the "poltergeist force" did not follow the standard inverse law, which holds for forms of electromagnetism, which are characterized by a linear field. The poltergeist energy faded faster, resembling processes such as radioactive decay.

The energy seemed most potent when Vasquez's back was turned to the objects. Often, the objects moved in a counterclockwise direction.

If it was a fake, it was certainly elaborate and fooled many people. Over the course of six weeks, no one, including the researchers, police, the magician, and fellow workers, reported that Vasquez was caught faking the incidents.

However, after Pratt went back to Virginia, Roll and Smith went over possible scenarios whereby someone could manipulate objects by trickery. For one experiment, they placed ashtrays on the edge of shelves, held in place briefly with dry ice (frozen carbon dioxide). When the dry ice dissolved, the ashtray would tip off and fall to the floor. But the dry ice left traces, and such traces were never found in the warehouse.

Unfortunately for Julio Vasquez, the owners could not take the chance of more damage and he was eventually let go from the Tropication warehouse. No damage was reported after he left.

By this time, Suzy Smith and Roll persuaded Vasquez to go back with them to the psychical research foundation in Durham, North Carolina. Under controlled conditions at the foundation, researchers say they saw a bottle fall off a table while he was nearby and in another instance in a laboratory, a vase allegedly moved while he was standing with researchers. He was also tested with a dice-throwing machine and apparently showed better-than-chance averages.

Vasquez also became sick — three months after the disturbances began, he came down with measles, chicken pox, and mumps.

When Vasquez returned from North Carolina to Miami, he was arrested for shoplifting a ring from a jewelry store and spent six months in prison. In jail, he was tested by a psychologist, who found him to have "early family tenderness", "love and training in high moral standards," but also "feelings of unworthiness, guilt and rejection, development of the personality traits of passivity and inaction, development of inner feelings of detachment and unhappiness and dissociated tendencies, especially in relation to expression aggression."

Two years later, he was working as a gas station attendant. When two armed robbers demanded that he turn over money from the register, Vasquez refused and was shot twice during a scuffle. He recovered from his serious wounds. After that, Roll reported, his "psychical and physical" lives settled down.

Skeptic Sammy: I think that in Roll's little chart, the reason there were fewer mysterious happenings further away from Julio was that he couldn't reach the objects. In my day, when an employee smashed the stock, he was arrested, not studied. And what about that hack magician? Nice turnabout for the defense—how he went from skeptic to a kind of believer. Maybe his ice show wasn't doing so well—you know, with all the heat and the melting going on in Miami. And what about that Suzy Smith? I might buy one of her books if it had some erotica. Another thing, what was the total bill for the souvenirs—ten bucks? I'm looking to pick up a cheap Elvis wall rug.

Rebutt Al: Sarcasm is not furthering this debate. Do you have *anything* to offer science?

MORE FROM AROUND THE GLOBE

Reports of other poltergeist cases from around the world:

- From 1925 to 1927, Rumanian peasant girl Eleonore Zugun excited researchers from Vienna to London. Witnesses say she moved jugs with her mind and turned her allegedly paranormal energy on herself, causing mysterious bite marks and other injuries. Many tests were done under 500-watt lamps, but superstitious people believed she was possessed by the devil.
- *The Hypnotist in Austria:* At Hopfgarten, near Weimar, Austria, in 1921, Minna Sauerbrey was dying of cancer and was said to be so weak, she could not move. However, there were strange knockings in her presence and the movement of objects beyond her reach. Police reportedly saw a wash basin move under its own power. According to officers, her stepson, Otto, was a hypnotist, who had put Minna into a trance to help her deal with her pain. When she died, he was charged with shortening her life through hypnosis, but he was acquitted. And the strange occurrences died with her.
- *Unwelcome Visitors in Brazil:* Think twice before inviting a poltergeist family over for a visit. In the summer of 1972 in Sorocaba, west of São Paulo City, Brazil, neighbors invited the Fernando Riberio family and their six children into their home because the family was allegedly suffering from strange noises and moving objects in their own house. But, according to the Brazilian Institute for Psycho-Biophysicial Research, the occurrences followed them and the neighbors quickly became irritated as their house was ransacked. One of the neighbors commented, "It looked as if a tractor had driven through the place." The Riberio family was sent packing and the events returned home with them.
- *The Cabinet in Virginia:* On December 19, 1976, at the home of Beulah Wilson in Pearisburg, Virginia, police were said to have seen a 200-pound kitchen cabinet floating through the air without any means of support. Other events reportedly involved the smashing of dishes, wooden chairs, and household items.
- *Indonesian Disturbances:* In 1974 in Timor, Timur, a small island in easternmost Indonesia, a young woman was suspected of creating psychic disturbances, including a series of loud rapping sounds and making a table wobble and flip onto its side. She was the half sister of two small boys and

was reportedly treated indifferently by her family because her skin was a different color.

- *Political Tension in Burma:* Can reports of a poltergeist stir up political tension? In 1998, cups and glasses were reportedly thrown around inside a house in Rangoon, Burma, which drew large crowds. Some area residents said it was the ghost of a police officer killed ten years earlier. A BBC correspondent said Rangoon police tried to keep people away from the house because they were worried the scene would stir up anti-government feelings.
- *The People in the Attic:* Some poltergeist cases are never resolved and leave investigators with an empty feeling. In 1987, investigative reporter Jim Henderson researched in detail the case of Ron and Doretta Johnson, whose Marion, Indiana, home was the stage for many unexplained events over the course of several years, including slices of bread that allegedly flew around the kitchen; strange noises; the appearance of shadowy apparitions, and electrical breakdowns. A parapsychologist believed that Doretta used her mind to cause some of the occurrences. Henderson, who had won many awards for his newspaper stories, including those on race relations and the atomic legacy of the United States, believed there was a rational explanation for 80 percent of the events, but he was perplexed about the other 20 percent. "I think the mind is capable of a lot more than we imagine," Henderson said. He coauthored a book with Doretta Johnson on the case, *The People in the Attic* (New York: St. Martin's Press, 1995).

Poltergeists in Pop Culture and the Future

This final section in the book ties up some loose ends, particularly revolving around the question, "If poltergeist activity really exists, can we learn to move things with our minds?" In Chapter 22, the believers and the skeptics check in, as well as a respected scientist, who believes he has been able to prove psychokinesis in laboratory conditions. Chapter 23 gives an overview of poltergeists in popular culture, while the last chapter is a rather light look at how poltergeists can be lucrative, as well as damaging, for some pub owners and parapsychologists.

CHAPTER 22

THE NEW FRONTIER: TAPPING PSYCHOKINESIS

"Whoever believes in psychokinesis, please raise my hand."
—PARANORMAL RESEARCHER/WRITER STEPHEN WAGNER

We hear stories from time to time about gamblers in Las Vegas who can make dice roll to lucky sevens just by focusing on them, or golfers like Tiger Woods who can move the ball into the cup through sheer willpower or brain power.

The alleged ability to consciously move things with one's mind is called psychokinesis (PK). Most scientists are probably skeptical that PK exists. Statistical findings from controlled laboratory studies have resulted in contradictory results. Some experiments have been criticized for their methodologies, or were tainted with accusations of fraud.

This book is full stories of suspected poltergeist activity, of people — mainly youths — purportedly moving things with their minds. Witnesses and parapsychologists lead us to believe that these so-called poltergeist agents summon a rare power called recurrent spontaneous psychokinesis (RSPK), in which they move kitchen utensils, chairs, and even heavy furniture with their minds, perhaps without even knowing they are doing it. RSPK differs from PK because is said to be harder to control, more spontaneous, and recurs over time.

Throughout this book we ask the question, "Do poltergeists exist?" Here are two follow-up questions: Can we consciously move things with our minds? Can anyone learn to do it?

Throughout history, there have been cases documented, however rare, of people who could reportedly move objects by focusing on them. Most of these people, such as psychic Uri Geller, who claims to bend spoons with his mind or by gently stroking them, have been controversial and subject to much skepticism.

But there was one woman in the twentieth century for whom usually skeptical Communist scientists had a great deal of respect. Nina Kulagina of Russia became so celebrated for her purported powers that the Soviet government wanted to keep her identity secret, so that her talents could not be studied by others during the Cold War with the West. And so she became known for a time under the pseudonym Nelya Mikhailova.

Her early life was full of challenge and trauma during the Second World War. Nina was fourteen when the Nazis began the siege of Leningrad and she joined the Red Army, serving on the front lines as a radio operator in a tank. She reached the rank of senior sergeant, but was seriously injured by artillery fire and her service ended. Kulagina recovered and went on to marry and have a son.

After the war, it was said she had unusual powers. Once, when she was angry in her apartment, a jug in a cupboard moved on a shelf, fell, and crashed to the floor, reportedly without anyone touching it. After that, many similar things purportedly took place, including lights that went on and off by themselves.

Unlike many other so-called poltergeist agents, Nina said she knew that she was the source of the power and that she could control it, at least some of the time.

The Soviet government, hardly known for embracing the paranormal or spiritual issues, had forty of its top scientists, including two Nobel laureates, study her for three decades. They believed they had found a new force in nature and wondered if it could be tapped.

Over the course of thirty years, not one of the scientists charged Nina with trickery or fraud. In some sessions, it seemed next to impossible for Nina to deceive anyone because she was enclosed in a metal cage and surrounded by cameras, or forced to influence things from a distance in Plexiglas cubes.

But hers was an inexact skill. Nina said she could not always produce her powers on demand, and she often needed up to several hours of focus and preparation. She said she had to clear her mind of all other thoughts and, when her concentration came to a peak, she would feel a sharp pain in her spine and her eyesight would become blurred. But that's when the miracles would allegedly start occurring — matchsticks would move, fountain pens would glide along a table, and compass needles would fluctuate.

The slow preparation time opened her up to criticism from skeptics, and one writer in the state newspaper, *Pravda*, called her a fraud, even though he had apparently never watched her in action.

Soviet scientists, including biologist Edward Naumov, who claimed she moved match sticks with her mind, believed in her powers.

In 1970, some scientists and parapsychologists from the West were permitted to come to the Soviet Union to see for themselves. American William A. McGary said he watched Kulagina move a wedding ring and the top of a condiment bottle across a dining room table. Another parapsychologist, Gaither Pratt of the University of Virginia, said he saw Nina move small objects under tightly controlled experiments. The investigators said they always checked for concealed magnets or threads, and for further "proof," sixty films were taken of the sessions.

A leading Czech scientist, Dr. Zdenek Rejdak of the Prague Military Institute, conducted his own testing on February 26, 1968, at the Kulagina family home, along with two physicians, Dr. J.S. Zverev and Dr. Sergeyev. After ascertaining that there were no magnets, threads, or devices, Dr. Rejdak reported: "After concentrating, she turned a compass needle more than ten times, then the entire compass, then the entire compass and its case, a matchbox and some twenty matches at once. I placed a cigarette in front of her. She moved that, too, at a glance."

In another test conducted by a group of celebrated physicists, filmed in Moscow, it was said that Nina moved several non-magnetic objects, including matches, which had been placed inside a large Plexiglas cube, out of her reach. They reportedly danced from side to side. A ping-pong ball allegedly levitated in another experiment, and then in 1970, it was said Nina was able to stop the heart of a frog that was floating in solution and then reactivate it.

A military physiologist, Dr. Genady Sergeyev, performed several years of research on Kulagina, studying the electrical potentials in her brain. He said her brain had very strong voltages and could expose undeveloped photos in a sealed envelope. And, curiously, he said that the usual force field around Nina was ten times weaker than the magnetic field of the earth.

Another observation the scientists made was that her abilities seemed to diminish during stormy weather.

The chairman of theoretical physics at Moscow University, Dr. Ya. Terletsky, said that Kulagina "displays a new and unknown form of energy."

With this focused energy, scientists said, she was able to move things as her pulse rate soared as high as 240 beats per minute.

Of course, many questions remained and Nina was not able to always produce the phenomena.

Three decades of scrutiny and moving things with her mind apparently wore down Kulagina physically and sometimes emotionally (in 1964 she suffered a nervous breakdown). She became exhausted, reportedly lost 4 pounds in one experiment, suffered an irregular heartbeat, and developed a disturbed endocrine system — all apparently due to intense stress. She died in 1990, along with the state formerly known as the Soviet Union.

OTHER PSI PEOPLE

Throughout history, there have been people who have claimed to have PK that they could control, at least partly, although they have not always claimed they knew how to do it.

In the mid-1800s, medium Daniel Douglas Home of Scotland put on demonstrations in which he seemed to levitate tables, a heavy piano, and even himself. Home submitted to intense laboratory tests by Dr. William Crookes, a Nobel Prize-winning physicist and president of England's leading scientific body. Crookes said he developed special devices to prevent fraud during the experiments. On one occasion, Home reportedly levitated himself right in front of Crookes, who said, "When he rose 18 inches off the ground, I passed my hands under his feet, round him and over his head when he was in the air." Many other witnesses say they saw Home levitate objects under similar conditions, including magician Robert Houdin (after whom the famous magician Houdini named himself).

Home and others who reportedly produced poltergeist-like effects were said to have had physical abnormalities (he suffered from consumption and eventually had to abandon his practices). In Chapter 2, we heard that some suspected poltergeist agents suffer from mental or physical maladies, including suspected epilepsy, and their brains may be hardwired differently than people who cannot perform paranormal feats.

Another high-profile case was Eusapia Palladino (1854–1918) of Italy, who reportedly levitated a 48-pound chair under the nose of Nobel Laureate for physiology, Charles Richet.

Austrian medium Maria Silbert (1866–1936) was apparently reluctant to develop what people called extraordinary talents, but her husband, a government official, pressured her. Author Adalbert Evian said he heard strange rappings when he was with her and "I felt as if a hand were being laid on my knee. I distinctly saw the impressions of the five fingers." Then he said he saw a table levitate. Rappings became so loud, he said, "the blows came as if with an axe on the table, and the wood began to split."

The most controversial PK figure of modern times is Uri Geller, who began as a psychic and became celebrated for reportedly making spoons bend by stroking them, moving objects without touching them, and fluctuating compass needles. Many scientists from around the world studied Geller under laboratory conditions and said he often passed the test to prove that PK was possible. But Geller did not always succeed and was labeled a fraud by skeptics, particularly James Randi, who proclaimed, "If Geller [bends spoons] by divine power, he does it the hard way."

Born in Israel, Geller has billed himself as a psychic, and reached the peak of his career in the 1970s. Geller was not a poltergeist child, but he said he discovered psychic powers when he was five years old; he said he saw a blue spark coming from his mother's sewing machine and when he tried to touch it, he reportedly received a severe shock and was knocked off his feet. After that, he said, he was able to read his mother's mind and could make the hands speed up on a watch by focusing on it.

In 1972 at the Stanford Research Institute in California, he impressed scientists by correctly identifying numbers he could not see, although tests to prove his mental-bending abilities were inconclusive.

In another test at Western Kentucky University, Dr. Thomas Coohill, of the physics department, declared, "There is no logical explanation for what Geller did here. But I don't think logic is what necessarily makes new inroads in science."

Geller said his power often could not be turned on and off. When he appeared on the *Tonight Show* with Johnny Carson, Geller was unable to produce any phenomena. For Geller's advice on how to develop paranormal abilities, check his Web site at www.uri-geller.com/howto.htm.

The late sociologist Marcello Truzzi, cofounder of the Committee for the Scientific Investigation of Claims of the Paranormal, said in 2001 that Geller "has not met the level of proof science properly requires to judge his psychic claims as valid. He has declined many invitations for tests...the burden of proof remains on him and not his critics."

However, parapsychologist William E. Cox, who organized a committee within the Society of American Magicians to investigate fraudulent claims of ESP, said that Geller had met the burden of proof under controlled conditions.

Many books have been written about Geller, who has dropped out of the public limelight in recent years. Throughout the 1990s to the present, Geller has made a living as a private consultant and a psychic geologist in search of precious metals buried in the earth. He says he also helps people develop their ESP abilities.

In general terms, Truzzi said he did not believe in the existence of extrasensory or psychic abilities, "and I scientifically take the view that parapsychology has not yet met the burden of proof for psi required by the general scientific community. Psi remains unproved, but not all evidence for it has been disproved. Evidence varies in degree, so I assert there is inadequate rather than no evidence for psi. Most evidence for psi, then, remains suggestive rather than convincing."

Here is another question: Is it possible that someone who has shown no poltergeist powers can learn to tap into PK?

Felicia Parise, an American hematologist, claimed she was able to develop PK in the 1970s after being inspired by watching old tapes of Kulagina in action.

Parise said that if she concentrated intensely, she could move small plastic containers and pieces of aluminum foil across a table.

Sometimes it took an emotional event to get her started, such as the time she heard that her grandmother was dying; when she then reached for a small bottle, it purportedly moved away from her hand. (According to British paranormal investigator Colin Wilson, this emphasizes the point that psychokinesis is often performed better by the subconscious mind. "We are all split-brain patients," he said. "The logical self interferes with the natural operations of the right brain. This is why the artist has to wait for inspiration, for the left brain to relax and allow the right to take over.")

On one occasion, said to have been performed under controlled conditions, Parise reportedly deflected a compass needle 15 degrees and exposed film with her mind. She said she gave up PK because it was too draining physically and emotionally and it took her long periods of concentration to move something. Her confidence would wane when the PK did not always happen and she missed helping patients with her other work.

THE PHILLIP EXPERIMENT

In 1973, eight members of the Toronto Society of Psychical Research tried to conjure up a ghost by using their minds. Instead, they reportedly summoned poltergeist activity.

Led by Dr. A.R.G. Owen, a psychic researcher and a member of the Department for Preventative Medicine and Biostatistics at the University of Toronto, they came up with an imaginary dead person and called him Phillip, then held a séance for him. Instead of bringing out an apparition, they reportedly produced rapping sounds, flickering lights, and made a table move and flip over. They recorded the sounds. Speculation was that the members had created a type of group consciousness, or perhaps a group hallucination.

They had suggestions for others considering their own experiment: use at least four people who have good rapport and a common motivation; be open minded; agree on details and history of the imaginary person; make him or her a friendly entity; suspend disbelief during the sessions; and expect a miracle, but be patient and enthusiastic.

MATTHEW MANNING: FROM POLTERGEIST TO HEALER?

As an eleven-year-old boy, Matthew Manning was said to be the agent for poltergeist activity in his family's home in Cambridge, England. Ornaments, chairs, and other objects moved mysteriously, so his father Derek, an architect, called the police and then the Cambridge Psychical Research Society. When Matthew was fifteen, the headmaster at his boarding school and several other witnesses testified that he had been the agent for paranormal phenomena at the school. Manning's classmate, Jon Wills, who became a housemaster at another school, said that "things just started to happen. Water appeared from nowhere. My bed moved and there was nobody near it. One night, a pile of dinner plates came down, apparently out of thin air, and shattered on the floor. Matthew was frightened and I was bloody terrified. It was the sort of experience that, unless you've been through it, you can't begin to comprehend."

Unlike most other suspected poltergeist agents, Manning was aware of his powers and denied to critics that he had cheated. "The chances of an eleven-year-old boy fooling all those adults is just impossible," he said as an adult. "My own feeling is that what I went through was caused by my own energy. It was nothing to do with spirits."

Manning decided to try to channel this energy into other areas. He started to practise automatic writing, which seemed to dissipate the energy he had to damage objects. By focusing on the names of dead artists, he was reportedly able to reproduce their drawings, particularly Durer, Picasso, and Goya.

When he was seventeen, Manning was tested in Toronto in 1972. Measurements of his brain waves while he was allegedly bending cutlery suggested that he generated unusual patterns of electrical energy, emanating from his limbic system.

Manning has written several books, including *The Link* in 1974, a best seller. He was interviewed by the eminent British broadcaster, Sir David Frost, and appeared on many television shows, demonstrating his abilities and sometimes causing electrical problems in studios.

Then Manning turned his energies to trying to heal people. While standing on a Himalayan mountaintop, he had a thought: "I realized that if I could exert control over machinery and electrical products, perhaps I could influence human bodies to help heal people." Now he claims that he can slow the rate of decay in red blood cells in a test tube and also destroy cancer cells simply by the power of thought.

Manning believes he has healed many people over the years, although it is difficult to prove. "He treats a lot of people, so statistically, it's likely some would have recovered anyway," said Richard Wiseman, professor of psychology at the University of Hertfordshire in England. "There is also the placebo effect; if we are in a positive frame of mind because we think we are going to get better, that undoubtedly can help recovery."

In his writings, Manning suggests that such psychic powers were once common to all humankind, but have been suppressed over the course of evolution.

AMERICAN TESTS

In the West, some suspected poltergeist agents have tried to perform PK feats in laboratories, but the results have not been as conclusive as they were with Kalugina in the Soviet Union. If they did indeed have paranormal abilities, in some cases they did not materialize, or they had weakened over time. Or perhaps the stresses in their household, which could have contributed to their RSPK in the first place, did not affect them when they were away from home.

In the Miami warehouse case of 1967, parapsychologist William Roll persuaded shipping clerk Julio Vasquez to go back with him to the psychical research foundation in Durham, North Carolina. Under controlled conditions, researchers say they saw a bottle fall off a table while Vasquez was close by and in another instance in a laboratory, a vase allegedly move while he was standing with researchers. He was also tested with a dice-throwing machine and apparently showed better-than-chance averages, Roll said.

In 1984, Roll was somewhat pleased with the tests he did with fourteen-year-old Tina Resch, the controversial poltergeist girl from Columbus, Ohio. After many reported RSPK events in her home, Roll brought Resch to the Institute of Parapsychology and to the Spring Creek Institute, both in North Carolina, for testing. According to Roll, a number of paranormal incidents took place at the institutes and at his home in Durham, but nothing was spectacular or conclusive.

Later that year, while Resch's powers were waning, according to Roll, she returned to North Carolina for more tests to see if she could move objects with her mind on command.

One day, Roll and two other researchers, neurobiologist Stephen Baumann and psychotherapist Jeannie Stewart, set up a table with a 12-inch socket wrench on it. According to Roll, Tina was not allowed near the table, but while Stewart and Baumann were standing between Tina and the table, there was a loud noise behind them and they saw that the wrench had moved off the table and about 18 feet along the floor, finally hitting a door.

Also in North Carolina, psychotherapist Rebecca Zinn said Tina created a number of paranormal incidents. In one incident, Zinn said she took Tina by the hand as they walked down a hallway leading to her office when a telephone suddenly came from behind them and struck the girl in the back. "There was no way anyone could have touched it," Zinn said.

As well in North Carolina, there were reportedly four movements of objects in Roll's house and ten at Spring Creek after Tina was hypnotized to try to recapture her mindset and emotions back in Columbus.

THE PRINCETON LAB

As mentioned in Chapter 1, a respected scientist, Professor Robert Jahn, dean emeritus of the School of Engineering and Applied Sciences at Princeton University, and his colleagues believe they have proven that PK is a reality, that ordinary people they have tested altered numbers and ping-pong balls just by thinking about them.

Jahn and others at the Princeton Anomalies Research Laboratory (PEAR) (www.princeton.edu/~pear/) claim to have produced experimental data to support the existence of PK. They say some people have influenced small balls and pendulums through willpower and the force of their mind under laboratory conditions at Princeton.

In the past, researchers used dice tossing and coin flipping to see if people could influence gravity, but now people are tested with high-tech machines called random events generators (REG).

In one PEAR experiment, researchers dropped 9,000 polystyrene balls down a network of pegs. They say that one of the experimenters was able to get more balls to go down one funnel of pegs by simply focusing on them. In addition, Jahn conducted more than 5 million tests of a pendulum and he said that an experimenter got it to swing in certain directions with his mind "beyond chance... the effect was tiny, but real."

The experimenters were reportedly not able to influence the tests every time, and they could not explain how they did it, so it remains an inexact science and open to criticism by people like skeptic James Randi. But the Princeton researchers suggest that, like people with paranormal powers, not all athletes are able to perform at their peak every night and that mood, confidence, pressure, and other conditions often affect results.

"We're not quite there, yet, but I hope one day we'll be able to show people how to influence things with their mind," Prof. Jahn said in 2005.

The Princeton researchers test ordinary people instead of psychics or mediums, the professor said, because "psychics and those who claim to have unusual powers bring a lot of publicity with them, they come trailing in with TV cameras and you find yourself being misquoted."

RSPK, or poltergeist activity, is even harder to prove than PK, Jahn says, because "such effects are extraordinarily rare and irregular in their appearance, usually arise at locations far removed from the experimenter's home base, and tend to persist only for short periods." By the time he arrives, Jahn added, "he typically finds the site overrun by law enforcement officers, medical and psychological practitioners, the clergy, media, family members, and skeptical representatives, who have so confounded and suppressed the effects that valid evidence is extremely difficult to obtain."

CHAPTER 23

THE POLTERGEIST IN POPULAR CULTURE

"The more civilized we get, the more we repress our sort of uncivilized nature. And one way to release that is through festival occasions, vicariously enjoying horror movies and all sorts of related things."

—LEON RAPPOPORT, PROFESSOR OF PSYCHOLOGY AT KANSAS STATE UNIVERSITY

Even if we do not believe in poltergeists, ghosts, and the paranormal, they certainly thrive in books and movies and on television. They've helped to make Stephen King (*Carrie*), William Peter Blatty (*The Exorcist*), and Steven Spielberg (*Poltergeist*) famous and quite wealthy.

Through big-budget movies and detailed books, the public probably has the impression that poltergeists are spectacular monsters from other dimensions. However, if poltergeists truly exist, they are more subtle than that. It seems we love to be scared out of our socks, and so writers and directors tend to embellish scripts.

We have made Blatty's 1971 book *The Exorcist* into a best seller, and a movie by the same title in 1973 has become a cult flick (starring head-spinning Linda Blair). Both were based on a poltergeist/possession case.

Perhaps it is because we want to know more about the shadowy side of the universe — if there is one — or because we are bored with the mundane.

Or perhaps we just want to get scared. "It goes all the way back to sitting around campfires, telling ghost stories and folk tales," said Leon

Rappoport, professor of psychology at Kansas State University. "It's a very prevalent, deep-seated, human characteristic to explore the boundaries where people can tolerate fear and anxiety, and then master that fear and anxiety by working through it. The more civilized we get, the more we repress our sort of uncivilized nature. And one way to release that is through festival occasions, vicariously enjoying horror movies and all sorts of related things."

Rappoport says that poltergeist and horror flicks are particularly popular with teenagers, partly as a way of rebelling because their parents say these movies are not fit for young minds.

In the contemporary Harry Potter books and movies, there is a poltergeist named Peeves, but he is not a classic poltergeist — more of a ghost — although the books' author, J.K. Rowling, says he is not the ghost of any person who has ever lived. Peeves is quite noisy and mischievous.

THE AMITYVILLE HORROR

The *Amityville Horror* reappeared in 2005 with a remake of the famous movie by the same name in 1979. It is based on what was supposedly a true story, although controversy remains about the authenticity of some of the paranormal events surrounding it.

In real life, the peaceful town of Amityville, NY, on Long Island's south shore, became known for what happened there in a three-storey, Dutch colonial home on Ocean Avenue in 1974 and 1975.

On November 13, 1974, the DeFeo family were slaughtered in their beds — Ronald DeFeo and his wife, Louise, their two sons, Mark and John, and their two daughters, Dawn and Allison. The killer was another son, Ronald Junior, who went from room to room with a high-powered rifle. Somehow, the victims never heard the other shots. In his trial, DeFeo, who was on drugs, said an evil spirit in the house forced him to do it. He pleaded insanity, but the prosecution said he was just trying to benefit from six life insurance policies. DeFeo was sentenced to 150 years in prison.

About one year after the horrible crime, a young couple, George and Kathy Lutz, bought the home for $80,000 and they claimed it was a hotbed for paranormal events — strange noises, an unearthly presence, and locked doors and windows reportedly opening and closing by themselves.

Following an exorcism by a Catholic priest, which did not work, scratching sounds and thumping noises intensified, objects moved about mysteriously, telephone service malfunctioned, apparitions were reportedly seen outside, and Lutz, a former Marine, seemed to become possessed by an evil spirit. The Lutzes packed up and left.

With the help of the Lutz family, author Jay Anson wrote the book *The Amityville Horror* in 1977, which was made into the movie of the same name by Dino de Laurentis and remade in 2005.

But many people believe the paranormal events were fabricated, exaggerated, or a complete hoax. Another family who moved into the home after the Luztes reported no occurrences. And a skeptical author, Stephen Kaplan, wrote a book *The Amityville Horror Conspiracy*, but it didn't seem to matter to the general public, who became fascinated with the story, hence the 2005 movie remake.

THE EXORCIST

Author William Peter Blatty based this famous 1971 book and movie on a story he read in the *Washington Post* on August 20, 1949, while he was a student at Georgetown University.

The *Post* story described an alleged exorcism of a thirteen-year-old boy in nearby Mount Ranier, Maryland, who was the only child of a dysfunctional family. But it is hard to ascertain the accuracy of the real story.

The boy's case took place in January 1949 when bizarre noises came from his bedroom walls, and furniture and objects moved. A Lutheran minister reportedly saw a bed move and a chair flip the boy onto the floor.

The boy apparently showed hysterical tendencies and, believing he was possessed, a team of priests performed a number of exorcisms, which were unsuccessful, but the occurrences stopped after four months.

Some of the information for the real case was passed down from sources as some of the priests refused to discuss it, and from a twenty-eight-page diary kept by Father Raymond Bishop, who reportedly saw the second exorcism.

Blatty also wrote the screenplay for *The Exorcist*, which starred a fictional girl, played by actress Linda Blair. Blatty's book reportedly sold more than 6 million copies.

For more information on the real case, check the *Fortean Times*, no. 123, page 34; *Strange Magazine* no. 20, 1998 (www.strangemag.com), and the article "Exorcism! Driving Out the Nonsense" in the January/February 2001 *Skeptical Inquirer*.

POLTERGEIST

There were three films in the *Poltergeist* series: *Poltergeist* (1982), *Poltergeist II* (1986), and *Poltergeist III* (1988). Steven Spielberg directed the first. They were about a fictitious family, the Freelings, who lived in homes inhabited by spirits.

Some of the events in the movies resembled several poltergeist investigations, including a 1972 case involving the Fischer family in Rothschild, Wisconsin. The family reported mysterious ringing bells, footsteps, electrical malfunctions, and strange shadows. They said they abandoned the home when a flying razor reportedly flew at Mrs. Fischer while she was in a bath.

Some people believe that the *Poltergeist* trilogy was cursed because four of its actors died.

Dominique Dunne, who played Dana Freeling in the original film, died at age twenty-two the same year the film was released, after being choked into a coma by her former boyfriend.

Heather O'Rourke, who played Carol Anne Freeling in all three movies, died in 1988, before the third movie was released, of septic shock on an operating table after bacterial toxins got into her bloodstream. She was twelve years old.

Two others, who appeared only in *Poltergeist II*, suffered less dramatic fates. Julian Beck, who played the evil spirit Kane, died at sixty in 1985 after a long fight with stomach cancer. Will Sampson, who portrayed a medicine man, died at fifty-three in 1987 of postoperative kidney failure and fungal infection.

THE ENTITY

The Entity was a 1983 film starring Barbara Hershey and loosely based on a case in 1974 in Culver City, California.

The real case was investigated by parapsychologist Kerry Gaynor, who became an adviser for the movie. A woman told Gaynor that a ghost had beaten and raped her. He was skeptical, but then he said he saw doors and pans moving under their own power and strange lights.

THE SMURL POLTERGEIST

A book and a television movie, both entitled *The Haunted*, were based on the middle-class lives of Jack and Janet Smurl, a real-life couple in West Pittston, Pennsylvania, who claimed they were haunted over a thirteen-year period, from 1974 to 1987, by apparitions and poltergeist-like events — footsteps on the stairs, unplugged radios blaring, a German shepherd terrorized by an unseen force, and toilets flushing themselves.

Several exorcisms apparently did not help, and some of their neighbors were skeptical about the claims of paranormal events. Demonic claims were not corroborated by independent observers.

Some viewers were skeptical of what they said were cheesy special effects in the movie, although it did get some good reviews.

SOME PARANORMAL FLICKS

The Village (2004, Bryce Dallas Howard)
The Ring (2002, Naomi Watts)
Signs (2002, Mel Gibson)
The Others (2001, Nicole Kidman)
13 Ghosts (2001, Tony Shalhoub)
The Sixth Sense (1999, Bruce Willis)
The Blair Witch Project (1999, Heather Donahue)
Friday the 13th movies (1980–, Kane Hodder as Jason)
Nightmare on Elm Street movies (1984–) Robert Englund as Freddie)
Ghost (1990, Patrick Swayze)
Beetlejuice (1988, Michael Keaton)
Poltergeist (three movies) (1982, 1986, 1988, JoBeth Williams)
The Shining (1980, Jack Nicholson)
The Changeling (1980, George C. Scott)
The Fog (1980, Adrienne Barbeau)
The Amityville Horror (1979, James Brolin; 2005, Jimmy Bennett)
Halloween (1978, Jamie Lee Curtis)
Carrie (1976, Sissy Spacek)
The Ghost and Mrs. Muir (1947, Gene Tierney)

TELEVISION

Television has not really embraced the poltergeist, although there have been some shows dealing with it on *The X Files* and *Night Stalker*. The series *Poltergeist: The Legacy* (1996 to 1999, created by Richard Barton Lewis) was not really about the traditional poltergeist, but a secret society that began many centuries ago to accumulate knowledge and artifacts to help fight against evil. John Edward's psychic show, *Crossing Over*, deals with the afterlife.

The X Files (1993–2001)
The Outer Limits (1963–1965, 1995–2002)
Poltergeist: The Legacy (1996–1999)
The Twilight Zone (1959–1964)

REAL LIFE EXPERIENCE

Veteran actor Brian Cox, who starred in the thriller *The Ring*, said he had a poltergeist experience at age eighteen in his native Scotland.

Cox said he rented a room in a house in Edinburgh and was lying in bed one night when he heard an unusual tapping noise. "It was a big room and I looked to the other side of the bed and there, by a big old Victorian dresser, was a chair," he said. "It was shaking, then it started to move. It moved along the room and then came in front of my bed. I was already gripping the sheet and when this happened, I pulled it over my head and passed out. It was scary."

The next morning, to make sure he had not been dreaming, Cox said he checked the chair. It had indeed moved away from the dresser and "there were scuff marks along the floor."

Cox believes the incident may have been related to children with a family upstairs. "They say poltergeist activity often centers around young children," said the actor, who appeared in *The Bourne Supremacy*, *Braveheart*, and *Manhunter*.

CHAPTER 24

SHOW ME THE MONEY

If poltergeists truly exist, they seem to cause a lot of damage and heartache. In Runcorn, England, a poltergeist reportedly caused £20,000 damage, a hefty bill for 1952. (See Chapter 17.)

And yet there is apparently money to be made on things that go bump in the day and night. Hollywood, of course, has raked in billions of dollars over the decades with poltergeist and ghost tales, mostly fiction. And hundreds of books have been written about the subject.

"Everything today is for a buck," said a man, who was suspected of being a poltergeist agent in a case in 1970 in St. Catharines, Ontario. At the time objects and furniture moved mysteriously around his parents' apartment, some authors, museum officials, and even some of his old neighbors had tried to make money on the strange happenings, he said. "I thought about telling my story, but it's not worth the price [to his privacy]."

On a lesser scale, no self-respecting English pub is without a ghost or poltergeist and they are often advertised to attract business. There's Bob the Poltergeist at the Hobgoblin Public House in Maidenhead, Berkshire; supposed poltergeist activity at Shipman's Public House in Northhampton, which is thought to be the spirit of Harry Franklin, a former manager who committed suicide; and an exorcism that was held to remove a stinky spirit at The Royal Oak in Huntingdonshire. And yet, poltergeists may not necessarily always be good for the customers or staff at pubs and stores.

In Scotland in December 2004, barmaids at the Castleview in Dundonald, Ayrshire, complained they were having their bums pinched by a poltergeist. "I won't even go to the toilet on my own because I'm scared he'll be there," said waitress Tiffany Luxton, eighteen. "It's as if you're being stalked. You feel him brushing past you and touching you. It's really quite scary. You can hear footsteps, but there is nobody there."

Pub manager Terry Quinn, forty-nine, said that on one night, "12 huge water jugs sitting on a solid wooden gantry all flew off the shelf at once and smashed." In addition, Quinn added, "the Co2 that powers the beer lines just turns itself off. What's going on is a mystery."

Quinn has summoned the Dunfermline Paranormal Research Fellowship, which was to carry out an investigation in 2005.

In September 2002, in a shop in Trowbridge, Wiltshire, a poltergeist named George allegedly tossed stock around the Millets Store. On one morning at 5:30, George was suspected of setting off a burglar alarm, although police could find no evidence of a break-in and nothing had been stolen.

"His name is George and we think he's Victorian," said the store's assistant manager, Renate Parvin. "Some people get a strange vibe when they go into the stock room. None of us find it frightening... we're certainly not going to get an exorcist in."

GHOSTBUSTERS

There are many parapsychologists, ghostbusters, and psychics, who investigate poltergeist cases for money, or for the love of it as volunteers through parapsychology organizations.

Many are like William Roll, who has been paid by universities to investigate paranormal claims and will come to a home free of charge. Others make cash by lecturing at conventions.

Some psychics and groups make a living by helping people with their paranormal abilities or problems. Their fees can range from several hundred dollars to $7,500 for an in-depth investigation. People who simply want to be tested for clairvoyance should expect to pay about $1,500, according to the International Society for Paranormal Research, based in Marina Del Rey, California.

Or, if you simply want to go with a psychic medium on a group paranormal investigation in England (www.ukhaunted.com) one evening, a team of mediums, photographers, and historians offers a commercial ghost-hunting venture. In 2005, they had an all-night vigil at Jerusalem Pub, beneath Nottingham Castle, for £99, which included, of course, a quality buffet meal. According to Nicola Froggett, cofounder and trainee medium, "We want the public to join us so they can see and experience what the team does. It adds credibility if unusual activity occurs."

Many cities in Europe and the United States have ghost tours.

Be wary of other ventures, however, as there are fakes. In New England, a man and wife said they had a poltergeist breaking dishes in their home and began charging admission for the public to see for themselves. A paranormal private investigator (PPI), Patrick Leonard, posed as a gullible tourist and discovered that the couple was hurling the dishes themselves when people were not looking.

POLTERGEISTS IN COURT

Some people have been accused of claiming they had poltergeists in order to get out of their council house. In 1995 in Rochdale, England, Jim and Vera Gardner said their council officials accused them of faking unusual water disturbances in their home so they would be moved to another council house. "That's ridiculous!" Vera said. "I've lived here 14 years and was perfectly settled until this started. Now I can't wait to leave." (See Chapter 17.)

In many countries, sellers of homes are required to tell prospective buyers if the home has a history of poltergeist or ghost activity. According to Peter MacDonald of www.homeloancenter.com, in the realty business they are referred to as "stigmatized homes." That could also mean a home in which there has been an unusual death or murder or one that has been built atop a graveyard. But proving that in court is another matter.

In 1999, an English couple refused to pay the final installment of £3,000 on their £44,000-cottage because they said it was inhabited by a spirit that caused objects to move and walls to weep. Josie and Andrew Smith ended up in Derby County Court. They explained to Judge Peter Stretton that they bought the house in Upper Mayfield, Staffordshire, in 1994 and were not informed by the previous owners, Susan Melbourne and Sandra Podmore, that it was haunted.

A priest, Rev. Peter Mockford, who specializes in the paranormal, told the court he had been in the Smith house, which was also inhabited by the Smiths' three children, and had felt a paranormal presence.

But Judge Stretton ruled in favor of the previous owners. "I do not accept that it is haunted now or has been at any other time," the judge said.

A lawyer for the previous owners, Thomas Dillon, told court that the Smiths invented the story to avoid paying the outstanding money.

Through the years, judges and lawyers have occasionally sifted through poltergeist evidence. In 1850 in Normandy, France, Felix Thorel reportedly sued his local priest, Father Tinel, for defamation, after the priest called Thorel a witch.

The priest blamed Thorel for poltergeist activities in the parsonage of Cideville, which allegedly was plagued with "every category of poltergeist phenomena." Father Tinel said there were thirty-four witnesses to unexplained knockings, rappings of tunes, furniture moving, knives being thrown, desks rising and falling, winds rushing, and bedclothes moving.

According to Sacheverel Sitwell's 1940 book *The Poltergeist*, the case was unsolved despite intensive investigation. There was no word on the defamation suit. Perhaps they settled out of court (lawyers thrived thence, as well).

In Braintree, England, in 1971, a thirteen-year-old boy was accused of burning down his school. His lawyer in juvenile court, Peter Perrins, claimed that an "evil poltergeist spirit" also made the boy cause considerable damage in his home.

POLTERGEIST INSURANCE, ANYONE?

Believe it or not, there is insurance you can purchase to protect yourself against poltergeists and ghosts.

An English pub landlord pays a premium of £500 annually for an insurance policy because he is worried that the "resident poltergeist" at his Royal Falcon Hotel in Lowestoft, Suffolk, will injure customers.

"I saw glasses move across the bar one night and thought what happens if it does something to hurt somebody?" pub landlord Terry Meggs said in 2004. "I never believed in ghosts before I came here."

Some people believe that the pub is haunted by a monk who hanged himself after being caught having an affair with a pupil or teacher when the building was a school.

"We get sounds of moving furniture, the glasses move, we get very loud banging, as if someone is banging with a hammer," said Meggs's wife, Shirley. "We get bells ringing and sounds of someone walking across the floor and things get moved to different places."

The couple has taken out the "Spooksafe" policy with the Ultraviolet insurance company, of Bristol, England, which says it will pay up to £1 million if staff or customers are killed or permanently disabled by poltergeists, ghosts, or other paranormal phenomena.

Ultraviolet said that in 2000, it paid £100,000 on "Spooksafe" after investigators looking into the death of a woman, who had been thrown over the banisters at her home in the US, concluded that a ghost was responsible for the crime.

"We had a specialist firm of investigators look into it and they were convinced," said Simon Burgess, chief underwriting officer, who did not identify the woman.

Ultraviolet said that it sold about 500 "Spooksafe" policies in 2004, mostly in California. The policy also covers damage committed by "poltergeists."

One famous couple, Hollywood reporter Joe Hyams and his actress wife Elke Sommer, who were never reimbursed by an insurance company, claimed they had a noisy spook or poltergeist in their Beverly Hills, California, house in 1964, which reportedly pushed chairs around and slammed doors. Hyams said he recorded the sounds on tape. Then the couple discovered that the previous owner had sold him the house because, he, too, had been haunted by the noises.

THE POWERFUL AND THE PARANORMAL

Many famous and influential people have believed in the paranormal.

Abraham Lincoln consulted with spiritualists and mediums. His wife, Mary Todd Lincoln, often arranged séances for him. Of course, he was not without criticism; the *Cleveland Plain Dealer* said he "consulted spooks."

Union general and US President Ulysses S. Grant turned to spiritualism later in life.

Former US President Ronald Reagan had an astrology adviser, while current President George W. Bush says God speaks to him and told him to invade Iraq in 2003.

SOURCES AND RECOMMENDED READING:

Auerbach, Loyd. *ESP, Hauntings and Poltergeists.* New York: Warner Books, 1986.

Broughton, Dr. Richard. *Parapsychology: The Controversial Science.* New York: Ballantine, 1991.

Chambers, Paul. *Paranormal People.* London: Blanford, 1998.

Clarkson, Michael. *Intelligent Fear.* Toronto: Key Porter, 2002, and New York: Marlowe and Co., 2002.

Colombo, John Robert. *Mysterious Canada: Strange Sights, Extraordinary Events and Peculiar Places.* Toronto: Doubleday Canada, 1988.

Ellison, Arthur. *The Paranormal: A Scientific Exploration of the Supernatural.* New York: Dodd, Mead, 1988.

Fodor, Nandor. *On the Trail of the Poltergeist.* New York: Citadel Press, 1958.

Gault, Alan and A. D. Cornell. *Poltergeists.* Boston: Routledge and Kegan Paul Ltd., 1979.

Guiley, Rosemary Ellen. *Harper's Encyclopedia of Mystical and Paranormal Experiences.* San Francisco: Harper, 1991.

Hines, Terence. *Pseudoscience and the Paranormal.* New York: Prometheus Books, 2003.

Kurtz, Paul. *Skeptical Odysseys: Personal Accounts by the World's Leading Paranormal Inquirers.* Buffalo: Prometheus Books, 2001.

Kurtz, Paul. *A Skeptic's Handbook of Parapsychology.* Buffalo: Prometheus Books, 1985.

Manning, Matthew. *The Link.* New York: Holt, Rinehart and Winston, 1975.

Owen, Dr. A. R. G. *Can We Explain the Poltergeist?* New York: Garrett Publications, 1964.

Playfair, Guy Lyon. *The Flying Cow.* London: Souvenir Press, 1975.

Playfair, Guy Lyon. *This House is Haunted.* New York: Stein and Day, 1980.

Rogo, D. Scott. *The Poltergeist Experience.* New York: Penguin, 1979.

———*On the Track of the Poltergeist.* Englewood Cliffs: Prentice-Hall, 1986.

Roll, William G. *The Poltergeist.* New York: New American Library, 1971, and a special edition New York: Paraview Books, 2004.

Roll, William and Valerie Storey. *Unleashed: Of Poltergeists and Murder: The Curious Story of Tina Resch.* New York: Paraview Books, 2004.

Spencer, John and Anne. *The Poltergeist Phenomenon.* London: Headline Publishing, 1996.

Steiger, Brad. *Real Ghosts, Restless Spirits and Haunted Places.* Canton: Visible Ink Press, 2003.

Taylor, Troy. *The Haunting of America.* Decatur: Whitechapel Press, 2001.

Wilson, Colin. *Poltergeist!* New York: Putnam, 1981.

PERIODICALS

The Skeptical Enquirer

Journal of the Society for Psychical Research

Journal of the American Society for Psychical Research

The Journal of Parapsychology

The Journal of Scientific Exploration

The European Journal of Parapsychology, Fate Magazine

The Fortean Times

ON THE WEB:

Prairie Ghosts site (www.prairieghosts.com)

Haunting Places Directory (www.haunted-places.com)

The Trickster and the Paranormal (www.tricksterbook.com) (this includes the papers of George Hansen, who was employed in a parapsychology lab and also wrote about fraud and deception)

PARANORMAL RESEARCH GROUPS

United Kingdom

Society for Psychical Research (www.spr.ac.uk)

The Association for the Scientific Study of Anomalous Phenomena (ASSAP), (http://www.assap.org/)

Manchester's Association of Paranormal Investigators and Training (MAPIT) (http://www.maxpages.com/mapit/home/)

Parasearch, investigates cases in the West Midlands of England (http://www.parasearch.org.uk/)

The Ghost Club (http://www.ghostclub.org.uk/)

Koestler Parapsychology Unit (http://moebius.psy.ed.ac.uk), a branch of the psychology department at the University of Edinburgh in Scotland.

Scottish Society for Psychical Research (SSPR) (www.sspr.co.uk/)

Institute of Paranormal Research (www.iopr.org.uk)

Scottish Society for Psychical Research (http://www.sspr.co.uk/)

UNITED STATES

The Parapsychology Foundation (www.parapsychology.org)

The American Society for Psychical Research (ASPR) (www.aspr.com)

Princeton Engineering Anomalies Research (www.princeton.edu/~pear/) pursues scientific study of the interaction of human consciousness with sensitive physical devices and systems common to contemporary engineering practice.

American Institute of Parapsychology (www.parapsychologylab.com)

Rhine Research Center Institute for Paranormal (www.rhine.org)

The American Ghost Society (http://www.caiprs.com/Mission%20Statement.htm)

Exceptional Human Experiences Network (http://www.well.com/user/bobby/ehe/eheorg.html)

The James Randi Educational Foundation (www.randi.org)

Pacific Neuropsychiatric Institute (www.pni.org and www.pni.org/research/anomalous)

Society for Scientific Exploration (www.scientificexploration.org)

OTHERS

The Association for Skeptical Investigations (www.skepticalinvestigations.org/) promotes skepticism, enquiry and doubt within science.

PRISMTEAM International (Australia) (http://free.hostultra.com/~adminprism/)

Australian Institute of Parapsychological Research (www.aiprinc.org/) is a non-profit community association based in Sydney but with an Australian-wide membership base.

Centre for Parapsychological Studies, Bologna (http://digilander.libero.it/cspbologna/)

Centre for Fundamental and Anomalies Research (www.c-far.com)

Survival Research Institute of Canada (www.islandnet.com/sric/)

The Ontario (Canada) Ghosts and Hauntings Research Society (http://www.ghrs.org/Ashley/links1.html)

Psi Mart (www.pst-mart.com/) offers books, videos and publications on parapsychology.

Links to Paranormal Research Groups:

http://freespace.virgin.net/polter.geist/groups.htm

http://granicus.if.org/~estelle/paranormal.html

http://www.survivalafterdeath.org/info.htm

Note: For the chapters on the Columbus, Ohio, case, I would like to thank William Roll for granting permission to use parts of his 1993 paper, *The Question of RSPK Versus Fraud in the Case of Tina Resch*, Psychical Research Foundation and Parapsychological Services Institute, Atlanta, Georgia.

For more information on Michael Clarkson and his books, see www.michaelclarkson.com